EMAIL MARKETING BY THE NUMBERS

EMAIL MARKETING BY THE NUMBERS

How to Use the World's Greatest Marketing Tool to Take Any Organization to the Next Level

Chris Baggott

with Ali Sales

John Wiley & Sons, Inc.

Published by John Wiley & Sons, Inc., Hoboken, New Jersey.
Published simultaneously in Canada.

Wiley Bicentennial Logo: Richard J. Pacifico

For general information on our other products and services or for technical support, please contact our Customer Care Department within the United States at (800) 762-2974, outside the United States at (317) 572-3993 or fax (317) 572-4002.

Wiley also publishes its books in a variety of electronic formats. Some content that appears in print may not be available in electronic books. For more information about Wiley products, visit our web site at www.wiley.com.

Library of Congress Cataloging-in-Publication Data:

Baggott, Chris.
 Email marketing by the numbers : how to use the world's greatest
marketing tool to take any organization to the next level / Chris Baggott.
  p. cm.
 ISBN 978-0-470-12245-7 (cloth)
  1. Internet marketing. 2. Electronic mail systems. I. Title.
HF5415.1265.B29 2007
 658.8'72—dc22

                                        2007002737

Printed in the United States of America.

10 9 8 7 6 5 4 3 2 1

CONTENTS

v

CONTENTS

INTRODUCTION

BY THE NUMBERS: WHAT'S IT ALL ABOUT?

Marketers, it's time to let go. Say goodbye to intangibles and opinions. Wave *adios* to feelings and gut instinct—you know, that reason your boss used when you asked him why the color green would work for your brochure.

Repeat this adage with me: "Half my marketing dollars are wasted. I just don't know which half." Okay, it's the last time you'll ever say those words. It's the last time you'll take a leap of faith or look into your crystal ball and make a wild prediction.

I know that making marketing decisions based on feelings and intuition seems natural. And that traditional marketing, branding activities, and expensive professional services can be alluring. They're comfortable. So comfortable, in fact, that they *seem* right to a lot of organizations. Here is one of my favorite lines from Thomas Paine's *Common Sense:* "A long habit of not thinking something wrong gives it a superficial appearance of being right."

Yet, there is a new era of marketing unfolding. One based on data, analysis, and what people actually *do* rather than what they feel or say. It's time to say "no" to what may feel comfortable and "yes" to the facts.

As humans, we like to think we are interesting. Complex. The reality is that we typically repeat the same behavior over and over again. Take me, for example. This morning, I read the paper. I drank

Starbucks coffee. I listened to my iPod while doing both. And guess what? I'll do the same thing tomorrow.

That's why action and behavior are such great predictors of future behavior. As a coffee drinker today, I'm a lot more likely to drink coffee tomorrow. Or, at least a lot more likely than my neighbor who never drinks coffee.

I'm continually baffled as to why so many coffee companies waste their time and money talking to noncoffee drinkers. That's the problem with traditional mass marketing advertisements. Every time you run one of these campaigns, you're spending most of your effort in the wrong places; hoping that if you expose yourself to a big enough audience, you'll find a few new coffee drinkers to make it all worthwhile.

Successful marketing means compelling people to act. We don't run ads for our health or to keep the publishing industry alive. We do it because, as marketers, we are responsible for making people *do* something.

Fortunately for us, this new era of marketing means lots of room for progress and improvement. It is based on the principles of relationships, metrics, and analysis. And tools like email marketing make it easy to embrace these principles.

The transition to this new marketing mindset will be tough for many marketers. Just think—by reading this Introduction, you already have an advantage.

I hope you're ready to learn and improve. No matter what size organization you come from, how big a budget you have, or what your specialty is, all of the strategies and tactics in this book are 100 percent doable.

Ever followed those "Paint by Numbers" instructions? Even the worst artist can get awfully close to painting a Picasso. This book is the "Paint by Numbers" of email marketing. It contains the step-by-step instructions you need to accomplish your goals, create better relationships, and move your organization to a higher level.

Because this book is designed to educate marketers from all types of organizations—large companies, small companies, nonprofits, associations, religious and educational organizations, and more—I frequently refer to your audience as "constituents." I'm hoping the term is a catchall for everyone you're hoping to influence and build better relationships with.

As much as I like providing my own perspective in the coming chapters, I've also reached out to individuals at a variety of organizations who will share their personal perspectives and experiences, too. At the end of most chapters, you'll find their unaltered words in the section titled "What Are Other Marketers Thinking?"

If you're anything like me, you crave proof as much as you crave Starbucks coffee. That's why I've also included some case studies that clearly demonstrate the power of email. What I love about case studies is that, regardless of industry or size, the tactics are relevant to nearly every organization. So take a deep breath and relax . . . let go of your past marketing mentality. Are you void of feelings, intuition, and preconceived notions? Good. We're ready to begin.

CHAPTER 1

WHAT IS MARKETING'S GOAL?

Relationships. The goal of all organizations is a better relationship with their constituents.

We (marketers) are all looking for long-term, mutually beneficial relationships. We want relationships in which our constituents overlook our minor imperfections, appreciate our subtle differences, and commit to us as much as we do to them. Sounds sort of like the ideal spouse, right?

It is impossible to do a better job explaining how we should view our marketing relationships than Seth Godin did in his amazing book *Permission Marketing* (New York: Simon & Schuster, 1999). With all due respect, I'll paraphrase him: As marketers, we usually don't approach our customers like we would approach a potential spouse, do we? No, we're more like a drunken frat boy at his first freshman mixer. Most marketers approach customers and prospects more intent on the one-night stand than the long-term relationship. We know it's wrong . . . but we do it anyway.

A lot of good things happen when you build better relationships. People tend to stay around longer, they become more engaged, and they tell their friends about the great relationship that they're in.

Want to argue this simple premise? Do you think marketing's goal should be customer acquisition? Higher sales? Lower turnover? Successful campaigns to sell more widgets?

Guess what? If you focus on the relationship, all of those good things will happen.

The funny thing is that relationship marketing has more traditional roots than many of us care to admit. It's mass marketing that is the recent corrupter.

In a letter from Rory Sutherland, vice chairman and creative director of OgilvyOne, he states: "It is the intervening age of broadcast, interruption-based communication that is out of step with today's consumer controlled media world, and it is the people who've grown up in that world who find themselves most wrong-footed."

Excellent point. Our grandfathers knew the value of relationship marketing, whether it was door-to-door selling or acting like Sam (the butcher) from the *Brady Bunch*. Take the time to get to know your customers as individuals. Pay attention to them. Talk to them like human beings (and show them you are a human being rather than an institution).

We know that these tactics work because each and every one of us is also a consumer. Who doesn't appreciate being called by name or having the right drink put in front of him or her without having to ask? We all want to be recognized and appreciated for our contribution and the value we are bringing to the relationship.

But mass marketing is so ingrained in our practices, despite having the most revolutionary tools ever available to us, we still measure success around analytics that should be tertiary at best (i.e., impressions, visitors, opens).

Like any addict, we as marketers need to take a step back and analyze our behavior. The goal isn't based on "hits," is it? The goal needs to be something that really drives your business. The goal is to build long-term relationships (Lifetime Value).

At this point, you really have no choice but to change your ways. You can keep blasting away, hoping that if you yell loud enough, a few people will actually pay attention. The problem is that it's getting harder and harder to yell and be heard. The audience is gaining more control; consumers have the upper hand in the relationship. They have multiple choices for almost every product, service, nonprofit, religious institution, and more. Why should they choose you? Lower prices?

Better location? A higher level of service? Maybe you can establish those as real differentiators, but how long until a similar product or a lower price or a better-located competitor comes along?

As your constituents gain more control, they are turning away from mass marketing tactics and learning to ignore them. Instead, they're talking to each other; going to social networking sites, emailing their friends—you know, good old-fashioned word-of-mouth.

What's really funny to me is the fact that when you talk to organizations about what makes them different (worthy, if you will), this answer always lands somewhere in the top three: our people.

So why do you hide your people behind the facade of a brand or an institution? At the end of the day, people associate themselves with other people that they like. Your constituents want to like you and have a relationship with you.

As a marketer who focused on people, you wouldn't run "campaigns." You would build better relationships. You would treat every conversation as if it were critical to the future of the relationship. You would try not to do anything stupid and would be quick to apologize and make it right if you did.

Valentine's Day should be the national holiday for all marketers. After all, as marketers, our job is centered on playing the cupid between our organizations and our constituents. You want your constituents to love you, right?

This special time of year gives us all an opportunity to reflect and focus on what is really important in our (marketing) lives. So, in the spirit of the season, I offer the following five ways to bring love to your constituents:

1. *Make them feel special.* People don't fall in love with people who make them feel ordinary. We all want to hear things that make us feel original and unique. This goes beyond calling your constituents by the right name and extends to everything you can find out about them.

   If you're serious about a relationship, you weave your significant other's likes into your conversations. If he loves football, you would try to learn something about the game. If she likes fine wine, you would take her to a great restaurant and show off your vast knowledge. The same goes for your constituents.

2. *Be human.* People don't fall in love with institutions, and they are not inclined to fall in love with a brand (Apple and Starbucks excluded, perhaps). Your chance of landing in a great relationship increases exponentially when you show a human side. Introduce your constituents to a real person. For 60+ years, we marketers have focused on institutions, which is an outdated approach. This year let's focus on person-to-person.

3. *Don't smother.* Just like a real relationship, you have got to be respectful of the proper pace. I love the commercial where a woman cooks her date's favorite food, knits him a sweater, and introduces him to her parents . . . all on the first blind date. (I have no idea what this commercial is selling, by the way.)

   All relationships develop at their own pace. Some people will only want an occasional date for a period of time before things really heat up. Come on too strong—and they're gone. Other people want to get married right away. Move too slowly and they are going to find more promising relationships.

   As marketers, it is up to us to sense the right pace for each and every one of our constituents. This is referred to as *frequency control* and it's a critical element for marketers to get right.

5. *Acknowledge when you make a mistake.* Apologize. Be humble and sincere. Ask for forgiveness and offer some token to win the person back. In a relationship, you learn the signs that tell you something is wrong with your partner. Whether it's the cold shoulder, silence, or yelling treatment, you're probably sensitive to these indicators and take steps toward forgiveness if you've done something wrong. Most of us are forgiving of others. We recognize that people make mistakes and an apology goes a long way.

   Smart marketers learn to recognize the problem and alter their communication to get the relationship back on track.

6. *Accept that relationships end.* It is a sad, sad fact: Some relationships do not last forever. Sometimes, they never should have started in the first place. If football is critical to your exis-

tence, and she hates it, you may have to acknowledge that perhaps this relationship isn't in the cards and let it go.

Other times, you make a mistake and the apology isn't accepted. Or your significant other might just find someone he or she likes better. If step four doesn't work, then you need to let it go.

As marketers (like all desperate lovers), we keep coming back. We can't bear the loss or the thought of rejection so we call, show up unexpectedly, and hang on to the relationship. In the real world, this is called stalking.

The problem is that rather than leaving the dumping party with a fond feeling about how mature we are, we become the subject of cocktail party jokes or of a restraining order. Either way, it's bad.

When it's over, it's over. Let it go. Adjust your attitude or find someone else who is more receptive to your communication style. In relationships, there are no guarantees. But there is hope that we will learn from the past and resolve to build a better relationship that extends far into the future.

What are some other aspects of a relationship? How about dialogue or respect? The ability to tell the other party the truth?

Are you afraid of your constituents?

I've been getting a lot of questions about a comment I recently made about companies (and people) being afraid of their customers. It's easy to deny, but true.

There are two facts about your constituents:

1. They are people (some even think of themselves as individuals).
2. You usually know more than they do.

Point 1 is obvious, but ignored. We know our constituents are people, but we don't want to communicate to them on that level. We are afraid they will ask a question we can't answer or afraid they might not like us.

The evidence is all around us. Even in email, my chosen media, most of us choose to hide from our individual customers behind some facade such as info@ or Cust_Serv@ instead of bringing forth our true selves.

Point 2 really hits on how afraid we are of customers. We are afraid to *tell* them anything. We don't want to step on any toes by making a suggestion or telling them when they are wrong.

The fact is that your constituents are loyal to you because there is some perception of *expertise*. If I could (or wanted to) program an enterprise customer relationship marketing (CRM) system or make a delicious pizza, I would. The fact is that customers hire us to be the experts. They take confidence in our confidence. If all we are doing is taking orders from customers, we don't build much value, do we? Where is the loyalty? Customers are loyal to people they can't do without, not organizations that just take orders or scream at them with irrelevant junk.

The time has finally arrived when organizations are getting serious about marketing for what it does best: driving value. Do we *really care* about relationships with customers? Of course not. We care about Lifetime Value (LTV). Relationships are how you can increase the value of your customers and convert your prospects. I hope that's not too cold for you.

I'm going to spend some time covering the basic metrics to consider when thinking about LTV.

LTV LESSON ONE

Don't pay too much to acquire a customer. The easiest way to get behind the 8 ball on Lifetime Value is to overpay in the first place.

Let's say you're spending $500 a month on a phone book ad. That means you need $500 a month in new business to cover that cost, right? It's so easy!

Wrong! Add in margin and defections, and that number is probably more like $5,000.

One problem is that brand new customers cost a lot more than existing customers to service.

Think about even the simplest example of a pizza shop. Assume the average cost per call in the pizza business is approximately

$1.50. For that first-time caller, it's around $2.50. Think about what that added cost does to the margin on an $8.00 pie. (Now you know why all those pizza places are pushing you to order online.)

There is also order size to consider. Often, the first-time buyer spends less than a returning customer. First-time buyers just want to try you out. You now have a margin squeeze from an order that is both more costly to service and worth less.

You may think, "I'll just average that acquisition cost over multiple orders and make it up."

Do you know your retention rate? In the average business, 50 percent of first-time customers never buy from you again. Are you average? Do you even know your defection rate?

That's the core of LTV—you must know simple stats such as average order size for first-time customers, defection rate, and cost of servicing that first-time customer.

Online, this picture can get even worse. If you are paying for clicks and not converting to a sale, all those costs have to be accounted for in the number of people who actually do convert. The problem is that most of the people who visit your site don't do what you want them to do.

LTV Lesson Two

Most of us are in the habit of measuring profit by product or service. We know that the large extra pepperoni is more profitable than the medium cheese.

But do you know that this thinking is wrong? We've been brainwashed into believing that marketing is all about products. The truth is, profitability needs to be measured by *customer*. Which *customers* are the most profitable? How do you calculate that?

1. Sort your constituents by the amount they spend over a period of time (a simple Excel spreadsheet will work just fine).
2. Group them into buckets for the sake of time (i.e., all customers who spent $40 to $55 over a period of 12 months).

3. For each group, subtract all costs so that you're left with the difference between that and the amount spent. That amount is individual profitability.
4. Taking overall revenue and dividing by individual profitability will give you a profit percentage for each of your buckets.

Here is a simple example: Assume that the Johnson family spent $10,000 on pizza last year. They order every week by calling in. They never know what they want, so it takes an extra minute on each call. They always use a coupon and live on the outer edge of our delivery area.

A second customer, 22-year-old Bill, lives in the neighborhood and spent $3,000 on pizza last year. He responds to your email and orders online. He always gets the loaded meat pizza and picks it up at the store.

Who is the most valuable customer? I don't know. But you need to know for your business, right? When you know profitability by segment, you can then determine how much to invest in acquiring each segment.

And you need to think about how you market to the different audiences based on their actual margin. If Bill starts calling instead of ordering online, or has delivery even half the time, you might see your profits slip.

If you can drive better coupons to the Johnsons based on their individual profitability, get them to place their orders online, or get a few of their neighbors to order so you can spread your delivery costs, the entire profit picture might change.

LTV LESSON THREE

How do you increase your customer margins? First, consider customer share of wallet. Are you getting all the pizza business from certain customers? Can you entice them to spend more per order? Can you convince them to come to you for other meals? McDonald's taught us all a lesson when it introduced its breakfast menu.

Disney has been highlighted in several books for its success in increasing wallet share. Disney realized that although it was getting lots of people to the parks, it was only getting a fraction of the dollars spent. The answer? Open Disney hotels and restaurants. Genius.

It's going to be interesting to follow Starbucks' entry into the music business. Does it need to be as big as Virgin? Of course not, it just has to show increased margin per customer.

Same with Apple. Asking simple questions like: "What is a computer?" Or, "What is software?" opened Apple up to a great new world where it enjoys the highest margin per customer in the business.

What about you? Do you know your share of wallet? Before you can increase it, you need to know where you currently stand.

LTV LESSON FOUR

I'm going to keep saying this: Chances are, you lose money on every new customer. We all know that it is a certain few who are profitable enough to cover the costs of all the losers. Who are they? What do they look like? Can you make sure you hang on to them? How about targeting some of the losers who have characteristics similar to the high value customers early in the relationship in an attempt to move a higher percentage onto the more profitable side of the equation? Of course, there is also the opportunity to convert more into second or third-time buyers.

We once did a study in the dry cleaners market. We found that 89 percent of first-time customers never came back. We also found that customers who came in a minimum of three times stayed more than two years. So what's the short-term goal of a dry cleaner? Get to that third visit!

LTV LESSON FIVE

Before we talk about retention, we need to consider its goal: to make more money and grow the company.

This is where it is so critical to know your customer margins. Often, it is the least profitable customers who perceive the least amount of value from your offering. As a result, you invest a disproportionate amount of time in trying to convince them to stay. Doing so increases your costs customers and decreases your margins. Additionally, it's likely to dilute your focus on the most valuable customers. Companies often resort to special offers to convince this group to stay, which are then offered to the good customers so no one is "left out." This adds no value to the relationship, while hurting profitability.

If you focus on individual customer value, you can't help but want to leverage more relationship marketing. I once heard this analogy using a stolen printer: A business owner comes to the office one morning and finds his $200 printer missing. So he conducts an investigation. He changes the locks and generally there is a lot of angst about the stolen printer. With this attention, he never loses another printer again.

Meanwhile, customers worth a whole lot more than the printer are disappearing from his organization (and yours) every day. That is why the focus of marketing has to be based on building better relationships. View your constituents as if they are assets (like a printer) and you will naturally want to focus more on that relationship.

Case Study

A Real Margin Challenge for a Real Pizza Place

Pizza Place is a chain of neighborhood pizzerias with over 50 locations. After discovering that the average check for delivery orders placed via the online site was 50 cents more than a phone order, and pick-up orders placed online averaged $1.25 more, it was obvious that the company should attempt to move more of its business online to maximize customer margins.

The company decided on a goal of 10 percent of total orders per week as online orders. It first analyzed the online ordering process and categorized online customers into five buckets:

Bucket 1 customers had registered for an online account and asked to receive special offers and updates via email.

Bucket 2 had made their first online transaction.

Bucket 3 customers had purchased again.

Bucket 4 customers had successfully purchased online at least four times.

Bucket 5 customers were designated as the most valuable patrons. Customers reaching this bucket had ordered an average of 17 times a year.

The company was not only smart to identify different buckets, they also set an overall goal for their efforts: reach 7,000 online orders per week. First, they educated their customers on the online ordering process via personalized letters from their president. After seeing an initial boost in online ordering now that more customers knew it was an option, the company decided to launch its new menu and a "Free Pizza for a Year" contest in which subscribers could vote for their favorite new menu item and their favorite local pizzeria via an email survey. Recipients were able to vote on their favorites directly from the email.

Results: 4,000 Online Orders per Week

During the email program, online orders jumped by a whopping 47 percent, to 4,000 orders per week. Even after the contest winner was announced, the spike in sales sustained for four weeks.

The program resulted in $105,000 in new business, which was over 20 times return on the initial investment. Email registrations and online account holders skyrocketed to 58,000, thousands of which completed online transactions to move them into buckets 2, 3, and 4. Bucket 5—the company's most valuable customers—grew to over 12,000 customers, which translates into a hefty $3.6 million in sales per year.

WHAT ARE OTHER MARKETERS THINKING?

In their own words . . .

If email marketing were a dictatorship, everyone would be required to listen to me. Thank goodness, everyone has a right to his or her own thoughts and opinions.

That's why several chapters feature what marketers from all different size organizations and industries have to say about the matters at hand. As you are reading their words, keep in mind what I mentioned at the beginning of the chapter: Nearly any primary goal you come up with is likely the outcome of a great relationship.

WHAT IS MARKETING'S GOAL?

By Stewart Rogers
Director and architect of ISS system, IOS
Blog: http://www.ioutput.com/issblog

According to internationally known marketing guru Brian Norris, "Marketing is the ongoing process of moving people closer to making a decision to purchase, use, follow, refer, upload, download, obey, reject, conform, become complacent to someone else's products, services or values. Simply, if it doesn't facilitate a 'sale' then it's not marketing."

There's a lot of truth in that statement. To add to that, I believe there are only two types of businesses: those that have a sales force, and those that take orders.

For those that have a sales force, regardless of whether the sales cycle is one hour or one year long, and regardless of the value of the sale, they must be in the business of "consultative" or "solution" selling (probe, prove, and close). In that environment, it is marketing's goal to create real opportunities for the sales staff where they can follow up *buyers*. This means that the marketing team needs to qualify every prospect, and email can be a useful tool in that respect. As an aside, if their sales force doesn't need to engage in "solution selling," then they should consider sacking the sales force and start order taking instead!

For those that simply take orders, all the work is done in marketing. For these businesses, it's all about getting the phone to ring or the website to click over, and once again email is a kingpin for twenty-first century B-to-B and B-to-C marketing.

So, from an email marketing standpoint, marketing's goal is to send communications to a prospective client until that prospect is either handed over (fully qualified) to a solution salesperson or until that prospect calls in/visits the website to buy the product or service.

This means that marketing is responsible for a number of separate actions when it comes to email marketing. If they choose to outsource, they need to decide which provider will suit their purposes best. If they choose to keep the process in-house, then they'll be responsible for database management, deliverability testing, email client testing, copywriting, sending, tracking, follow-up, and, if a sales force is involved, prospect handover. It's a big undertaking and not something that can be taken lightly or paid lip service.

Email is also more important to marketing than many people think. One of the many "rules of seven" kicks in quite nicely here. Some people say it takes seven touch points with your prospect before they understand you and your brand well enough to take you seriously. I believe it is worse than that, and that it takes seven touch points with a prospect, through three different media types, before they will really involve you wholeheartedly in their buying cycle.

Sending email is a great way to communicate your message on a regular basis and hit those seven touch points, but you shouldn't ignore old-fashioned direct mail and telephone calls if you really want to build your marketplace. My new rule of "seven times three" means, in reality, you have to get in touch with them 21 times in all! It's tempting to use email on its own because it is a low-cost medium, but making it a part of an overall, multi-media campaign is a much smarter move.

WHAT IS MARKETING'S GOAL?

By John Wall
Producer, M Show Productions
Blog: http://www.themshow.com

Call me biased as a marketer (but not without first testing, please), but marketing has the most difficult goal in the company: We must translate how human needs, emotion, and behavior all interact with whatever it is we're selling. There are usually three areas of marketing that do this (an idea I've stolen and modified a bit from Pragmatic Marketing).

1. *Product marketing:* People who make sure that the next version of the Widget 5000 is one that customers actually want to buy, not something thought up by some insane entrepreneur better locked in a broom closet. This is the "translating the human need" goal.
2. *Marketing communications:* The folks shaping and getting the messages straight and out to the press and public. These people get told the human needs by the product marketing guys and figure out which emotions to invoke.
3. *Lead gen:* The marketers who get the actual names for the sales infantry to engage one-on-one. These are really just Super Salespeople. Instead of fighting one-on-one, they use their weapons against all the prospects at once. This gives sales the ammunition to begin their attack to mold the behavior of the prospects (i.e., get them to buy hundreds of thousands of Widget 5000s).

This is a pretty heavy definition, but I think it works well to explain all of the marketing process to those who want that much depth. It describes what a good marketing machine is. For discussions with people who know nothing about (or have no interest in learning about) marketing, it's simpler to define the Ms.

Before Sergio Zyman (former CMO of Coca-Cola) was rolling with his consulting group (http://www.zyman.com), I had already bought into his argument of marketing being all about the Ms. Classic college Marketing 101 textbook talk about the Ps—marketing is about a good Product, the right Pricing, proper product Placement in the marketplace, Promotion (as in advertising), and some new age ones would throw in People for good tree-hugging measure.

Mr. Zyman contends that it's all about the Ms—Marketing is about MORE: selling more products, more often, to more people, for more money.

I've found this to be very useful as it goes right along with the sales guys and their dreams (brand name jewelry, cars, and other items that marketing people tend not to be hoodwinked by). If "more" sounds shallow, I have a friend who calls it "Creating a life filled with abundance." That sounds better, doesn't it?

CHAPTER 1 REVIEW
- The goal of all marketers should be great relationships.
- Great relationships are the gateway to maximizing customer Lifetime Value (LTV).
- You can build great relationships by treating your constituents in a way that makes them feel appreciated, unique, and valued.
- You cannot be afraid of your constituents. You should always reveal your true self and your expertise, and leverage the information they've provided.
- Pay careful attention to metrics such as cost, revenue per individual, and profit margins.

- Measure profitability with respect to individual constituents, not products.
- Maximize wallet share and profitability by focusing on the customers who already like you and perceive your company as delivering good value.
- Remember that existing customers are much easier to build relationships with and typically cost a lot less than new customers.

CHAPTER 2

IS EMAIL THE PERFECT MARKETING TOOL?

It would be difficult to write this book if I didn't believe that.

The fact of the matter is that the greatness of email is not about email itself. It's about the ability to build relationships. If smoke signals were the best way to build relationships with lots of people, then this book would be about smoke signals. Email just happens to be one of the best mediums to build long-lasting relationships—especially given the constraints that all organizations must deal with.

Ask yourself this question: If you had endless funds, all the time in the world, and a staff with 100 percent consistency, how would you market to your constituents?

If you're like me, you believe that face-to-face meetings are the ideal way to build relationships. Meeting in person means seeing an individual's needs, preferences, and behavior firsthand. And the person you're meeting with is able to understand the same about you—what you stand for, where your values lie, and how sincere you are about building a lasting relationship.

As much as I like face-to-face meetings, they present a real problem when you're talking about an organization with more than a handful of constituents. It isn't scalable. There are only so many people you can meet in a day, and only so many representatives you can hire to handle these additional face-to-face chores. Representatives present additional problems due to expense and consistency. We all know that human capital is expensive, and good human capital is even pricier. The more you try to scale a representative force in order to build relationships, the more costly it becomes. Ultimately, the model doesn't scale, and you must sacrifice the value of true one-to-one relationships with your constituents because of the associated expense.

Consistency is another problem all together. You know how *you* will interact with your constituents when building a great relationship. But do you know how Chris Salesperson will interact with them? Will he be as quick on his feet as you are? As smart? As ready to provide value and answer questions? Unless Chris is a close personal friend of yours, you probably aren't sure. And as you hire more and more people to manage these relationships in your absence, it becomes more and more difficult to maintain consistency. Eventually, you must hire a staff to manage and control all of the people you've already hired to manage relationships for you.

Oh, and did I mention what a pain it is to schedule face-to-face meetings? You check schedules, check your partners' schedules, do a lot of back-and-forth checking, and finally pick a meeting day (only to show up a half hour late due to traffic). The back-and-forth and additional nuances make scheduling meeting time difficult. And therefore, such face-to-face meetings are likely to become inconsistent.

Okay, so we agree that money is an issue, as is consistency. So now how are you going to reach your constituents?

Another way to build relationships is over the phone. Without having to worry about transportation and other logistics that must be factored into face-to-face meetings, you can have several more phone calls in a day. It's also easier to deal with the expense and consistency problems that arise when it comes to in-person meetings. Phone representatives are less expensive than representatives in the field and can typically be located in the same place, which means better control. Marketing and sales managers can manage consistency through shared training, recorded sessions, and internal team meetings.

But in the end, the phone still presents the issue of time constraint. There is still a lot of back-and-forth communication in order to set up a meeting. And once the meeting is scheduled, how many people show up to the call on time? I am continually baffled as to how different time zones can be such a pain point. If you've never missed a call due to time zone confusion, go ahead and pat yourself on the back. You are one of the few and very lucky people who can say that.

So we've considered the good and the bad that comes with live meetings and phone interaction. Now let's compare them to mass marketing tactics such as print, TV, radio, billboard, websites, direct mail, and banner ads. Do any of these marketing tactics enable us to build one-to-one, unique relationships? I'm hoping that you're shaking your head, saying, "No." These tactics may work for branding, but they will not accomplish the types of individual relationships that we want to build.

Let's dig into branding for a minute. Do you believe in the power of it? Before you answer, I suggest that you read what follows.

Maybe you think branding is justified by "increased awareness." My questions for you are: Can you track how much money that awareness translates into? Are you able to measure it? Branding is the most expensive aspect of marketing and the least measurable. It gets marketers wrapped around metrics such as "impressions," which is just a fancy word for how many times someone sees your brand. Do you think that the more your audience sees an untargeted, blast advertisement, the more likely they are to buy? While this might have worked back in the heyday of television, we know this is a broken tactic in the new marketing era.

Despite its lack of trackability, there is one aspect of branding that gets my attention. That aspect is "permission."

Remember your high school football quarterback? Even if he wasn't the best looking guy on the team, he was likely to get a lot of dates. Why? Because the quarterback is a persona. Quarterbacks all over the world have formed a brand. When the quarterback calls to ask you out, you at least know who he is. He has an advantage over that poor unknown calculus whiz, because at the very least, you recognize his title (quarterback). And recognition is part of building a relationship. Ever seen that movie *50 First Dates?* Poor Adam Sandler can't build a relationship with Drew Barrymore because she has amnesia and can't remember who he is. Every day he has to reintroduce himself to Drew Barrymore's character. Branding is essentially recognition that can get you over the, "Wait—who are you?" hump. With recognition in place, you can focus on the activities and conversations that actually build the relationship.

At that, I don't believe that branding is about awareness. It's about consideration. As marketers, we still have to invest in branding activities to drive that initial consideration. Such activities might be a trade event, advertising, public relations, or even community involvement. Although small businesses may struggle to appear large, one great advantage they typically have is the opportunity to get involved locally. On the other side, big companies tend to struggle to appear more "local."

In any event, I'll warn you that branding does not build relationships. There are very few instances where branding is strong enough that people truly develop a relationship with that brand (Google, Apple, and Starbucks all come to mind as exceptions to the rule). It is nearly impossible for anyone to build this kind of loyalty or relationship based on branding alone—although millions (perhaps even billions!) have been spent trying. After all, people are fickle. One day Blockbuster is the greatest thing that's ever happened, and the next day we've moved on to Netflix. Or maybe you prefer your local video store, where the owner greets you by name and recommends new movies based on your past rentals. Ironically, the video store doesn't do any branding activities (can you believe it doesn't have a logo?). But what it lacks in branding, it makes up in relationships.

WHAT DOES ALL OF THIS HAVE TO DO WITH EMAIL MARKETING?

Everything. The reality is that (most) marketers are good people. We want to do the right thing. We would like nothing more than great relationships with all of our constituents. So what keeps us from getting there? Obstacles that include processes, time, money, and people. Traditionally, we've been forced to spend so much time and energy overcoming obstacles in order to execute, we have no time to take a step back, evaluate, and adjust. Even the simplest campaigns and activities require lots of setup, legwork, and manual steps that get in the way of the idea itself. How many times have you found yourself starting down one path and adjusting due to constraints (i.e., we aren't setup to handle that, we can't track that, it's going to take too much time)? Often what you're left with is a fraction of the initial idea or campaign.

This execution problem especially relates to technology. You have the data captured in your customer relationship management (CRM) system. You have an intelligent marketing team that can develop the insight and the strategy needed to drive better relationships. You have the technology needed to execute the campaign. But wait . . . the tools are too difficult to use. In fact, so difficult to use—the opposite of user friendly—you're unable to leverage your data and your strategy.

I have great news for you. When it comes to email marketing tools, the most important element is ease of use. If you can get sophisticated, automated tools into the hands of the marketer, you eliminate the pain associated with execution. This means you now have the time and energy to focus on actual marketing. Ease of use facilitates an incredible amount of change. Marketing becomes faster, more relevant, less expensive, and more valuable. That's why email is the greatest marketing tool in history.

Four Reasons Why Email Is a Phenomenal Marketing Medium

1. Email Is Easy

With the kinds of software and tools available today, it is easy for any organization to develop effective email programs to help build relationships. The best part? The tools are so intuitive, there's no need for technical geniuses. Earlier, we discussed the obstacle and execution pain that typically stands in the way of great marketing. Take traditional marketing, for example. It's slow (there's a reason it's called snail mail). You have to involve all kinds of people, like the printers, post office, IT people, and others. You have to wait . . . and wait . . . and wait . . . before seeing any tangible results.

Email eliminates the extra steps and middlemen who don't add a lot of value and create friction by slowing down the process. And while email marketing tools can be sophisticated, they can still be easy enough to use that marketers can handle a campaign from start to finish.

My philosophy is that if good marketing isn't easy, it doesn't get done. There are only so many hours in a day. Marketers, like anyone else, want to do a good job. But without the right tools, limitations arise. In the past, relevant, data-driven, relationship marketing was easy to plan but difficult to execute. Email makes it easy, without sacrificing quality of activities or campaigns.

2. Email Is Inexpensive

I mean, really, really inexpensive. There is no marketing medium that is less expensive than email. Print, television, and telephone can range from a few dollars per touch to several thousands or even millions (think of those Super Bowl commercials). The price of an email can be as inexpensive as a penny or less. This means that organizations of any size save money over traditional mass marketing tools. For small organizations, email is a great equalizer. You don't need a monstrous budget. To be successful with this medium, all you need is desire.

3. Email Is Interactive

Now we're getting to the real magic of email. Interaction. You can track email. You can see exactly where an individual clicks within an email (and which links are ignored). You can measure overall effectiveness and integrate email with other systems in order to measure actual behavior (purchases, etc.). In the interactive world, this is equivalent to *listening*.

In a face-to-face conversation, you can see if you're holding someone's attention. Is your audience rolling their eyes or glancing at their watches? Or are they smiling and nodding enthusiastically? Email interaction gives you the same kind of insight. That sort of trackability is what makes it very different from a postcard or television. Best of all, with email, your constituents can talk back to you. It's as easy as hitting the reply button. When was the last time you were able to talk back to a commercial and have your voice be heard? Exactly. You can even take email interaction to the next level by adding forms and surveys.

4. Email Is Data Driven

A lot of marketers don't know what to make of data. They understand that customer data is good to have, but they aren't sure how to use it. Maybe it's too time consuming to leverage the data. Or expensive. One blast print insert is much cheaper and easier to execute than 50 versions based on profile data, isn't it?

With email, you can easily use data to tailor a unique message and dialogue for the individual recipient. Data is an absolutely critical part of relationship building. You need data to show that you recognize uniqueness, to prove that you are listening, and to become more and more relevant with your messaging over time. Marketers should be focused on gathering data at every customer touch point. Touch points can be anything from web interactions, to phone calls, to sales, direct mail, or even over the counter. Retailers focus on point-of-sale (POS) systems. Restaurants use reservation systems, and businesses have CRM systems. The key to email is that it makes all of this data actionable.

To recap, email is easy to use, inexpensive, interactive, and data driven. The combination means a really powerful marketing tool that makes great relationship building possible. And remember, aren't great relationships with our constituents what all of us are striving for?

I want to reiterate that email marketing is not just for the big players. Many small organizations think that marketing requires a budget the size of Mount Everest. It doesn't. It requires the right tools and mediums. Although many large organizations have received attention for email accomplishments, smaller players may actually have an advantage here.

EMAIL IS A GREAT EQUALIZER—SIZE AND BUDGET REALLY DON'T MATTER

According to an article from *eMarketer:*

In the past, small companies could never hope to compete with the *Fortune* 100 in terms of direct marketing dollars. But compared to other forms of direct marketing (e.g., direct mail and telemarketing), email is extremely inexpensive. In other words, the mom-and-pop convenience store now has a potent marketing tool to compete with the huge conglomerate at the strip mall.

The key to email's power, particularly at the local level, is that it is targeted and personal. Indeed, no marketing communications medium exists that is more targetable, customizable, and flexible than email. That is why email is revolutionizing direct marketing. Email direct marketing, when done correctly, can overcome the limitations of traditional direct marketing by offering limitless targeting ability at pennies per email and allowing marketers to have a one-to-one conversation with each of their customers.

With proper targeting, tracking tools and a carefully built opt-in list, email can be highly personalized to the needs of individual customers. Communications sent on behalf of companies from messaging solution providers can be targeted and customized using sophisticated database marketing techniques. The technology can capture and track individual responses throughout the campaign, "learn" more about customers from response and purchase behavior, and refine customer profiles for future communications.

Packaged email-marketing software and outsourced email-marketing services leverage customer and CRM databases, allowing companies to create and send highly targeted and customized email campaigns for maximum response. For personalizing messages, these programs not only use standard mail merge operations, but can also make all or part of the entire content of marketing messages conditional on one or some database attributes, such as the interests, transactional behavior or personal characteristics of list members. Dynamically assembled email based on past purchase and response profiles promises to bring marketers closer than ever before to one-on-one marketing capability.

It seems that with email marketing, we may finally be approaching that heralded goal of one-to-one marketing. This has been bruited about in marketing circles for some time but, as with many great ideas, it was more talk than reality. But now the technology is in place to bring this to fruition. And it appears that small businesses will be leading the way.

One other important aspect to keep in mind is that nearly everyone uses email. It is practically universal, meaning that your constituents are likely to accept email, know how to use it, and like it. Contrary to what you might have heard, email engagement remains consistently high relative to other media. Sure, people hate irrelevant junk and spam, but if the marketer does her job correctly, the email is well received and appreciated. People still get excited when they log in to find an email from Mom, don't they? That's because the message is targeted (e.g., Hi Cindy, it's Mom. I remembered that recipe for the pie you liked so much.). It is from someone they want to hear from. It includes something of value. You should strive for your constituents to react to your marketing messages the same way that they react to emails from dear friends and family.

Case Studies

Case Study 1: Start Small and Move Quickly

An insurance company needed to quickly communicate with its 400+ annuity brokers in an attempt to generate new contracts. Rather than rely on the phone—which could possibly take months to personally reach out to support each broker—the company knew that email would be more time friendly and a great way to offer support brochures and documents covering a new "10% Commission to age 85" program. The company worked with an agency that refused to expand any other marketing budgets until the initial investment of $8,000 (for the entire email platform and services associated with the program at hand) was exceeded in ROI.

Results: ROI of 200 Percent and Sales of $1,000,000

Within a mere 60 days, the campaign generated ROI of 200 percent, with $1,000,000 in sales from nine new contracts. The success enabled the company to present a business case for co-op marketing funds from other insurance companies they represented. With a fast moving, result-producing (and trackable) program under its belt, the company was able to easily expand the investment for future email programs.

Case Study 2: It's Interactive . . . and It's Going to Save Money?

A major convention and visitors bureau was skeptical when their agency said that an email brochure would not only help with interactivity . . . it would actually save money. The organization was willing to try anything due to the fact that if a potential visitor were bitten with the travel bug, he'd have to wait up to *eight weeks* to receive requested information (talk about snail mail)! By the time the brochure had arrived, either the trip was over or the desire was gone.

With help from its agency, the convention and visitors bureau set out to pare the current eight-week time frame down to near real time by developing a way for visitors to create their own e-brochure. On the organization's website, tourists could click on a "Free Guides" icon, where they were given the choice of ordering printed brochures (uh, no thanks) or creating their own instant e-brochure. To create the customized e-brochure, the visitor simply checked boxes for different interest categories, such as shopping, outdoor/adventure, arts and performances, and golf. After entering an email address and zip code, a custom e-brochure was emailed—within minutes.

Results: 70 Percent of Recipients Request More Info

Of those who received the e-brochure, 70 percent clicked to request more information. The results indicate that the convention and visitors bureau is now catching potential visitors at the appropriate stage in the cycle. Not only is the e-brochure delivered at the right time, it's easily customized based on the individual visitor's preferences, it's interactive, and has reduced printing and postage costs. Due to the success of the e-brochure, the bureau immediately began brainstorming additional programs for meeting planners.

Case Study 3: Handling Time-Sensitive Content

No one likes to be considered "old news." Especially not a company whose bread-and-butter offering is a subscription-based newsletter detailing the performance of seven sector funds and offering recommendations based on performance.

The company's paying subscribers, who just two years ago were willing to patiently wait to receive this weekly communication via fax and direct mail, were getting antsy. Back in the old days, the company sent raw investment data in a PDF file to a printing service. A few days later, the documents were sent to subscribers via snail mail. Time-sensitive investing information took days to reach subscribers, severely decreasing its relevancy and usefulness. Furthermore, the communication was full of hard-to-decipher data.

With the assistance of an agency, the company was able to forever alter the way these communications reached subscribers. The team was able to deliver the time-sensitive email updates in minutes, not days. And even more importantly, the quality of the content remained intact.

How did the process change? Every Thursday at 6:30 P.M. (when the market closes), the individual behind the company posts recommendations to the agency's FTP site. That data is then converted into usable HTML tables and graphs and PDF documents. Working from standard templates, the team arranges and tests the email, while simultaneously updating website content. An email draft is then sent back to the company for review and approval. After a few minor tweaks, the message is sent.

Results: Emails Deployed within 40 Minutes of Market Close

Within 40 minutes of the market close every Thursday, subscribers receive their email packed with timely, relevant investor information. Yes, 40 minutes start to finish. Compare that to the earlier process, and it's easy to see why the company now sustains 90 percent renewal rates due to satisfied subscribers.

WHAT ARE OTHER MARKETERS THINKING?

In their own words . . .

IS EMAIL THE PERFECT MARKETING TOOL?

By Duncan Shand
Founder, InsideOut
Blog: http://www.iout.co.nz

One of the most overlooked marketing tools has to be the simple email. It's fast and cheap to deploy; it's instant and easily absorbed by the consumer. Just as email has developed over the past 10 years from a novelty to something that we can't live without, over the past 5 years marketers have moved to include email marketing as part of their budgets.

There are a number of different ways you can deploy email marketing, from a simple, offer-based execution to a very complex, segmented campaign. The beauty is that you can start with an easy, basic program and develop it over time to make it more efficient. There are a surprisingly large number of businesses that still don't take full advantage of this tool, but the good thing is that it's easy to get going.

One of the biggest drivers of email marketing is its return on investment. DoubleClick's Touchpoints III survey (http://www.doubleclick.com/us/knowledge_central/) underlines the importance of email and online marketing as part of the marketing mix. The influence your website has on sales is becoming increasingly recognized. In 8 out of 10 industry sectors, the company website was in the top four resources used for research before an eventual purchase. Email, of course, is the link for your customer to find your website.

However, email is more than just a delivery device to bring people to your website. It offers the chance to keep in touch, to interact, to tell a story, to introduce an idea; you can use it to build loyalty for your brand. Coupled with a good database, you have the potential to segment you customers down to an audience of one, creating emails that are not only personalized, but that deliver content tailored to their needs and preferences.

Email, unlike most marketing activities, is completely trackable. That means you'll know what's working and what isn't. You can test different subject lines, different headlines, different offers. Test on a small subset, see what works best, and then roll it out to the whole target market so you can fine-tune your messages and work to increase your response rates and sales results.

And what other marketing media can you deploy at a cost of about 2 cents per person? What else can be spread so easily? What else can be measured and tracked right through to a sale? What else allows you to personalize the content right down to an audience of one? What else gives such a fast response? Email is truly unique in that if fulfills all of these needs.

One thing you need to be careful about is the fact that *because* email is so cheap and easy to use, it can be prone to over use. You can burn your list by sending too many emails that aren't carefully segmented and lack a clear purpose. Be sure you manage your email database as an asset, respect it, and nurture it.

So is email the perfect marketing tool? In many respects, you could make a very strong argument that it is. However, you must manage the whole process. Email may be the best tool in your toolbox, but make sure you use the right tool for the job at hand.

IS EMAIL THE PERFECT MARKETING TOOL?

By John Wall
Producer, M Show Productions
Blog: http://www.themshow.com

Of course not.

I'm looking at my email account right now—5,000 emails in the spam folder. If there's anything in there that's important, there's no chance I'm going to see it. Spam trapped down there will never influence me in any way.

But despite email's warts . . . . it is the best marketing thing going. The results are the marketer's fantasy. Anyone who has launched a campaign has sat in front of the monitor wasting too much time watching the percentages creep up . . . watching to see if the Champion template will continue to reign or if the new Challenger has finally stumbled upon the magical formula.

There is one thing about email that makes it stand apart from any other marketing activity (and that is a testament to the power of the medium): Every single marketer I know, and myself included, freely admits that the final click to send out an email is the most terrifying, pants-crapping moment they have ever faced in their career as a marketer. Usually when you do a print campaign, so many people have seen the blue line proofs, everyone is glad to see it crammed into a FedEx tube and sent off to the printer. Live video and audio usually have a whole crew of engineers, and most of them have fallen into a lazy habit and groove of perfection through hard won experience.

In contrast, there is the lone marketer, sitting at his desk and beginning to sweat over the last click. You're as terrified as if you were a sniper with an enemy in your sites, knowing that at the best you are firing into the crowd, at worst you are really going to screw something up. At least now with web-based tools you can do it from the comfort of your cube.

And yet this fear is not a bad thing. How many among us would admit, even under oath, the times when (in a fit of panic) we've realized that something is just not right with the list—maybe the wrong test group that would tank the whole campaign data, a bad link in the message rendering everything worthless, or worse yet, a forgotten suppression list. Of course, we discover these things as our finger is creeping over "send."

After all is fixed and the final click comes, there's still the panic, even more if you get a weird message or phone call in the first hour. But soon your own message comes through, the clicks and conversions start to show up, and all is well in the world.

GAZE INTO OUR CRYSTAL BALL: THOUGHTS REVEALED THROUGH EMAIL READING

By Sarah Eaton
Managing Editor, BeTuitive Publishing
Blog: http://betuitive.blogs.com/betuitive

Imagine you're in possession of a crystal ball that, when you gaze into it, allows you to tell just where your customers and prospects are in their buying cycle. You would know what they were thinking and when they were thinking it. Sales would be child's play.

Crystal balls and other clairvoyant methods aside, you can apply the following ideas to make your sales proactive and savvy:

- Identify the behavior of your prospects and customers when they are early in their decision-making process.
- Figure out a way to identify that behavior before your competitors do.
- Build a relationship by giving your prospects or customers something of value—usually this means information or consulting in the B-to-B sphere. Then you can count on the strength of your relationship to tip the scales in your favor when the time comes for your customers and prospects to buy.

Challenge: Discovering your customers' and prospects' interests through a systematic, scalable, noninvasive, legal, and value-added methodology.

Fact: Reading patterns are a great leading indicator of future purchasing.

Solution: Trend analysis of what topics your e-newsletter subscribers are reading.

Changes in reading behavior are precipitated by a number of things, including shifts in interest and trends, budget approval, pain, and need. Just as you interpret complex signals sent by body language and expression in order to understand and nurture your personal relationships, you can learn to be intuitive about your customers' needs by observing their reading patterns.

For instance, I have a pattern I follow when I'm buying a new car. Three months before I make a purchase, I'll start going to auto websites, buying car magazines, and doing initial sweeps of lots and showrooms. As I gather more information and feel more secure about my intended purchase, I'll do test drives and narrow the field. I'm not going to buy the car on impulse, or within the first couple of days of my search. Because it's a major purchase, I need information and time until I feel I'm making exactly the right decision.

These patterns are generally the same across the board for purchasing. The first step is seeking out information in the form of the written word. Think of a human resources administrator who is changing insurance carriers for her company, which has well over a thousand employees. The first step is research. She scours the Web for information, signing up for newsletters, reading articles, and making side-by-side comparisons. Only after she feels secure in her research does she begin making calls to potential new companies to discuss her needs.

Question: What will happen if one of those companies is aware of her research activities and can proactively contact her?

1. The company knows which specific aspects of a policy are important to her because they know what she has been reading.
2. The company is able to send her extra information in the form of email and invitations to informative webinars (helping her with her research).

As a result, she will see this company as one that recognizes her needs and provides her with valuable information. She will see them as contenders for her business. That company has the edge over the others that don't receive the benefits of trend analysis.

Email Is Dead! Long Live Email!

By Patsi Krakoff, Psy.D.
President, Krakoff Wakeman Associates, Inc.
Blog: http://www.coachezines.com

Email is dead. We can still use it to communicate with one another on an individual basis, but as far as content is concerned—RSS holds infinitely more value and promise. . . . I'll likely continue to "do" email newsletters.

—Chris Pirillo, interviewed by Lee Odden

Portrayal of the demise of email reminds me of the British chant whenever there is a death of a monarch, "The King Is Dead! Long Live the King!"

Let's get real. In response to the above interview, email marketing is not dead. It's just evolving rapidly and only the strong will survive.

In February 2004, Jakob Nielsen reported that a study of email marketing showed that targeted e-newsletters continue to show strength:

> E-newsletters that are informative, convenient, and timely are often preferred over other media. However, a new study found that only 11% of newsletters were read thoroughly, so layout and content scanability are paramount.
>
> Email newsletters continue to be one of the most important ways to communicate with customers on the Internet. Newsletters build relationships with users. . . . Still, users are highly critical of newsletters that waste their time, and often ignore or delete newsletters that have insufficient usability.

The bottom line? Improving the quality of your content will ensure your email marketing and newsletters survive, get opened, get read, and work for your business.

Get Opened, Get Read . . . and Get Found on the Web

How do you increase the chances that your email messages will get read, get click-throughs, and work for your business?

Just like all other forms of communication, in the past 10 years, email content must deliver promised benefits to the recipient—quickly, clearly, and in a way that entertains while informing. Now that's a lot to live up to!

In addition, online content must also meet two additional requirements to be effective:

1. It helps elevate your search engine rankings.
2. It attracts qualified traffic and holds the attention of your prospects and customers (Jonathan Kranz, Kranz Communications, www.kranzcom.com).

To be clear, online content can refer to any web-based page published on the Internet (blogs, website pages, articles in directories, newsletter archives). Email marketing refers to those messages that are emailed, as in e-newsletters. In order for e-newsletters or other emailed promotions or messages to be effective, they must also be published online—on your website, in web-based press releases, in article directories, on blogs—anywhere your content remains posted "live" on the Web. This is the way a business e-newsletter gets Google "juice" and contributes to your business getting found more easily by clients and customers. One of the biggest mistakes professionals make is not posting their e-newsletters on their website or blog. If an email newsletter isn't posted on the Web, it disappears and has no lasting value.

As to the second point—attracting qualified, targeted traffic—this comes from being strategic about keywords in your titles, subheadings, and body of the content. To be effective, you must spell out who you are writing for, what problem you are solving, and how your visitors can get access to your solutions.

Common Sense, Uncommon Practice

But everybody knows that already, don't they? Write to solve a problem or relieve readers' pain, show your expertise, create trust, and then leave them with a compelling offer.

Then why do so many e-newsletters and email messages miss the boat?

I started doing newsletters for other executive coaches and business consultants in 1998 (www.CustomizedNewsletters .com). At that time, most professionals preferred to mail out a printed newsletter. In 2000, we began offering an email version, cutting down costs of printing and mailing. And in 2003, we stopped offering printed newsletters altogether, instead offering plain text, PDF files and HTML formatted e-zines. Those clients who still use PDFs like to print them out for workshops and mailings.

Recently there has been a decline in PDF newsletter requests and an increase in HTML formats among my clients. Another change has been for shorter content: from 2000-word to 1,000-word, and now to 600- to 700-word lengths.

The key to writing good e-content is to make the most sense with the fewest possible words, while making an impression/connection with potential clients—to the point that they respond to your call to action.

What Are the New Rules for Successful e-Content?

Here are a few new rules shaping effective email content today:

- *Keep an eye on headlines (they're more crucial than ever).* A cleverly crafted headline (or subject line for email) will determine whether your email gets opened and read. Headlines appealing to a reader's desires on an emotional level will be more effective. "Insider secrets," or, "5 tips you can apply now to save time/money/energy," and "What they don't want you to know," are examples of titles that work because they are compelling. They offer a promise to solve a problem. They leave the reader with great curiosity. They seduce the reader to open and read the email.
- *Use keywords in the headline.* Use them again in the first paragraph, and repeat several times in the body of the content. When somebody types keywords into a search

engine looking for information, will your content be found?

- *Keep content length short and to the point.* Once you write your message, review it and delete as many words as possible. Ask, "So what?" at the end of each sentence. Keep the focus on your core intention for that email message.
- *Use bulleted lists to provide readers a means to scan your points.* Remember the Jakob Neilsen survey that showed only 11 percent read an email thoroughly? Make your messages user-friendly. Oh, and use keywords in both your bullet points and your subheadings.
- *Use stories to make it real to readers.* Use your own experiences, or those of your clients. One tactic is to use your own mistakes and then describe a lesson learned. This is because you want readers to trust you.
- *Write with readers in mind.* Focus on providing solutions to their pain.
- *Demonstrate a clear purpose.* Each email should have one intention only. One subject, one call to action.
- *Use statistics, testimonials, case studies, and expert references to support your point.* Never forget that readers have sensitive BS antennae and a finger poised on the delete key. Don't waste their time.
- *Make a clear offer.* Be transparent and up-front. Give them a "reason why" and a reason to act now. Whether you are selling a product or a service, help reduce the reader's fear of risk. Stand behind what you offer.
- *Go easy on the hype.* A good tip is to read your content out loud. If it sounds like a commercial, rewrite it to sound like part of a conversation. Be friendly, yet professional. Overuse of power words will trigger the delete finger.

Do You Make These Common Mistakes?

Out of the hundreds of email promotions and newsletters I review each week, here are the most common errors:

- Either too personal, informal, and friendly, or—too formal, too impersonal, with too much jargon or corporate-speak
- Too much content, too many topics, and multiple calls to action
- Boring content, nothing compelling in the subject line or headline
- Talking about the person or company too much, with no regard for what's in it for readers
- Too much hype, too many bolded or all-cap words, aggressively calling for action with no real benefit spelled out for readers
- Not enough compelling reason to do anything other than scan, read, and delete . . . in some cases, no call to action whatsoever

Remember, your email must inform, educate, entertain, and give something of value to your reader. Otherwise, you are taking up valuable time and energy from your readers who will eventually delete and unsubscribe.

Your content should work to get you found on the Web, by the strategic placement of keywords, and posting your content on the Web.

CHAPTER 2 REVIEW

- Face-to-face meetings and phone calls are great relationship builders but are restrictive due to time, monetary, and consistency constraints.
- Branding activities (typical of traditional media) are a good way to receive initial consideration for your product or service but are not relationship building tools due to their mass messaging.
- Email is an incredibly powerful marketing tool because it is easy, cheap, interactive, and data driven.
- Email is a great equalizer. Budget, organization size, or staff size mean very little. The most critical factor is the desire to leverage what you know about your constituents in order to drive targeted messages.

CHAPTER 3

WHAT'S WRONG WITH EMAIL?

Even the best things in life have drawbacks. Maybe you take a vacation but have loads of work waiting for you when you get back. Or maybe you can afford a luxury car but are forced to spend more money on gas. I know you get my point. While email is the greatest marketing tool of all time, unfortunately, there's a four-letter word that can skew its effectiveness: spam (the technical term for unsolicited commercial email, not the tinned meat kind).

Before we get into further detail on email and spam, I'd like us to first cover two mass marketing tactics: reach and frequency.

Reach marketing refers to how many different individuals you can touch. The marketing theory is that the more people you touch, the more successful you will be. That's why mass marketers look for advertising with the highest traffic counts possible. Obviously, this is what's made prime time television such a valuable property. By putting your commercials on television, you're assured they are going to be seen by millions of people. But we should probably change the last part of the sentence to: You're assured they are going to be *shown* to millions of people, and those who pay attention will actually *see* your commercials.

If you really have a big budget, you can afford to run these ads more often and on more channels. You'll be everywhere, which means your audience will always be thinking about you, right? In other words, you'll be able to increase the frequency of your marketing, which refers to how often your ads are shown to your audience. The theory here is that the more often you hit people with your advertisement, the more likely they are to follow through on the desired action. So if a viewer saw your commercial five times within a week, the assumption would be that the individual is five times as likely to respond as someone who saw the commercial only once.

When email hit the scene in the late 1990s, organizations soon realized its potential as a marketing tool. It quickly became the preferred medium for internal communication and crept into external campaigns. Unfortunately, since most of these marketers had reach and frequency techniques engrained in their minds, they relied on these same tactics with email marketing. Organizations looked at email as if it were simply another form of cheap paper. Rather than trying to blanket the world with commercial messages and direct mail, which cost *dollars* per touch point, suddenly you could spend pennies using email. That meant huge opportunities for reach and frequency.

The most incredible part is that reach and frequency tactics actually worked with email. People engaged with email. It was immediate, new, and exciting. It enabled engagement like never before. Unfortunately, another term hit the scene shortly after the preliminary success of email as a marketing tool. You know the word I'm coming back to: spam.

While consumers were busy getting angry about the unsolicited emails filling their inboxes (and Internet service providers [ISPs] such as Google and Yahoo tried to figure out how to combat it), another type of spam emerged.

This spam actually came from "legitimate" marketers who never considered themselves spammers. The result is known as "permission spam." Permission spam encompasses both explicit opt-in and implied opt-in, where an organization assumes if you have a relationship, you want to hear from them via email. And although a relationship does exist in the case of permission spam, it doesn't prevent these emails from qualifying as junk. Why? Because they are completely irrelevant messages that bring little or no value to the recipient.

A great example of permission spam is most airline email. I travel frequently, which means I've accumulated lots of points with several airlines. I'm like most people in that I always fly out of the same airport, which is near my home in Indiana. Every week (around Wednesday), I get an email from my airline offering a weekend escape. These weekend escapes are last minute flights with empty seats. The airline assumes that since I have flown with them before, I'll be open to hearing about one of those seats. The unfortunate part is that these are all trips they should know I'm not going to take. Why? Because they don't originate from my hometown. Do they really think I'm going to drive to Massachusetts to catch a flight to Texas?

So what do I do when I receive airline emails? I ignore them. I've already decided that the messages are irrelevant to me. When the airline actually does send an email that's of some value to me, I'll miss it because the relationship is ruined. I haven't unsubscribed because it's more fun to write or blog about all of the horrible deals I keep getting (and hope that someone at those airlines takes note). This results in a missed opportunity on both sides.

The example brings up another potential email drawback, which is the tendency to focus on campaigns rather than relationships. The purpose of a campaign is to convince people to buy or do something. If enough people take action, you offset the cost of the campaign and drive a high return on investment. The purpose of a relationship is to maximize Lifetime Value.

We know that the weekly airline emails are intended to be campaigns, not relationship builders, right? The airline's goal is to sell a certain amount of flights, although they have nothing to do with the individual recipient. If the goal was a relationship, they would send offers that each individual was likely to care about rather than the same laundry list of flight combinations. That's why airline email epitomizes reach and frequency campaigns. The more recipients, and the more times they see an offer, the more likely they are to sell. At least that's what the airline thinks. And the campaign is cheap. Little expense and effort are involved with batching up a list, cranking out an email, and blasting it out to everyone in the database.

SO WHAT'S THE BIG PROBLEM WITH FREQUENCY AND REACH CAMPAIGNS?

Maybe they make money in the short-term, but they sabotage long-term relationships by ignoring the opportunity to talk to the appropriate individual about the appropriate things. In Chapter 2, we didn't do lessons in short-term customer value. No, we did five lessons on customer Lifetime Value. Too often, frequency and reach campaigns reach near-term goals at the expense of long-term relationships.

How can airlines improve their campaigns? (Okay, I know I'm picking on airlines here. But they are an easy target, because they strike me as one of the industries most afraid of having a real relationship with their customers. And they have a lot of potential for improvement due to the nature of dependency that frequent flyers have on them to fulfill a need). Here are my suggestions for how airlines can improve their email marketing efforts. What suggestions would you add to the list? Which of these strategies might work for your email marketing program?

How to Improve Airline Emails

- *Send me trips that depart from where I actually live.* Enough already with the weekend getaways and Thursday specials that I can't use. You know where I live (Indianapolis), so how about an email with a special deal from the Indianapolis airport to Cancun, rather than Los Angeles to Cancun? Or even worse, I've seen deals from El Paso to Kansas City!

  Imagine if airlines only spoke when they had something relevant to say. Sure, we might talk less frequently, but I would care about what they were saying. This one's a no-brainer that may actually compel me to take more spontaneous trips.
- *Apologize for delays.* When you're late to a lunch meeting, you probably apologize. It's simple human decency, both for personal relationships and with respect to business. Airlines, you

know what flights I'm on. You know when those flights get delayed. You know whether I've been inconvenienced or not. Apologize, please. It is a simple gesture (a courtesy, actually) that will be appreciated.

- *Thank me.* Every once in a while, it would be nice to see a note to the effect of: "Hey, Chris. I noticed that you've flown our airline five times this month. Thanks a lot for your business. You're a very valued customer. Is there anything else we can do for you?"

- *Ask me questions.* A database is going to tell the airline that I typically take brief trips lasting a day or two. I also like taking longer family trips that may not be reflected in a particular airline's data. If they asked some questions about my broad vacation habits (i.e., how many other people I would travel with, where I'd like to go), they may find some cross-sell opportunities that interest me.

- *Help me use my banked points.* How about a few suggestions? If I fill out a survey and an airline now knows that I have a wife and four children, why not make suggestions for them to accompany me to a specific destination where I've already booked a flight? I love taking my kids on business trips. Airlines should drive perceived value by reminding me that it's an option.

Truth be told, there is a lot of bad email out there. That's the biggest drawback, in my opinion. Email is so accessible and inexpensive, it can be abused by both spammers and trustworthy organizations. We know the signs of bad email because we all experience it. What are your least favorite emails? Why do you dislike them? Have you taken the time to unsubscribe? Think about these questions and answers with respect to your own email marketing efforts.

In fact, there is a lot of email, period. How many emails do you receive to your inbox every day? Just think—as an email marketer, you are essentially competing with several other emails in your audience's inbox. How do you get noticed? How do you compel someone to pay your organization ongoing attention? Email can present a catch 22 at times: It is so easy to execute, it takes very little time to get a message out the door; it is so easy to execute, it is very easy to throw a thoughtless message together and get it out the door. Quantity means nothing. Quality of your messages means everything.

I encourage you to free yourself of the word "campaign." I know, I know. It's the hundredth thing I've asked you to do, and we're only three chapters in. But by forgetting your campaign orientation, you'll broaden your focus and naturally begin thinking of email as the powerful relationship building tool that it is.

You may be wondering how you'll know whether your email recipients find your messages relevant (or if they perceive you as a permission spammer). One of email's biggest strengths is its precise trackability. We're ready to tackle our next chapter on subscriber engagement, which is your key to understanding how your constituents view your email.

Before moving on, I'll leave you with some very basic tips that will help you triumph over spam and permission spam. We'll get into a lot more detail in a separate chapter, but this will be a great foundation to build on.

WHAT ARE OTHER MARKETERS THINKING?
In their own words . . .

STAY IN THE INBOX

By Chip House
Vice President, Marketing Services, ExactTarget
Blog: http://etdeliverability.typepad.com

Chris asked me the best way to make sure your mail doesn't look like spam. Well, first, you should make sure it *isn't* spam. You can do so by getting explicit opt-in permission. Then, the next best thing you can do is avoid things that make your email look like spam. Of the 15,825 spam emails I've received in my personal email account in the past week (really), they all violate one (or all) of these five guidelines:

1. *Keep the "from" address consistent.* It shouldn't change every time you do a mailing. There's nothing wrong with maintaining different "from" addresses for different newsletters. But if you change your address with every send, it won't do any good for recipients to add you to their address book. You're denying recipients the opportunity to whitelist you.
2. *Is the message clearly from your company?* Are the recipients going to recognize the person or company in the "from" address? If you're not sure, you could have a problem. A lot of spam has forged "from" addresses that try to look like you're receiving a one-to-one email. Make sure the "from" address and subject line work together to clearly indicate you and your brand.
3. *Don't tell people your mail is not spam.* If they remember you, they'll know it's not spam. If they don't remember you, they'll think you're lying. If you do this, your mail is going to be junked MORE often because you just made your message look like spam.
4. *Use a spell-checker.* Spam is often riddled with typos. Besides making your message look unprofessional, some spam filters actually notice misspelled words and will increase your spam score because of them.
5. *Don't add an old or bad list into your good, clean email database.* If you do, your bounce rates and spam complaint rates will jump. ISPs will notice. You might get away with it . . . for a day or two. Then your mail gets filtered (or blocked), and you'll have a deliverability problem to deal with.

The things that help get your emails to the inbox are necessary to *keep* your emails arriving to the inbox. Keep in mind, getting to the inbox is a *journey,* not a *destination.*

What Is Wrong with Email?

By Richard Gibson
Chair, Email Marketing Council's Benchmarking Hub
Commercial Director, Direct Marketing Association (UK)
Limited & RSA Direct
Website: www.dma.org.uk

With so much written about the success of email marketing, does it help to summarize the disadvantages?

Yes, but only if it can help us learn to become more effective email marketers. So what is wrong with email, exactly? Has there ever been a more successful channel to communicate en mass with a group of customers? Part of the reason why email is so successful is the low cost, but it also has several implications for email marketers.

Fact: The volume of email is rising. There are several reasons why:

- The low cost, general effectiveness, and higher adoption rates mean that more companies are using email and sending more campaigns.
- Customers choose email because *they* often prefer email over direct mail and phone calls.
- Finally, there is spam.

Add all of these elements together into one big pot (inbox) and it becomes apparent that while on one level, the volume is a significant issue in itself, the more important issue associated with the increase in volume is the ability to remain relevant.

If your email marketing program consists of sending the same message to all segments of your customer database when *you* want to promote your goods and services, then you will always be trying to add volume to your customer and prospect list as opt-out rates increase.

Every time a marketing email gets sent to a customer or prospect, we as email marketers have the chance to learn something, to make improvements, and to decipher data in our reports. The disadvantage of not making our marketing messages relevant to the recipient is more than just the initial annoyance factor. Can you as a marketer quantify the brand damage for sending an irrelevant message to your list? Can you quantify the potential loss of revenue over your customers' lifetimes if they unsubscribe? Do you know the cost to acquire a similar customer?

So what is *wrong* with email? So long as email marketing is viewed as a cheap means of communication, the amount of irrelevant email will continue to rise. Without proper effort invested in this medium, marketers risk adding to email volume rather than delivering a relevant communication.

WHAT'S WRONG WITH EMAIL?

By Colin Delany
Founder and Editor, E.politics
Blog: http://www.epolitics.com

What's wrong with email? Let's look at some of its intrinsic weaknesses and some ways you may be tripping yourself up (problems that you can avoid, if you're careful).

- *Email is intrusive.* Yes, email is intrusive, which is both a strength and a weakness. Intrusiveness is a strength in that your messages demand attention from the recipient, but it's a weakness because a constant barrage of emails in the inbox can be very annoying. As I'll discuss next, you need to make sure that your list members WANT to receive your messages. "Delete" is a very easy button to push. Because of email's in-your-face nature, the effects of small mistakes can be greatly magnified.

- *Legitimate email can be confused with spam.* Spam is the enemy of everyone who uses email as a communications tool, for business, for politics, or just to keep in touch with family and friends. At many companies and organizations, more than 95 percent of the messages hitting the email server are spam. Even with the best filtering software, this volume of garbage can manage to gum up the works.

  As an email marketer, spam can stop you in your tracks in two ways. First, spam filters seem to take a fiendish delight in diverting email newsletters. The characteristics of legitimate email newsletters and marketing offers are very close to their unauthorized cousins, and spam-blocking software is always going to have trouble telling the two apart.

  Second, many people simply get annoyed at the volume of unsolicited messages they receive and come to see ALL commercial email as spam—even those marketing lists that they initially requested to be on (assuming they remember that they even signed up in the first place. Consider the fact that people often forget which lists they join). You may easily lose subscribers through no fault of your own.

- *Oversaturation.* I am on dozens of email lists—some related to my professional life, some purely for pleasure, and some as a result of products I've bought in the past. I don't think I'm alone. The longer you're online, the more lists you're going to end up on. Eventually, it can become too many emails to manage. Even if the message explosion doesn't force you to actively unsubscribe, you're likely to start deleting unread mail.

How Do You Avoid These Issues?

Don't "look" like spam, both in terms of your content and in terms of your technology. Make sure that your content is relevant to your list members. If you send them things they aren't interested in, they're going to unsubscribe or delete. Keep them involved! Give them things to do—link to games to play, puzzles to solve, articles to read, product discounts to use, and videos to watch.

Above all, make sure that your content is on target. Your readers care about what THEY care about, not necessarily what YOU want them to care about. Play on their needs and interests, and you're much more likely to be read. Finally, don't annoy your subscribers by sending messages too frequently. Your frequency should be enough to keep your relationship with your readers intact, but not so often that you burn them out.

Now for the technology: Work with a good email provider to make sure that you stay off the email blacklists. I can't stress how important a good technology company is. And if you do end up being blocked, immediately work with the watchdog organizations to clear your name.

Is Email on a Long-Term Decline?

According to recent studies, college-age Internet users regard email as a tool to use when contacting adults for officialdom, not for communicating among peers. These users tend to use Instant Messaging, social networking sites such as MySpace, and cell phone text messages. To them, email is about as cool as starched collars.

As more and more of this generation of online users graduates and moves into the workplace, will they convert to email users or will they keep their old habits? If email becomes equivalent to a certified letter and not a tool for personal communication, email marketing may gradually die. I predict that this isn't likely to happen anytime soon, but it is a trend to watch.

CHAPTER 3 REVIEW

- While many marketers believe that reach and frequency are the best ways to compel people to act, relevancy of the message is still the best way to compel action.

- Reach and frequency tactics may make your organization money in the short term but can sabotage longer relationships due to general distrust after receiving irrelevant messages one too many times.
- Just because you have permission to email someone or have a relationship with your audience does not mean you are free from being interpreted as a "permission spammer." Again, relevancy is your only safety net.
- Try to rid yourself of the term "campaign." The purpose of a campaign is to convince people to buy or do something. The purpose of a relationship is to maximize Lifetime Value.
- Understand that email can present a catch 22 at times: It is so easy to execute, it takes very little time to get a message out the door; it is so easy to execute, it is very easy to throw a thoughtless message together and get it out the door.
- Remember that quantity means nothing. Quality of your messages means everything!

CHAPTER 4

SUBSCRIBER ENGAGEMENT: WHAT MATTERS?

Many organizations wonder how they should measure email success. The long and short of it is: Either your recipients do something when they receive your email, or they don't.

I understand that sometimes, interpreting engagement is not that black and white. For example, assume that your organization sends an email to a few thousand people. Thirty percent of the recipients who typically interact with your email do nothing with this specific message. Thirty percent who typically ignore your message interact for the first time. So was the email successful or not? I'm a big fan of suspense, which is why we'll come back to this at the end of the chapter (in your head, you should hear mystery theme music playing right now).

Back to the customer engagement question at large. To address it, ExactTarget conducted a comprehensive study consisting of thousands of past email programs across a wide variety of vertical industries and millions of subscribers. Additionally, with a few select clients, we conducted a structured six-week test to proactively experiment with the theories developed through the study of the historical data.

The goals of these studies were to determine (based on data):

- What does customer engagement "look like?"
- What factors help drive customer engagement?

One of the most glaring issues for email marketers today is dwindling engagement. For whatever reason, people who at one point opted-in and engaged with the email by opening it, clicking it, and purchasing, have stopped engaging. They ignore the message.

Figure 4.1 demonstrates what our study concluded is happening to email recipients over time:

- Nonresponders are less and less likely to become engaged again.
- On the positive side, a sudden engagement will break the trend and increase the chances of future engagement.
- As a result, identifying nonresponders and implementing reengagement strategies is key.

By measuring, segmenting, and responding, organizations are able to get in front of the engagement curve. Before we take a deep dive into measurement, let's cover some basics.

Figure 4.1
Monitor Response to Evaluate Engagement

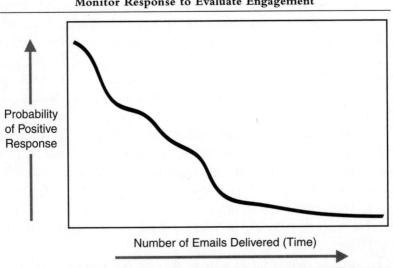

In general, there are four major areas that drive higher engagement. They are, in order of importance:

1. *Past behavior:* Yes, it's basic, but it's also one of the most forgotten elements of engagement. People repeat behavior. In my introduction, I mentioned that I read the newspaper and drank coffee this morning. And guess what? I'll do it the next morning. And the next morning . . . people repeat behavior in life. People repeat behavior with respect to email. If they engaged with your last email, then they are highly likely to engage again. I know how obvious this seems, but too many marketers ignore past behavior as an indicator of future behavior. If someone who has typically clicked on four links in every email she's ever received suddenly stops clicking, what is she telling you? Are you still sending her relevant content? You also need to ask yourself (and perhaps even her): "What am I going to do to get her to start clicking again?" There is no magic answer here, but I'll share some of my ideas later in the chapter.

2. *Relevance:* The second most important factor in driving successful email engagement is relevance. Think of it this way: If you go to a dinner party and the person sitting next to you continually talks about hockey (assume you hate hockey and know nothing about it), then you're probably going to tune out—fast. This person will be saying names like Wayne Gretzky and you'll be dreaming about chocolate cake for dessert. Hockey is irrelevant to your personal interests and, therefore, you ignore the person sitting beside you. And the next time you see each other— maybe at the grocery store—you're going to walk on the other side of the aisle so that you don't have to greet this person and waste your time talking about hockey. It's the same thing with email. If you're talking about the things your recipients care about, they're going to listen and respond. If the conversation becomes one-sided and you're only talking about the things your organization cares about, your audience is going to disengage.

3. *Frequency:* Frequency simply relates to how often you mail: daily, weekly, monthly, or other times. It has a great deal to do with successful engagement. Many people want to know what

is the "right" frequency. The truth is: It varies by individual and segment. We'll get into the details of frequency in another chapter because it's so important. For now, keep in mind that how often you send makes a big impact on your success.

4. *Creative:* Surprised to find creative fourth on the list? Many organizations think that creative is the most important factor in driving engagement. That's why such a hugely disproportionate amount of marketing effort is invested in email design. Why? It traces back to mass marketing. If several organizations are blindly emailing the same mass audience, the belief is that strong creative is the only way to stand out in the clutter. But if an email has a great design and totally irrelevant content, isn't that the same thing as nice looking junk mail? Granted, I'm not saying that you should intentionally create unattractive emails. I'm saying that in the big scheme of success, creative is not where to spend the majority of your effort.

What you should also keep in mind is that many of the rules governing email are no different from the direct marketing rules that have been established for more than 60 years. Have you heard of the 40, 40, 20 rule? That means 40 percent weight on the audience, 40 percent on the offer, and 20 percent weight on creative.

EMAIL ENGAGEMENT CHECKLIST

While there isn't a formula that's going to ensure that your recipients engage with every email you send them, there are questions you can ask yourself prior to sending your email that will give a good indication of your success:

- *Is this the appropriate audience?* I can't stress the importance of audience enough. Sending to the wrong audience is like showing up at an email marketing conference and talking about chess. No one cares. You must spend the appropriate time defining the audience most likely to react. Then you must do the segmentation necessary to get to that audience.

You should also ask yourself if you have permission to send emails to the audience. If you're blasting off emails to every address in your CRM system and assuming, "Yes, these people want to hear from me!" you are wrong. And the response to your mailing will prove it (there will be an usually high percentage of bounced emails, ignored emails, and unsubscribes for non-permission campaigns).

- *Is my message targeted, personalized, and relevant?* Targeting goes hand-in-hand with proper audience identification. It also enables you to leverage what you know in order to personalize the message (e.g., "We know that you recently bought a new mattress and wanted to let you know that all of our bedding is 10% off").

  Personalization will humanize your communications and draw attention to their relevancy. It includes everything from name to purchase history (I'll note that name is an expected field and including only this as a personalization field can be insulting to a subscriber if the rest of the content isn't relevant). A general rule of thumb is that the more personalization, the better. Most email marketing systems make it extremely easy to personalize so you can leverage the benefits of an individual and humanistic message.

- *Does my message communicate a clear incentive or benefit?* No matter what you define as the ultimate goal of your email communication, part of what will make it successful has to do with the initial offer. The best offers tap into the core desires of the target audience. For example, people like to feel recognized, valued, and part of an exclusive group. You must always keep in mind that your job as a marketer is to compel people to *do* something. Many times, this means clearly spelling out the benefits— especially why your audience wants to act now. Other times, this means including a special incentive that may be as simple as a discount, coupon, or a contest.

  Good email marketers realize that their constituents' time is precious. Another general rule of thumb is that recipients should be able to open your message and understand what they are to do and why within three to five seconds. Test this on your spouse, significant other, kids, or a department that isn't as familiar with the email. Let them open the message and look at it for five seconds. Then have them close the message and tell you what they think they're supposed to do. It's a simple test that will tell you a great deal.

- *Does my message make the recipient want to take action NOW?* A great message with a clear call to action includes *urgency*. You've seen those segments on Home Shopping Network that tell you the 20-piece set of pots and pans is available for only *five* more minutes, right? They have a little clock counting down those five minutes and show you all of the people who are ordering those very pots and pans that you must have. This is a traditional offline approach that also works well for online. You should give your recipient the exact way to reach you and the time by which they should respond. Internally, many organizations know that their employees won't respond to something unless there's a deadline. It's the same thing with external email. Deadlines are crucial. Don't beat around the bush here. Tell them by when. Tell them why it's important to meet the deadline.

- *Is my message the appropriate length?* Contrary to popular belief, short is not always better. Testing has proved that long copy versions can generate a better response rate. Yes, that's a key point: You must test. Without trying messages of various lengths, you won't know if your recipients prefer short, succinct messages, or longer emails with more content. Regardless of the length that works for your organization, you must still get your overall message across in the first few lines. Don't make people hunt for it, or you're wasting the precious time that they could spend *doing* something rather than looking for what it is you want them to do.

- *Is my subject line powerful?* The subject line is important because if it's a bore or totally irrelevant, your constituents aren't going to bother opening your message. That's why the subject line should read like a billboard, clearly calling out the "what's in it for me?" specifics. Subject lines should also be continually tested, which we'll cover in more detail later.

- *Will my message even reach my audience?* Email deliverability presents problems for many organizations. One easy way to increase your chances of deliverability is by asking your subscribers to add you to their email address book. Once you're added, you can generally be assured that you will not wind up in the junk or spam filter. If your message gets caught in a folder that your recipients never check, you've already lost your chance for engagement with them.

- *Am I paying attention to the right metrics?* Your open rate is simply the percentage of all the email you send, divided by the number of those emails that are opened. The calculation is straightforward, but presents problems concerning how it relates to measure of engagement success.

  First and foremost, the open rate indicates an impression. That's it. By registering an open, you assume that the subscriber has had a chance to see the message. However, you have no idea if the subscriber has actually engaged with the message. The only way to measure an open rate is by including a tiny image (usually 1 pixel by 1 pixel gif or jpeg) within the email. Since the text and graphics are served at different times (and only combined when you click on the email to open it), tracking devices constitute a "call" to that tiny image as an open. For impression advertising, this may be an okay metric. For someone trying to get a close read on initial engagement, it's a really poor measurement.

  You should know that as we sit here mid-decade, approximately 50 percent of all email clients (such as AOL, Outlook, and Gmail) don't display any graphics. That means if you're relying on creative design to drive engagement, you have a big problem. The problem has only been worsened by handheld devices, which we'll delve into with our next checklist.

  While open rates aren't a great read on engagement, I do think it's important to pay attention to click rates because they will help you determine initial engagement. You should pay *very close* attention to conversions, ROI, and revenue. So what if you get 90 percent unique clicks on an email if no one signs up for what you're promoting? That means you created initial interest but did not seal the deal.

Email Engagement Checklist: Handheld Devices

More and more of your constituents are likely to receive, review, and respond to email via handheld devices (PDAs) such as Blackberries and Treos. As a handheld user myself, I use my Treo as an inbox cleanup device. Every day, I get a few hundred emails. When I have down-time—waiting on a plane, on the phone, sitting in a meeting—I use my Treo to decide which emails I can delete right away and which I want to keep for later, when I have access to my computer. With that said, the rules here are a bit different from when you're delivering to a computer. Here are some of the questions you should ask yourself:

- *Is my design flexible?* Now that handheld devices have become ubiquitous, subscribers have a lot of choices as to how they interact with your email. Your design must be flexible enough for you to deliver your message to various media formats. This extends beyond HTML versus text format considering that handheld devices that are supposed to render HTML oftentimes mangle the message. You'll need to do some testing to see what happens in that case.
- *Have I handled images appropriately?* What looks great on a computer (images, formatting, etc.) is often turned into ugly links and codes on a handheld. The quandary is that graphics can be very successful in driving engagement. I'm not saying that you should send text email all the time, but you should manage your creative so that you at least have a chance of engagement if your email is rendered on a handheld devise. That means you should be wary of an email that is top heavy on images. If you make subscribers scroll through long links that would appear as nice pretty images if they were on a computer, they will hit "delete."

  Along those lines, you should also add an alternative text (ALT) tag. Without an ALT tag, the PDA will default to HTML and will show image codes and programming strings. Alternative text tags will enable your PDA to render the email in a simple, readable format without affecting how the email will look on your computer. You'll need to ensure your email vendor can support ALT tags.

- *Do I get right to the point?* Put copy as close to the top of your email as possible. You must get to the point quickly in the text format. The key is to get your main messaging on the first screen. The more a handheld user has to scroll, the lower the likelihood that he or she will engage.

  Stop asking to be added to the address book. I know this is contrary to earlier advice. The problem on a handheld is that this message will take up the entire content area! Once a subscriber has added you to her address book, stop asking. This data should become an attribute, with dynamic content driving the message back to only those who have not yet clicked to add you to the address book.

The bottom line is that handheld devices are gaining huge acceptance among your constituents. This is especially true if you are a Business-to-Business (B-to-B) marketer. But the issue won't stop with B-to-B in the coming months and years. Today, there are over 2.5 billion handheld devices in the world. Among the Generation Y crowd, handheld devices are more frequently interacted with than computers. You must be prepared to consider handheld devices with respect to your email programs.

SOME EMAILS ARE MORE PRONE TO ENGAGEMENT THAN OTHERS

Of course you want to know what kind, so you can deliver more of these messages and optimize what you include in them. Here they are:

- *Transactional email:* Transactional email is a huge wasted opportunity when it comes to marketing. Many people associate transactional email with a purchase, but it can be a follow-up to any type of interaction. This could be a response to a phone call, a meeting, event attendance, or other contact. Recipients are nearly guaranteed to engage with the email (as long as it is timely and relevant) because it is a follow-up to something pertinent to them.

A few months ago, I bought a 42-inch plasma television online. It was from a company I found on Shopping.com, and one I'd never done business with. This company did a good job acquiring me for this one time purchase . . . but then what? Shouldn't they want to have a further relationship with me? Well, let's judge that by the transactional email they sent me.

I received three lines of text in an email confirmation acknowledging my order. It gave me a tracking number. It asked me not to reply to the email. That's right—it said, "Please don't respond to this email." This company has no information about me other than the TV I just purchased. Don't they find this frustrating? They spent all this money to find me, and they've missed a huge opportunity for a potential long-term relationship.

What if they had included a survey within the confirmation email? What about an up-sell? (Perfect considering I forgot to order the wall mounting bracket and wound up buying that from another vendor.)

Think about your organization. Are you sending transactional emails? If you open your eyes, you'll see all kinds of transactional opportunities ranging from a follow-up to a customer service call, to a lunch. Are you leveraging them to fulfill a purpose and deliver targeted marketing opportunities? Take a look in your inbox and the type of transactional emails you receive from other companies. I'm sure you'll see some opportunities for improvement there as well.

Go ahead and take advantage of the fact that most people appreciate confirmations and follow-ups, thus lending themselves to huge relationship and engagement opportunities. Oh, and don't ask someone *not* to respond to you. If you must, provide another email address that explains how your organization can be reached.

- *Emails with forms and surveys:* By nature, forms and surveys are interactive. You must answer a question by providing an answer. You are required to engage.

As you evaluate your email efforts with your constituents, think about what you would want to know about them if you were having a conversation. By inserting a simple form or survey, you make it easy for your recipient to quickly and easily provide that very information. And as we all know, the more data you have on each individual constituent, the more you are able to segment in order to deliver a highly relevant message.

Here are some factors you may want to consider with respect to survey and form success:

—*Ask questions* within *the email.* We see a lot of email that relies on third-party survey applications to handle the questions. These surveys rely on web page(s) outside of the email, forcing you to click, arrive at a new page, and fill out the questions from there. Surveys and forms found within the email itself are going to have a higher response rate. Why? Think about friction. Every extra step you require of your recipient adds a level of friction to the process. The greater the amount of friction, the lower the response rate from participants.

—*Don't ask a question you already know the answer to.* I know, I'm pointing out the obvious again. But I'm sure you've seen emails addressing you by name that ask you to fill in your name as the first form field. There's no need for this, right? Your recipients should spend their time providing answers you don't know. Asking obvious questions not only makes you appear foolish, it also adds a layer of friction that can hurt your conversion rates.

—*Use the data that you collect.* Nothing is worse than collecting data on an individual and then not using that data. Remember the airline examples? The airline knows where I live and what home airport I always depart from. But they ignore it. Which makes me hesitant to provide any additional info. It is incredibly frustrating when personal details that you know about your constituents go ignored. In fact, it's a form of trust abuse.

—*Keep it short.* I repeat: Do not ask me for answers that you already know. Ask one or two new questions that will help you target your messages in the future. Remember, more questions mean more friction. I don't mind clicking a few boxes that are multiple choice. I'm a lot less likely to spend 10 minutes going through 20 questions. If you must ask that many questions, ask them over time. Expect that this relationship is going to progress, so there's no need to overwhelm in the beginning. Just like when you meet a new person, you refrain from providing every detail of your life. Ask a *series* of relevant questions over time to ensure continued engagement.

- *Lead management emails:* In 2005, a CMO Council report tied missed revenue to mismanagement of new business development activity. A joint report by the CMO Council and the Business Performance Management Forum found that U.S. companies experience *huge* losses in potential revenue as a result of mismanaged new business development activity. (The study was based on an online survey of approximately 800 C-level executives in the third quarter of 2005.)

  The study found that an estimated 80 percent of leads are typically lost, ignored, or discarded. That means that 80 percent of your organization's leads may be falling through the cracks.

  According to the report, nearly three-quarters of respondents said they could increase revenue by at least 10 percent with better business development practices; 37 percent said they could increase the top line by more than 20 percent.

  Also, 73 percent of respondents said that their company has no process for requalifying and revisiting business leads (this explains why such a great percentage are lost in the shuffle).

  Lead mismanagement is a fact in all companies. But it doesn't have to be a dead end. All you need to do is look for the right inflection points in your lead process. Yes, imagine how you would talk to these leads if you were having a live conversation. The emails should use the appropriate personalization and references to past conversations that set the stage for the next step.

For example, if your leads have already had a conversation with a specific salesperson, it is appropriate for that email to come "from" the person rather than the company at large (and yes, it is completely possible for a marketer to send consistent and controlled emails on behalf of the company's representatives). Similar to the transactional emails we discussed before, early stage leads (i.e., those acquired at tradeshows) are likely to show the signs of high engagement in the beginning. They're brand new to your organization and you haven't had the chance to ruin the relationship yet. Okay, all joking aside, there's an enormous opportunity when it comes to these leads.

Let's dig a little further into event attendance (whether online or offline). Typically, a fraction of the people who commit actually show up for the event. How do you follow up with the people who do attend? How do you follow up with the people who don't attend? Perhaps it's appropriate to deliver attendees a relevant white paper or the slides used for the presentation. Nonattendees probably deserve another chance to attend if it's an option. A targeted email helps both groups progress to the next step.

Does your organization have a system for database clean up? There are likely to be hundreds—even thousands—of untouched leads that a representative has not followed up with. Dividing and conquering these leads among an inside team (you can even designate a "lead clean up day") could make a big difference.

- *E-newsletters:* There's a lot of controversy surrounding the term and concept of an email newsletter. On the one hand, most businesses—especially small businesses—use e-newsletters as a significant part of their communication strategy. I'm not trying to stop your organization from sending an e-newsletter. They can certainly have value if created and implemented the right way. But I'm going to make a case against the traditional newsletter.

After reading this, you may rethink your current newsletter approach.

In the old days, marketers had a very had time talking to people like individuals. Cost and complexity tied up the execution of our communication. In this paper-based world, newsletters were great. You could round up a bunch of content and hope that your audience would take a look at some of it. You also had the efficiencies of batching, because it really didn't change the amount of work it took to get the newsletter out the door. Whether it was three articles, five articles, or eight articles, the labor component didn't change much because you were still sending one communication.

The reason why I don't like the term *newsletter* has to do with this very process. First, an e-newsletter also implies batching. Newsletters are typically monthly, quarterly, or yearly. I understand that limitations of paper, printing resources, and postage drove the batch mentality with respect to paper newsletters. The great thing about email is that you don't have these same limitations, which frees you from adhering to the historic concept of a newsletter. You can send your messages whenever you like. Wow, talk about freedom. Have something important and relevant to share? Share it. Don't have anything to share? Keep quiet until you do. There's no need to distribute junk just because it happens to be the 15th of the month.

Okay, here's my last problem with the term *newsletter*. It's comprised of the words "news" and "letter." I think that this implies the sharing of new information in a letter format. There are no implications of immediate interaction and engagement. And remember, these are the very strengths of email—the ability to engage your constituents and start a dialogue. This is a revolution that was never possible with paper newsletters. That's why organizations that think of their publications as simply a replacement for their paper newsletter really miss this opportunity to take advantage of human-to-human interaction.

So I'm officially making a commitment to replace the term "newsletter" with "relationship builder" or "conversation starter." You get the point.

WHAT TO DO WHEN LIST QUALITY IMPACTS ENGAGEMENT

List quality absolutely affects engagement rates. If you have a subscriber list compiled from several old sources or perhaps that didn't follow best practices at one point (i.e., you prechecked the "Newsletter sign-up" during registration), you should consider a re-opt-in email confirming that this person does in fact want to hear from you.

Many people consider re-opt-in emails too risky to try. They start trembling at the thought of it and say things like, "But . . . what if we lose half the people on our list?"

Well, the fact is that it isn't about quantity. It's about quality. Is it better to have lots of people on your subscriber list who ignore you, or a few that hang on to every word you say? Why would you want to keep wasting time and money on an audience that continually ignores you and may not have asked to hear from you in the first place?

ExactTarget recently ran a re-opt-in campaign for those very reasons. Allow me to note some of the strengths of our reengagement efforts:

- We made it easy for the subscriber to understand why ExactTarget sent the email.
- The call to action was above the fold in every version.
- There were eight different versions tested in sample audiences (rather than blasting off the same variation to everyone and hoping it worked). The winner was mailed to the entire list.
- Each version contained a "TIME DATE" field that told the subscriber the reply deadline, thus adding urgency.
- The subscriber was made aware of the fact that by not confirming a subscription, he or she would no longer receive emails.

With an email like this, you want to spend some time testing and putting together a good, compelling call to action. When these people are gone, they are gone for good. So it's worth spending time to get a strong message together that may reengage some individuals who went dark. When sending a re-opt-in email, you are accepting the fact that the purpose is not for everyone on the list to confirm a subscription. Attrition must be expected.

THE FINAL ENGAGEMENT RULE YOU MUST REMEMBER

People are busy. Busier than ever, actually. And no one likes to waste time. If you have something to say, say it. If not, don't waste anyone's time. The "little boy who cried wolf" scenario absolutely applies to your email messages. If you talk to your constituents enough, without anything valuable to say, they aren't going to believe you when you finally deliver something of value. That means your engagement is sunk until you can convince them to forgive you for crying wolf in the first place.

I've said it before and I'll say it again: One of my favorite things about email is that any size organization, with any size budget, can execute on these principles. It all comes down to the right content, execution, and tracking tools. If your tools aren't easy to use, you'll face so much execution pain, you'll never have the time necessary to focus on engagement and maximize your interaction with constituents.

Much of what we've covered so far hinges on segmentation, which we will delve into in much greater detail in an upcoming chapter. In fact, assume that every recurring theme that hasn't been explained in great detail will be explained in a later chapter.

Earlier, I asked whether you'd consider an email with the following characteristics successful: 30 percent of the recipients who typically interact with your messages did nothing; 30 percent who typically ignore the message interacted for the first time.

The answer is that it was successful in some cases. The audience who typically interacted but did not interact this time should be reevaluated. Perhaps the message was irrelevant or inappropriate for them? The group who interacted for the first time should receive similar messages in the future since they engaged in a positive manner. The key here is that there's no magic formula for subscriber engagement. What will work to engage some of your constituents will not work for others. Everyone is different. Look, I'm back at the segmentation and testing points I made earlier. It's a giant circle of themes.

I hope you leave this chapter with plenty of ideas and the commitment to yourself and your organization to push the interaction envelope, test, experiment, and focus on what really works to accomplish your goals.

Case Studies

Case Study 1: Give-and-Take Boosts Engagement

A financial group specializing in annuities, life insurance, and long-term care insurance wasn't sure how its emails to over 5,500 independent insurance brokers were performing. How could they know? They were relying on Outlook to send batch emails, with absolutely no tracking available.

The group recognized that they were missing a huge piece of the puzzle in engaging with their brokers. (There was no way to improve if they didn't know where they were, right?)

So the group switched to an email system that enabled them to personalize the message and track success. After sending a few emails and taking a look at the results produced in the new system, the group realized that they we asking each broker for information, but failing to give anything in return. If they wanted to engage their brokers in actually requesting an immediate annuity quote, they needed to provide something in return.

Each email now includes sales information, personal incentives (such as 20 free prospecting letters), and selling tools. In fact, with a real-time tracking view, the group is oftentimes able to immediately connect with the agent while he or she is still browsing through the letters.

Results: Increased Monthly Quotes over $12 Million

With an estimated ROI of $4,400 for every dollar spent on its email platform, the financial group saw quotes increase by over $12 million in one month alone, $5.5 million of which quickly converted to sales. The group is confident that they can sustain this kind of success due to the fact that they can now take a proactive approach to find out what's engaging their brokers and what isn't.

Case Study 2: *A Smaller List May Have More Kick*

A beauty retailer had engaged in acquisition methods that resulted in initial success but presented long-term list hygiene issues. The email program suffered declining open rates, click-through rates, and conversion from email to online and in-store sales. The problems compounded when a major ISP blocked all sends from the retailer due to spam complaints and spamtrap hits. Their challenge was twofold: Restore delivery to top ISPs and implement a strategy to regain—and surpass—sales numbers generated from their past email marketing efforts.

With help from a deliverability specialist and an account specialist, the company ultimately decided on the following strategy to remedy list hygiene issues and regain strong deliverability:

1. Identify all "engaged" and "disengaged" subscribers. "Engaged" was defined as any subscriber who had opened or clicked on an email promotion within the past 90 days.
2. Send reengagement email to "disengaged" subscribers. Because "disengaged" subscribers were more likely to make a spam complaint, the retailer sent an email asking these subscribers to reconfirm their interest in receiving additional email promotions.
3. Design and implement a "contact strategy" that included ongoing reengagement campaigns.
4. Introduce plans for full-scale list cleanup. In the long-term, messaging could eventually be drafted based on opt-in source and purchase data.
5. Continue deliverability reporting.

While the company was hesitant to deploy a reengagement campaign, they knew it was a must. List size would inevitably drop, but without the campaign, ISPs would continue to block their emails. The marketing team decided that it was appropriate to include an incentive as part of the reengagement emails in an attempt to grab subscriber attention.

Results: Smaller List, with 350 Percent ROI Improvement

As expected, the opt-in campaign resulted in a smaller overall list size, but the open rate, click-through rate, and sales after the campaign were astounding. In addition, the retailer's email campaigns were unblocked by the major ISPs.

Because the subscribers on those lists were all "engaged," the retailer saw an impressive 30 percent increase in total sales with their 15 email campaigns post-opt-in. Given a 60 percent decrease in total emails sent after the opt-in and an open rate increase of 119 percent, the company achieved a 350 percent ROI improvement.

Case Study 3: Engagement Keeps Going . . . and Going . . . and Going . . .

Perhaps that is the mark of great marketing: engagement doesn't end after the immediate actions are complete. The custom homebuilder in this case study understands what it's like to see engagement that lasts.

A direct mail and phone advocate no more (Realtors tended to be inundated with junk mail and phone calls as it was), the homebuilder's marketing team needed to find a way to drive attendance to an upcoming event. And not just attendance in general—they needed attendance from the right people. In the past, when the company succeeded at getting Realtors to attend events, oftentimes the high-end Realtors sent associates in their place. However, it's the big-deal Realtors—not their associates—who bring in sales.

The event was a Realtor sneak peak for the Holiday Wish Home, a $2 million luxury home constructed by the homebuilder.

The marketing team sent two email invitations to Realtors: one several weeks before the event and another several days before the event. The emails used elegant script and minimal copy. Realtors were given four options:

1. View an exclusive invitation.
2. Click to RSVP.
3. Print a map.
4. Call for further details.

Clicks brought Realtors to a special landing page designed to convert interested parties into attendees. The landing page featured a 45-second audio of the homebuilder personally inviting the Realtor to attend the event and giving *just enough* insider detail to pique interest.

On the landing page, Realtors could click to RSVP, download a map PDF, and view enough photos of the home to make them want to see it in person. In other words, the marketing team wouldn't take "I'm considering it" as an answer. They used tactics on the landing page to push the Realtors to go ahead and commit.

Results: 25 Percent of Targeted Realtors Attended

Remarkably, 25 percent of targeted Realtors attended the sneak peek event. And the benefits didn't stop there. At the event, McKenzie sponsored a prize drawing. The business cards gathered for the drawing were used to send a "Thanks for participating" email and links to a landing page including video of the home and a "forward to a friend" mechanism.

Several of these Realtors sent the page on to other Realtors. Some Realtors even brought other Realtors back to the house to show it. In other words, the homebuilder always gave the Realtors a clear task and made it easy for them to follow through with it.

What Are Other Marketers Thinking?

In their own words . . .

Subscriber Engagement: What Matters?

By Kelly Rusk
Communications Manager, cardcommunications
Blog: http://www.cardcommunications.com/blog

So you got people to opt-in to receive your emails. Now you can go ahead and send them whatever you want, whenever you want, and they will just love you forever, right?

As ridiculous as that sounds, the truth is that email marketers often worry more about growing their database than keeping existing subscribers engaged. Like any kind of business, it's more cost-effective and valuable to keep existing subscribers rather than find new ones.

Email marketing is all about relationships. And like any relationship, it takes work to keep your subscribers happy. In order to develop your email subscriber relationship, it's important to know who your subscribers are and what type of information they want to receive from you.

While there can be hundreds of methods, facts, and opinions about keeping subscribers engaged, it really all comes down to testing with your own list. After all, I think you know your own subscribers better than I do.

But what do you test? The joy (and pain) of email is that there are so many variables. The possibilities are endless, and I've included what I believe to be the big ones:

- *Determine frequency.* Sending emails too often might annoy your subscribers and cause many to unsubscribe. While there is no rule of thumb for email frequency, unless you are sending very relevant information, more than once a week may be too much. If you send too infrequently, however, subscribers may forget about you and lose interest. Once a month is usually a good fit, but again, it depends on who you are talking to and the nature of your relationship.

- *Develop a mouth-watering content recipe.* Are you sending a good mix of timely, relevant, and meaningful content to keep your subscribers engaged? Like perfecting a cooking recipe, you may need to experiment before getting it right. Carefully examine your click-through results and make note of what works and what doesn't.

  Your content recipe will depend on what your business offers, your relationship to subscribers, and what resources you have, but some suggestions are:
  —Ask an expert
  —Feature articles
  —Contributed articles by industry experts
  —Tips
  —Case studies
  —Success stories
  —Industry news
  —Q&As
  —Interesting stats
  —Industry trends
  —How-to articles
  —Did you know?
  —Short surveys or polls
  —Announcements
  —Learning experiences
  —Awards and merit
  —Career opportunities

- *Don't forget segmentation.* Probably the most effective way to keep subscribers engaged is segmentation. Segmentation can be as simple as splitting your list by preferred email format (HTML or text) or as complex as segmenting by geographic location, interests, purchasing behavior, gender, click-through habits, and more.

The easiest way to start a segmentation strategy is with your opt-in sign-up form. It's important to carefully choose which subscriber details you ask for. You don't want to ask for too much as it may defer some from signing up. At the same time, you want enough information so that you can start segmenting effectively from the start.

Segmentation should be an ongoing strategy that is reviewed and revised as your subscriber relationships grow. After you've split your lists, you need to determine the best way to speak to each group. Will you use different graphics? If you're segmenting by geographic location, maybe you will use a different image that represents where each segment lives. The possibilities are endless.

- *Set the tone with the right welcome message.* Like the crucial first date, your welcome message sets the tone for the subscriber relationship. Studies show that the welcome message has the highest open rate of all—this is a well-read message so make the most of it! First, and obviously, you want to make your new subscribers feel comfortable and welcome. It's a good idea to reiterate what they're getting into (what type of content you'll be sending and how often) and cover some housekeeping items (ask to be added to their safe sender/address book and link to your privacy policy and instructions about unsubscribing in future mailings). Also, you may want to offer a little bonus for signing up—a free download, a complimentary white paper, an entry into a contest, or whatever may be valuable to your audience.

  That being said, it's very important to keep the welcome message short and sweet. Leave them wanting more!

- *Test, measure, refine. REPEAT!* Subscribers' interests change over time, so be prepared to change your strategy. Review your strategy throughout the year to ensure your emails are maximizing their potential. If they aren't, it's time to start testing something else and making refinements to keep your e-marketing program on track.
- *Think small for big results.* Think quality, not quantity. Forget about getting millions of barely interested people on one big list. Instead, focus on getting all of your subscribers anticipating your every email. With our fixation on ROI and the bottom line, it's hard to step back and think quality over quantity, but consider this: Is it better to have 100 subscribers engaged in every email, or 10,000 subscribers deleting it regularly? Maybe that's a bit of an exaggeration, but having qualified, interested, and engaged subscribers will definitely do more for your business than being able to brag about your huge database. And if your list is big, think about how you can slice and dice it. That's when you'll see the magic of segmentation in email marketing begin.
- *Show a little respect.* Ask anyone how life is these days and you'll probably hear "busy!" Also, think of all the email you receive. Do you read each one? Be respectful to your subscribers' time by keeping your emails short and to the point. That doesn't mean you have to throw away content for the sake of brevity, just provide the important stuff in the email and link to additional information. Think scanability—your email should look easy to digest at first glance. Keep sentences and paragraphs short; leave lots of white space and add graphics to support your story.

   And on that note, I think I've said enough. Email marketing is a powerful tool and, when used strategically, can provide amazing results. I see it every day! I'm Kelly, and I'm an email-aholic.

CHAPTER 4 REVIEW

- Four factors influence the success of emails: past behavior, relevancy, frequency, and creative. They are listed in order of importance. You should weight them accordingly in each of your email messages.
- If you'd really like to tick off your constituents, go ahead and talk to them like you've never heard from them before. Collect personal data and then *don't* use it.
- Spend time on audience selection because it will help you deliver the right message to the right people.
- Always ask yourself if your email is targeted, personalized, relevant, easy to understand, and urgent. Have someone who isn't as close to the message take a five-second look and provide an unbiased opinion.
- Remember that email opens are the same thing as impressions. Pay attention to unique click-throughs to determine initial engagement. Pay even more attention to conversions, ROI, and revenue to determine overall engagement.
- Leverage transactional emails, forms, and surveys, and lead management emails—by nature, they are very conducive to high engagement.
- Evaluate whether or not the term "newsletter" is appropriate given when you email your audience. You should speak to them when you have something to say and hold your breath when you don't.
- People are busy. Make engaging with your organization worth their time.

CHAPTER 5

BUILDING A KILLER DATABASE

To leverage the benefits of email segmentation, you need a good database. And to build a good database, you need to understand what data is going to drive your business and email marketing programs. So let's start with an email address and permission to mail to it. I know it seems obvious, but the most basic and fundamental building block of email is permission to send someone your message. It's so important, in fact, that we'll spend a whole chapter on it later. For now, we'll focus on email address alone.

As you think about your organization, how much of a priority is collecting email addresses from your constituents? My guess is not nearly high enough. I want to clarify that email is not an acquisition tool—it's a retention tool. Email is a nurturing tool. Email is a credibility-marketing tool. It seems as if 90 percent of marketing dollars are invested in acquisition programs, including keywords, banners, direct mail, TV, radio, billboards, and so on.

What I want to focus on is leveraging those acquisition tactics to *acquire permission* to continue the relationship. See the difference? For many organizations, leads come via the Web. Some marketing activity drives a prospect to your site or landing page, where a choice is presented: yes or no; buy, or go away. This is called *macro-conversion*. You buy a keyword to drive a prospect to a landing page to buy a DVD, or download a white paper, or schedule a demo, depending on your business.

It is a fact: Most of the people who visit your site go away. They leave (anonymously, because they haven't told you anything about themselves) and may never return. Most people are browsers, who are merely seeking information or comparing you to your competitor. In other words, they aren't ready to make a final decision. But does this make them less valuable? You already spent the money to bring them in. If they leave anonymously, that investment is gone.

Imagine if 10 percent of the individuals who typically leave gave you permission to keep in touch with them. They said, "I'm not ready to make a decision, but I'd like to hear from you again." So how are you going to capture those people? Eureka! Collecting an email address is the perfect way to continue the relationship. Capturing an email address in this situation is considered a *micro-conversion*. The concept of the micro-conversion is to prioritize registration over the sale. Minimally, you need to constantly test your landing pages for both macro- and micro-conversions. An email address is a valuable enough micro-conversion that it should not be tossed into the corner of your homepage, with an invitation to "sign up for our newsletter." I'm cringing at the very thought. Why would people want to do that? What's the value to them?

You have to decide *right now* if collecting permission email addresses is a priority or not. Since you've made it this far into the book, I'm guessing you think that email is a valuable marketing tool. But how valuable is it to your organization? That's right, put a price on it. I'm getting all sorts of demanding here, aren't I?

Earlier, we talked about acquisition costs. You have to know how much a new constituent costs. How big is your overall acquisition budget? Go ahead and do some rough back of the envelope calculations. I don't mind waiting.

Okay, now how much did you spend on marketing last year, last month, or even last week? How many new constituents did you capture? Since most of your marketing dollars are likely to be spent on acquisition, it's a safe bet to say that whatever number you get by dividing total budget into new constituents will give you an idea of your acquisition costs. If you're a web business, you can compare this to your site visitors. The point here is to consider what would happen if you were able to email some of the defectors, who then became customers, which translates into money. You know where I'm going with this . . . there is a value to your email addresses. It may be $1, $10, or even $1,000.

Now do you think email address collection and permission are worth your time? I knew you'd come around. We're ready for proven tactics to acquire those email addresses.

Email Collection: What NOT to Do

The first step to successful email marketing is permission. I have a core rule here: *Permission is not transferable.* Others in the email industry may disagree with me. They assume that if we have any relationship at all, I'll be open to receiving their emails. I disagree. The only way you can get permission to email market to someone is to ask directly. I know it's contrary to both phone and direct mail practices. The last thing you want is to assume that you have permission to send email to a group of people who (1) don't like you or (2) don't remember you, which is a recipe for getting perceived or reported as spam. In the direct mail world, spam and junk mail land you in the trashcan. In the email world, it lands you in big, big trouble with ISPs such as Yahoo, Google, and Hotmail. Assuming permission is not worth the expense of your email deliverability.

Here are a few other email address collection no-no's:

- *Selling or renting your lists:* Does your organization need to make a quick buck or two? Selling your list is *not* the way to do it. Email marketing is different from catalog marketing. Catalog marketers will make money from you in two ways: by your sale and by selling the fact that they made a sale to you. They provide this data to a list broker who is happy to pay the fee to the catalog so that he can in turn sell your data to other catalog companies who sell similar products. We've all experienced it. You buy one little thing— a new kitty litter box as a Christmas present for your aunt—and suddenly you're getting offers for similar products from every other pet catalog company under the sun (oh, and little do they know, you don't even own a pet). It's violating, isn't it?

It doesn't matter if it's an accepted direct mail practice. You will never ever want to sell or rent your constituents' personal data. The permission is with you, no one else. Selling that permission will erode the trust you are building with your constituents.

- *Selling or renting someone else's lists:* It's a two-way street: You should never sell your data to another company, and you should never buy data from another company. Ever see those little checkboxes at the bottom of an online registration page that say something to the effect of "want to hear valuable information from our partners?" Well, check the box at your own risk. Typically, it means your data is going to be sold or rented. Don't let your organization be the renter or the seller. Remember, email is not an acquisition tool—it's a conversion and retention tool. If you're renting a list, I'm guessing you'll see response rates indicating that the recipients have a relationship with someone else, not you (lots of unsubscribes, spam reports, and low opens and clicks). You can't take advantage of someone else's permission. I repeat: Permission is not transferable.

- *Email appending:* A subtle spin on the point above is called an *email append.* The thinking goes something like this: You have constituents. You make the assumption that since you have a preexisting relationship with these folks, they obviously want to be added to your email list. The problem? You don't have any of their email addresses.

  Email appending services are companies that have purchased huge databases of email addresses with some other corresponding data. Their business is built on matching up your data with their database of email addresses, with the hope that enough match up to make the exercise worthwhile. Don't do it. The ROI is typically terrible (it isn't cheap to utilize an append service), the match rate is low, and I'm back at my earlier point: Just because you are able to find an email address (aren't you clever), does not give you permission to email that individual.

I know I'm being strict on this rule. But just like football players who consider their home field sacred territory, I consider the inbox sacred territory. At that, it's sacred territory abused by so many marketers, it's sometimes difficult to determine what is or isn't a best practice.

The final thing to keep in mind is that unlike reach marketing, you never want to mistake quantity for quality. Permission email addresses are a step toward the end goal of great relationships. Relationships come from targeting and relevance, not from frequency. I once attended a meeting with a potential retail client who pounded his fist on the table and announced, "Our goal is to have an email database of over 30 million addresses by next year." I took a deep breath before responding, "How about if we figure out how to make $30 million using email marketing." My point is that list size is not the goal—relationships that make your organization money is the appropriate goal.

PERMISSION AND OPT-IN ARE SYNONYMOUS

In the email world, an opt-in simply means that constituents have given explicit permission for you to email them. There are a few different types of opt-ins, which we'll cover now.

Single opt-in typically takes place from a simple email collection form. Your constituents fill in their info and bingo—they're on the list. The biggest benefit of single opt-in is that it's easy. There is very little friction, so you're likely to build a bigger list with this method. Of course we all know that bigger isn't necessarily better, so that's the drawback. The quality of the names is typically mediocre at best. For example, if you provide access to a white paper as a reward for an email address, many people will just put in gibberish so they get access to what they need. The result? High bounce rates and poor deliverability when it comes time to email these people. Another problem is that pranksters will put other peoples' email addresses into the form, which results in people receiving email that they didn't ask to receive. Many times, you wind up with spam complaints.

The last problem with single opt-in is that many people sign up unconsciously, without really wanting or appreciating what you are trying to accomplish. These people will often ignore your emails, or even worse, forget that they asked for the message to begin with and flag you as a spammer. Don't worry, there's a way around all of these drawbacks.

Double opt-in includes an extra step that ensures quality of email addresses before they are added to your list. The process doesn't end at form submission. It ends with a confirmation that your constituent must provide from the email address that was just submitted. (Note: Many email systems can handle this automatically. You must simply write the confirmation message.) The confirmation note can be as simple as this:

Dear Chris,

We are thrilled that you've subscribed to (insert name). You have my personal commitment that we will continually strive to bring you great content on (insert subject). Because we value this relationship, we'd never want to send you email that you didn't ask to receive.

Can you please click on the link below to confirm your subscription?

http://confirmationlinkhere

Thank you so much,
Bob

What a nice note from Bob! Did you notice that I slipped another concept in here? This note contains what is known as a *positive confirmation*. The subscriber has to take another action to be fully subscribed.

Some organizations use *negative confirmation* to handle double opt-ins. A negative confirmation is similar to the positive confirmation, but you must take action *not* to be added to the list. For example, the note above would say, "Please click here if you do not want to receive our emails."

Do you see the difference? In the negative confirmation, the subscriber has to take an action *not* to get the email. I wouldn't recommend this approach because you will still have a lot of junk in your email database. While the positive confirmation opt-in will likely yield the smallest database, it will be the highest quality and give you the least amount of trouble with bounce rates and spam complaints.

IT ALL STARTS WITH EMAIL ADDRESS ACQUISITION . . .

Without getting your constituents to supply their email addresses, you won't be able to market to them via email. Thus, we'll spend a lot of time on "how" you can collect email addresses. Our tactics are broken into three sections: online registration, offline or location registration, and Business-to-Business/networking/real world registration.

Online Registration

Online sign up typically occurs from a website, micro site, or landing page. There are some general rules of thumb to keep in mind here. If you already have an email sign-up program going, see if your current approach is in line with the following. If you are starting a new program, you'll want to ask yourself these questions prior to implementation:

- *Is your registration form easy to find?* I'm lazy. Most people don't want to look for your email address registration form. Make it easy! Don't bury it at the bottom of your homepage. Test different locations to learn what spot drives the most conversions without sacrificing your other objectives.

- *Is your form on every page?* You may be tempted to put your registration form on only your homepage because you don't want to take up "prime real estate" on other pages of your site. Big mistake. Permission to build a relationship is critically important to your organization. Email registration must be prioritized.
- *Do you provide compelling reasons for registration?* "Sign up for our newsletter" won't cut it any more. You need to paint a clear picture of the real value. Your subscribers don't care about the newsletter itself; they care about the coupons, special research data, or other great information and offers you'll deliver via email. Your subscribers must see a compelling reason that convinces them to add you to the 100+ emails they already receive. The good news is that despite crowded inboxes, people are still willing to opt-in when value is evident.
- *Do you ask too many questions?* I love the registration forms that ask me fifteen questions, including SSN number, date of birth, eye color, height, weight, and favorite color. Just when I think I've finally submitted, they ask me if it would be too much trouble to send in a birth certificate, driver's license, and DNA sample. At this point, my registration will be complete.

    Wow. Talk about friction! Your constituents are not signing up to become ER surgeons overnight. They aren't signing up to carry the Olympic torch. They are signing up for your *email program*. Let's keep this in check. Ask *only* those questions that you need to begin the relationship. There's a lot of data and qualifying information you can find from other sources. For example, if my zip code is 46204, do you want me to waste time filling in city and state (appending is perfectly acceptable here)? And you can also ask follow-up questions via email survey.

    So ask yourself: "Will that hair sample really give us the critical info we need on Chris?"
- *Are you leveraging other media to drive registrations?* If you've been reading closely, you know that email is not an acquisition tool. At the same time, you must leverage your offline and online acquisition activities to drive email registrations. Think about your other marketing activities. Maybe you invest

in keywords, postcards, and radio. Why not include an email registration call to action? The easiest way to have your constituents fulfill this step is by visiting a specific landing page online.

I keep coming back to the dry cleaner example, and I'll use it again to illustrate how this can work. In this case, the dry cleaner created a nice postcard coupon program that was segmented by neighborhood. The postcards were different from traditional dry cleaner postcards due to the fact that they were not an actual coupon. To get the coupon, the customer had to go to a specific, customized landing page that featured his or her neighborhood (i.e., "Welcome Maple Farms Customers"). In order to receive the coupon, the recipient filled in a simple email registration form and committed to getting regularly scheduled coupons sent "right to the inbox." As you can imagine, this was a very successful program.

Here are some things to keep in mind with respect to landing pages: navigation should be minimal in order to prevent distraction, the task should be clear, and the form should be above the fold.

- *Are you offering an incentive?* Contests and giveaways (such as an educational piece) may be good ways to encourage opt-ins or even build credibility. As you might expect, the problem with an incentive is that some subscribers may only be in it for the reward rather than the relationship. By keeping an eye on the quality of your registrants (is it a bunch of junk email addresses?), you'll be able to determine whether the lift in sign ups due to an incentive is worth it. I'll mention again that the quality of your list is a hundred times more important than the quantity of your subscriber list.

Offline or Location Registration

If you're an organization with both a web presence and a physical location, you have other opportunities for collection. Lucky you! Ask yourself the following:

- *Are you taking advantage of high traffic areas?* This could be the cash register, the counter space leading up to the cash register (where people wait in line), your tables (if you're a restaurant)—there are several places that your customers gravitate toward. Why not leverage these zones for email opt-ins?

Sometimes the best ideas are the simplest. There's a Mexican restaurant across from my office that's always packed. On the counter leading up to the cash register, there's a plastic box with a nice "Free Lunch" offer. To be eligible for the drawing, you just toss in a business card. The sign on the box explains that there is an email opt-in associated with putting your card in. This container is full every day. It's nothing special, but it's a compelling enough offer that people want to participate. Now the real magic with this restaurant's program is how they execute on the opportunity to begin the relationship once they have an email address.

Here is an example of the restaurant's follow-up email:

Dear Chris,

We really appreciate your business. Thank you for having lunch with us. I'm sorry that you didn't win the free lunch this week. That honor went to (insert name and picture).

We do have a weekly email that offers several opportunities to save money AND to place orders online so that you don't have to stand in line at the restaurant.

Would you like to subscribe? Just check the box and hit submit.

This kind of email is entirely appropriate. They aren't adding their drawing participants until they confirm. In other words, they are taking the double opt-in practices we covered earlier and applying them to offline email capture. Well done!

- *Are the collected email addresses added to your database?* Don't laugh at the obvious. I'm always amazed by how many cards I put into a fishbowl and never hear anything. Not a peep! So maybe I didn't win the prize, but wasn't an email opt-in associated with it? What a lost opportunity . . . it comes back to the fact that if you ask for information—use it! Double check to make sure you have a system for inputting email addresses captured offline into your online database.

- *Are your employees trained and motivated?* To maximize the opportunities associated with your physical location, it's imperative to properly train your employees about what's important to you and why your constituents benefit. No one likes a nag, but the more you discuss it as a priority, the more your employees will take it seriously.

Incentives can work well here. I've seen programs that reward waiters with movie tickets or gift certificates depending on who collects the most email addresses when delivering the bill. It's amazing how motivating four movie tickets can be. Think about it: If you do an employee contest that rewards four movie tickets every week ($10 per ticket), and your employees generate a thousand high quality email addresses valued at a dollar a piece, you have a pretty nice ROI.

Business-to-Business/Networking/ Real World Registration

Unless you've been placed in an isolation chamber, I'm guessing that you and your salespeople interact with others. It may be face-to-face, or on the phone, or via email. Guess what? Each of these touch points is a chance to gain email opt-in.

For this reason, Business-to-Business (B-to-B) marketers often have a significant advantage in effective database marketing. By definition, they require some form of customer and prospect contact through direct sales representatives, telephone sales, or customer service personnel. Let's discuss some of those interactions and what to consider in order to optimize them:

- *Do you have a centralized view of customer activity?* All organizations should strive to have some sort of collective database where they have a centralized view of all customer activity (it's possible with on-demand software companies such as Salesforce.com or

Microsoft CRM). When all employees have an equal view into the organization's database, everyone is empowered to take advantage of constituent interaction and gain permission and other pertinent data.

- *Are you handling trade show or networking leads appropriately?* One common starting point for B-to-B and other businesses are industry trade shows or networking events. I'll illustrate the example with a trade show.

  Prior to the show, there are attendees. Those attendees are appealing prospects because they're likely to share some of the basic attributes that you look for in a customer. That is why you are investing in this trade event in the first place. Those attendees are *prospects.* They are not leads yet.

  Your job at the trade show is to get as many people as possible to move to the next step. You are trying to get permission to convert them from prospects to leads. Some will remain prospects because only the first contact has been made. Others will become leads during a lengthy one-on-one conversation about their company's needs.

  In any case, you should come back from the event, add all of these new contacts to your database, and immediately start mailing, right?

  Wrong! Just because people let you scan their badge does not give anyone permission to add them to an email marketing database. Don't do it! What you have is a small crack of permission to talk to this person at least one more time. Call. Or send a very personal email note to schedule a time when you can talk over the phone or in person. Those are appropriate places to gain permission. If you're a business with a longer sales cycle, remember that you must nurture these leads into becoming clients. Email is the perfect nurturing tool, but you need explicit permission to use it.

- *Are you taking advantage of internal resources?* What if your receptionist or customer service representatives asked callers if they would like to receive information or updates via email (and clearly painted a picture of the benefits)? Again, it's important for everyone to have access to a central database so that employees are empowered to assist with gaining permission.

BEYOND THE EMAIL ADDRESS

So far, much of this chapter has been devoted to the development of permission and ideas on "how" to collect those email addresses. Keep in mind that an email address and permission to mail it are the tip of the iceberg when it comes to building an effective marketing database.

The great thing is that you can essentially use every one of these tactics to build data on the attributes that help you drive business. In the next chapter, we'll cover segmentation, which will also help you decide what sort of data is worth collecting.

I'll end my thoughts on a light note. You know those milk ads that feature celebrities with a nice white mustache, saying, "Got Milk?" My next book will feature me on the cover wearing a shirt that says, "CRM," and a caption that reads, "Got data?" Just as milk promotes healthy bones and teeth, data promotes healthy relationships in today's world of analytical marketing.

Case Studies

Case Study 1: Incentives That Work

A restaurant with a mere 102 customer email addresses knew that its email subscribers were more engaged, visited more often, and tended to spend more than other patrons. The question was: How could they find more patrons willing to provide an email address?

With help from an agency, the restaurant developed an incentive that presented a win-win for both patrons and the restaurant. In exchange for his or her email address, the patron received a $10 coupon redeemable Monday through Thursday. The same strategy was implemented offline, using a brief comment card with each check holder.

In the beginning, the restaurant sent only a general e-newsletter. However, the agency pointed out that an event-specific call to action caused reservation rates to spike. As a result, the restaurant eventually delivered an entirely separate event email. Reservation rates exploded with the promotion of a special Valentine's Day Dinner, 50 Percent Off All Wine Mondays, and various local entertainment events.

Results: 10,000+ Email Addresses in Ten Months and $58,000 in Revenue

Within 10 months, the restaurant's list had grown from 102 names to over 10,000 names. They estimate a direct ROI of $4.14 to every $1 spent for this time frame, which does not include the additional reservations made via phone or repeat visits. Other mediums that the restaurant engaged in (such as broadcast radio and print) cost up to three times as much and were impossible to track. On the other hand, a single event email generates as many as 140 reservation requests, which represents nearly $12,000 worth of revenue. To date, the program has generated over $58,000 in revenue.

By providing a compelling email registration incentive that actually drove revenue, this restaurant hit the nail on the head.

Case Study 2: Make It Easy for Your Constituents (Using Data)

There is nothing worse than having to enter in your information *every time* you visit a site. Isn't part of your job as a marketer to make it *easy* for your constituents to do what you want them to do?

A theater realized that it was time to move several business efforts online and give their patrons a convenient way to interact with them. Part of this interaction included an easy way to renew annual tickets online, as the theater realized that it was much easier to retain its current patrons than spend time and money seeking new ones.

The theater spent several weeks getting its database in order to ensure that the email message notifying the patron that it was time to renew was personalized, accurate, and prepopulated as much information as possible. For example, it provided the subscriber with seating and pricing options, reminded the subscriber what he or she had committed to over the past year, and allowed the subscriber to easily choose a payment option. After a few clicks, the patron was renewed.

Results: Highest Renewal Rate Ever

The result speaks for itself. Data makes a marketer's life easier because he or she can deliver more relevant messages that generate results. Data makes the constituent's life easier because it can be a big time saver (and we all know that time is money). It's as simple as that.

WHAT ARE OTHER MARKETERS THINKING?
In their own words . . .

OPT-IN NUTTINESS

By Marc Sirkin
Vice President, eMarketing, The Leukemia & Lymphoma Society
Blog: http://www.sirkin.com/nonprofit_emarketing

We recently did something that most marketers only read about in case studies. We made our entire list opt back into our email newsletters. Those who didn't were dropped from our lists. We also recently introduced double opt-in for new subscribers—and that's made a difference as well. Our list quality is way up and that's good. Even if our lists are a lot smaller.

The results are astounding and stunning. . . .

I have a lot to say about this, but will encapsulate my thinking as a top 10 list that explains why every NPO marketer should do this immediately:

10. Sure, it's controversial to lose more than 50 percent of your list size, but it's worth it—and worth talking about.
9. Our spam complaints have dropped dramatically.
8. Our email vendor thinks what we're doing is great and wants a case study from us.
7. We can effectively benchmark our lists and provide solid guidance to our chapters.
6. We renewed list excitement.
5. We cleaned up old and duplicate email addresses that were ruining our delivery and click rates.
4. Our lists are now chock full of folks who WANT TO HEAR FROM US!
3. Deliverability rates went from 80 percent to over 98 percent—wow!
2. Click rates went from 1 to 2 percent on average to anywhere from 15 to 30 percent.
1. Our open rates are up over 50 percent on average from less than 20 percent.

CALCULATE THE VALUE OF AN EMAIL ADDRESS

By David Baker
Vice President, Email Marketing and Analytical Solutions
Agency.com

Eager to learn how? With the help of one of my guru analysts, I will share an elegant formula to help you establish the financial value of an email subscriber over a given time period. Most marketers have moved beyond basic email analytics and now focus on process-oriented metrics such as conversion rates, ROI, revenue per email, segment, and ISP performance variations. These are important metrics, but they tend to force us into a campaign-level mindset. As marketers, we need to look beyond campaigns and take a longer-term, customer-focused view. Consumers opt-in to receive a flow of communications from you and tend to view your messages in the aggregate. This model seeks to do the same. It presents an easy-to-digest numerical value for those who do not have a granular view of email marketing (think of your vice president of marketing, who needs snapshots of all channels).

This is ultimately an analytical process because it incorporates results from various campaigns. While there are several ROI models, we felt this one would be most generally useful as it contains a direct mail cost variable as a factor. Here's the basic model:

$$\begin{aligned} \text{Annual value of} \atop \text{an email subscriber} = &[(\text{Average incremental revenue} \atop \text{from each email}) \times (\text{Number of annual} \atop \text{email campaigns})] \\ + &[(\text{Cost savings versus} \atop \text{direct mail}) \times (\text{Number of annual DM} \atop \text{campaigns displaced})] \end{aligned}$$

To generate a proxy for the total value of your email list, you can multiply the per-subscriber dollar amount by the total number of active subscribers. There are a few subtleties to the model that are important to note:

- We're considering incremental revenue generated by email relative to another channel, not just total email revenue.
- Variations in campaign types and audiences may lead to starkly different revenue results that need to be incorporated in some way. For example, some campaigns may be general sale messages to the whole database, while other sales may be highly targeted to a specific segment.

- The cost savings side of the equation relates more to awareness-type messaging, such as time-sensitive news and other non-revenue mailings, rather than true displacement of direct mail, since most marketers are multi-channel messengers.
- The meaning of active subscriber will vary by organization. It could be someone who has opened or clicked, or there may be a transactional component to the definition.

Example: We'll assume a marketer sends four campaigns a year, realizing an average incremental revenue of $1.45 per campaign. Further, the marketer uses email twice a year for time-sensitive news, saving 30 cents per piece by sending email rather than direct mail.

The basic value equation is:

$$\text{Value of an email subscriber} = (\$1.45 \times 4) + (\$0.30 \times 2)$$
$$= \$6.40 \text{ per active subscriber}$$
$$\text{per year.}$$

$$\text{List value} = 1 \text{ million active subscribers} \times \$6.40 \text{ per subscriber}$$
$$= \$6.4 \text{ million.}$$

Things to Keep in Mind

- First, the value is an average across all active subscribers. Some segments will have greater value, and the same methodology can be applied to determine the value of those segments.
- Second, the low cost of email will likely lead someone in the organization to say, "We just need to email more often!" Don't fall for that trap, as high frequency and message irrelevance can quickly drop your subscriber value.
- Third, this value is not meant to convey that direct mail should be dumped.

It's still a critical channel for acquiring new customers and reaching lapsed email subscribers who wouldn't otherwise be reached. One financial model doesn't suit all. There are numerous books about statistical models. Find one that is relevant to your business, adapt it to your email program, and then live and breathe it.

Business Card in Hand Doesn't Mean "Opt-In"

By Chip House
Vice President, Marketing Services, ExactTarget

The business card has long been an important instrument to a salesperson attempting to build his or her network, and in turn, success. This was true long before email marketing came to be, though the collision of the two hasn't always been pretty. Big surprises are ahead for the unwary salesperson (and company) who doesn't carefully manage contacts derived from business cards.

What's the Problem?

According to Jupiter Research, the average B-to-B delivery rate, not counting bounces, is 89 percent. What factors are driving businesses to block or eat emails at such a rate? In addition to the general rise in spam, the business community is to blame. At least in part, I think it has to do with the poor way that many businesses have managed their lead acquisition campaigns. In many cases, a significant amount of a company's prospects come from personal meetings, tradeshows, and other events where business cards change hands. This makes sense. But what doesn't make sense is adding all of the email addresses derived in this manner to the company marketing database and beginning to send weekly sales pitch emails.

How You Get the Business Card Makes a Big Difference

Certainly the way you capture the business card has a lot to do with how you might use it. If it is captured in a face-to-face meeting with a handshake, then you'll have implicit permission from recipients to contact them at least once via phone or email and try to strike up a conversation or spark interest in what you're selling. However, if the card was merely placed in a fishbowl at your booth for a chance to win something, then you'll be treading up hill a bit. In this situation, it should be only *one* email asking the recipient to opt in, sign up, fill out a trial form, or something else before you communicate again.

Approach It Like a One-to-One, Personal Email Communication

The golden rule applies here: Treat others how you would want to be treated yourself! With a personal email, you wouldn't harass someone every week until she yelled at you to go away. So why would you get a business card, add it to your marketing database, and force the recipient to unsubscribe if he or she wants to be removed from further communications? Let's be serious. Respect the wishes of your potential clients, and you're more likely to get a sale over time.

Capture Date and Time in Your Database

The ability to prove you have permission to email a name is critical. Ensure you keep a record of the date and time that you captured your subscribers' opt-in in your CRM database or contact file. If captured online, capture their IP address if possible. Permission marketing is the only way to improve the reputation for Business-to-Business email.

RETAIL EMAIL SUBSCRIPTION BENCHMARK STUDY: CURRENT TRENDS AND BEST PRACTICES FOR RETAILERS OFFERING NEWSLETTERS

By Chad White
Research and Editorial Director, RetailEmail.Blogspot
Blog: http://retailemail.blogspot.com

Methodology

Between June 13 and 21, 2006, RetailEmail.Blogspot signed up for the email newsletters of 101 of the top online retailers. The retailers included in the study were among the online retailers with the highest online sales as identified by *Internet Retailer* magazine.

We excluded retailers that required too much personal information. For instance, eBay required a credit card number to create an account through which you could sign up for a newsletter.

Introduction and Key Findings

First impressions are everything. When it comes to their newsletters, the top retailers largely fall into two camps: those that make the sign-up process as quick and painless as possible, and those that make it rich and personalized.

Half of the top retailers offered one-click sign-up for their newsletters, allowing people to sign up by entering their email address in a field on the retailer's homepage and clicking "sign up." It doesn't get any more pain free than that.

The second group, representing 24 percent of the retailers in the study, went for personalization, offering subscribers more than one newsletter or product focus from which to choose. In fact, these retailers offered an average of 9.5 different newsletters or product focuses to choose from. Barnes & Noble had the widest selection, offering 24 newsletters on a variety of subjects.

Unfortunately, there is also a third group of retailers, the 26 percent that make signing up for their newsletters cumbersome or intrusive. This group includes the 13 percent of the top retailers that require subscribers to create an account in order to sign up for their newsletters. It also includes the 7 percent that required the subscriber's mailing address and the 4 percent that required their phone number—both pieces of sensitive information that many people aren't comfortable giving out just to receive an email newsletter. These retailers risked not only losing potential newsletter subscribers but also hurting their brand reputations.

Other key findings from the study include:

- 27 percent of the top retailers offered subscribers some kind of incentive or reward.
- Beyond the person's email address, retailers most often required the person's name (31 percent) and zip code (23 percent) to complete the sign-up. All other pieces of personal information were required by less than 10 percent of retailers.
- 23 percent of retailers required a subscriber's zip code, proof that retailers are tying their web operations into their local store operations. Among other things, knowing the subscriber's zip code allows retailers to customize the content of their newsletters based on whether there is a store local to the subscriber, and if so, customize the content of their newsletter based on the products and services available at that store.
- 24 percent of retailers asked subscribers to confirm their email address by entering it in a second field at the time of sign up.
- Retailers overwhelmingly prefer to have visitors sign up for their newsletter via a field rather than a button, with 72 percent of the top retailers using that method. That said, only 50 percent offered one-click sign-up from the homepage, so nearly one-third of those using a field on

their homepage simply forwarded prospective subscribers on to a page with a sign-up form, just like the retailers using buttons did.

- The most popular position on the homepage for the sign-up field or button was the lower right-hand side, with 36 percent of the top retailers placing it there. The second most popular position was the lower left-hand side, with 32 percent. Fifteen percent placed it in the upper right, while only 8 percent placed it in the upper left. The lower quadrants included all portions of the website below the midline of the initial screen of the homepage.
- 11 percent of retailers in the study didn't have a sign-up field or button on their homepage.
- 13 percent of retailers had not sent their first email within three weeks of the subscription date. Given the lapse of time, it's possible that the sign-up processes failed at these retailers, which include iTunes, CDW, Sears, 1800flowers, Walgreens, DrsFosterSmith, Snapon, QVC, SamsClub, Shop.MLB, NFLshop, Niketown, and Reebok.

Best Practices

- *One-click sign up plus optional registration.* Don't scare off prospective subscribers with lengthy sign-up forms. Instead, follow the lead of Bluefly, Northern Tool, and others who allow one-click sign up from their homepage but then follow-up with a landing page that allows subscribers to select personal preferences and provide additional information if they wish. This approach enables you to work within subscribers' comfort zones, allowing them to give up more than just their email address if they're comfortable with that.
- *Not requiring addresses, phone numbers, and other sensitive personal information.* Some retailers apparently still think that customers who sign up for their newsletters

also want to receive their print catalog and mailers, which is why they continue to ask for subscribers' mailing addresses. It's unwise to make that assumption—first, because prospective subscribers who are wary about giving out their address may simply not sign up for your newsletter; and second, they may become irritated when they receive a catalog they didn't request. During the sign-up process or immediately after, a number of retailers included either a button or unchecked check box that would allow subscribers to sign up to receive the print catalog as well. If your newsletter drives subscribers to make purchases, then you'll have their mailing address soon enough. There's no good reason to ask for it upfront. The worst offenders here were Bed Bath & Beyond, Coach, Harry & David, J. Jill, Office Depot, QVC, and Victoria's Secret, all of which asked for full mailing addresses.

Four e-tailers—Harry & David, Office Depot, QVC, and Walgreens—also had the gall to ask for subscribers' phone numbers. Again, there's no justification for asking for that. People are attracted to email because it isn't intrusive. If people think they're going to get calls because they signed up for a newsletter, some of them may decide it's not worth the risk of being called.

Retailers should also reconsider their practice of collecting birth dates. Alloy, American Eagle Outfitters, and Reebok required subscribers' birth dates—and Amazon, Bloomingdale's, Macy's, Saks, ShopNBC, Spiegel, and Walgreens all requested it. Some said it was for age verification and a few said they wanted it so they could send a special gift on the subscriber's birthday. However, plenty of retailers verified that subscribers were over the age of 18 by having them simply check a box. Walgreens surely needs a person's birthday to fill prescriptions, not to sell general merchandise. It would be better to collect that information when a person tries to fill a prescription online. Considering that plenty of retailers have had data security breaches in recent years, and the fact that birth dates are almost as much of a liability as Social Security numbers, we're not sure why retailers would want to be responsible for keeping that bit of information safe.

- *Rewarding customers for subscribing.* Wanting to get off on the right foot, 27 percent of the top retailers offered subscribers some kind of incentive to subscribe. Most rewards were for discounts of 10 percent to 15 percent. For instance, AllPosters offered "10 percent off your next order," and Ross-Simons offered "15 percent off your next purchase plus free shipping." Macy's reward was a somewhat cryptic: *"Free shipping on your $100 purchase."*

  But there were also variations on the rewards theme. For example, Crutchfield and Musician's Friend both entered new subscribers into a raffle. Crutchfield subscribers were entered into a monthly Great Gear Giveaway (we were offered the chance to win a Toshiba MEGF20S 20GB Digital Music and Photo Player). Musician's Friend has a Weekly Gear Giveaway, which offered us the chance to win a Universal Audio UA-S110 SOLO/110 Precision Class A Mic Pre & DI Box (see Figure 5.1).

  The Gap Inc. brands—Gap, Old Navy, and Banana Republic—had their own interesting twist. They offered reward points on their credit cards. We think this is a nice way to tie newsletters to a loyalty card (although the 100 reward points are only equal to $5 off a purchase, which is pretty miserly compared to what the percentage-off deals are usually worth). We would even bet that a small number of people sign up for a GapCard just to get the extra 100 points (see Figure 5.2).

- *Offering plenty of content options.* Letting subscribers customize the content that they will receive vastly improves the relevance of that newsletter, and therefore

Figure 5.1
Musician's Friend Weekly Gear Giveaway

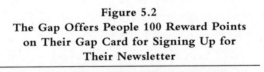

increases the chance that they will be long-term subscribers who recommend the newsletter to friends and family. Twenty-four percent of retailers offer more than one newsletter. These retailers offered an average of 9.5 different newsletters to choose from. Barnes & Noble had the widest selection, offering 24 on a variety of

Figure 5.2
The Gap Offers People 100 Reward Points on Their Gap Card for Signing Up for Their Newsletter

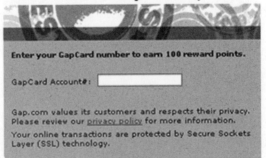

subject areas with delivery frequencies ranging from weekly to quarterly (see Figure 5.3).

Content customization was the most popular with computer and electronics retailers, with 31 percent offering it, and apparel retailers, with 25 percent of them offering it. For example, Palm offered a newsletter just on

Figure 5.3
Here Are Just a Few of the Content Options Given to
Barnes & Noble Newsletter Subscribers

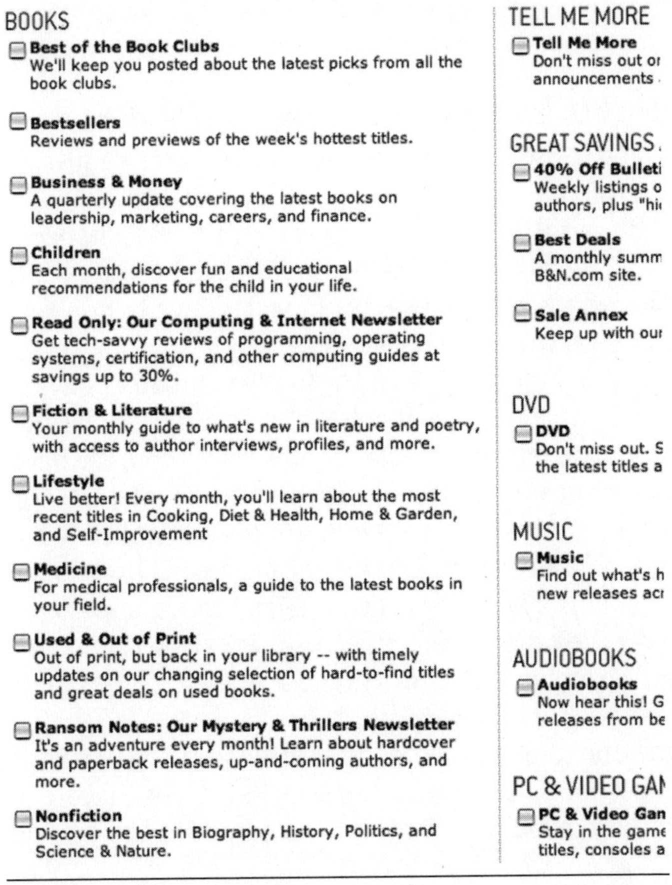

BOOKS

Best of the Book Clubs
We'll keep you posted about the latest picks from all the book clubs.

Bestsellers
Reviews and previews of the week's hottest titles.

Business & Money
A quarterly update covering the latest books on leadership, marketing, careers, and finance.

Children
Each month, discover fun and educational recommendations for the child in your life.

Read Only: Our Computing & Internet Newsletter
Get tech-savvy reviews of programming, operating systems, certification, and other computing guides at savings up to 30%.

Fiction & Literature
Your monthly guide to what's new in literature and poetry, with access to author interviews, profiles, and more.

Lifestyle
Live better! Every month, you'll learn about the most recent titles in Cooking, Diet & Health, Home & Garden, and Self-Improvement

Medicine
For medical professionals, a guide to the latest books in your field.

Used & Out of Print
Out of print, but back in your library -- with timely updates on our changing selection of hard-to-find titles and great deals on used books.

Ransom Notes: Our Mystery & Thrillers Newsletter
It's an adventure every month! Learn about hardcover and paperback releases, up-and-coming authors, and more.

Nonfiction
Discover the best in Biography, History, Politics, and Science & Nature.

TELL ME MORE

Tell Me More
Don't miss out or announcements.

GREAT SAVINGS.

40% Off Bulleti
Weekly listings o authors, plus "hi

Best Deals
A monthly summ B&N.com site.

Sale Annex
Keep up with our

DVD

DVD
Don't miss out. S the latest titles a

MUSIC

Music
Find out what's h new releases acr

AUDIOBOOKS

Audiobooks
Now hear this! G releases from be

PC & VIDEO GAN

PC & Video Gan
Stay in the game titles, consoles a

its Treo product. It also offered newsletters on several different software categories targeting particular industry verticals such as legal, real estate, and healthcare. On the other hand, apparel retailers offered content targeting the type of clothing the subscriber is interested in—men, women, boys, baby, maternity, and others.

We were surprised to see that only 18 percent of sporting goods retailers offered content that catered to the particular sports interests of subscribers. We would think that most people are focused on just a few sports, if not only one. But only BassPro and Reebok allowed subscribers to tailor their newsletters to the sports they are most interested in.

Retailer Study Follow-up: Pass CAN-SEND Now

We're very close to writing letters to our representatives in Congress to have them reopen the CAN-SPAM Act and add a rule that says that companies have to start emailing people within 10 days of them signing up for newsletters—a sort of corollary to the rule that says companies have to honor unsubscribes within 10 days. Here's why:

We did our initial research for this Benchmark Study back in mid-June, signing up for the email newsletters of 101 of the largest online retailers. In the months since then, we have received regular emails from just 86 of those retailers. Of the remaining 15 retailers, eight of them sent us welcome emails but nothing since (Amazon, American Eagle Outfitters, Barnes & Noble, Best Buy, Diamond.com, FTD, Lowe's, and Ross-Simons). The other seven retailers—1-800-Flowers, CDW, iTunes, Niketown, QVC, Sears, and Walgreens—have sent nothing at all.

Now one might conclude that after so many weeks that the subscription processes at these 15 retailers have completely failed, but we're not so sure that can be said yet.

The reason is that each week, a few more of the subscriptions finally kick in. For instance, within the last few weeks, we've started receiving regular emails from Sony, MLB, Reebok, Sam's Club, Staples, Drs. Fosters & Smith, and J. Crew.

While the sign-up processes at these retailers turned out not to be complete failures, they were anything but a success. Surely the average person expects to start receiving email newsletters within a month, if not much sooner—which means that they were probably perturbed when the emails finally started rolling in (we figure that some went back after a few weeks and signed up for the newsletters again). Either way, the experience was less than impressive.

So with all that said, we call on all retailers to make email friendlier by passing their own email sign-in bylaw—call it CAN-SEND—whereby they pledge to fulfill email newsletter subscriptions within 10 days of sign up.

CHAPTER 5 REVIEW

- You must put a price on what an email address is worth to your organization. It's the only way you'll make a compelling case to make it a priority internally. It's the only way you'll be able to make use of email marketing.
- For worthwhile results, you need to get permission the good old fashion way (by asking). Selling or renting your lists, selling or renting someone else's lists, or email appending are all unacceptable practices.
- When confirming permission, double opt-in includes an extra step that requires the potential subscriber to click and activate the subscription. While it yields a smaller list than any other kind of opt-in, it ensures quality of email addresses before they are added to your list.
- Leverage all email collection points available to you: online, in-store, and networking and tradeshow opportunities. You are

investing in customer acquisition tactics outside of email (because as we've already discussed, email is an ineffective acquisition tool), so you might as well use those touch points to build your database!

- When collecting any sort of data via a form, keep questions minimal and friction low. I already told you that I'm not sending in a hair sample to register for your emails.

CHAPTER 6

SEGMENTING FOR RELEVANCE

In a previous chapter, we discussed subscriber engagement. We established the fact that your constituents are busy people and don't want to be bothered if you have nothing relevant to say. When you *do* have something relevant to say, you must say it to the right individuals.

Segmentation is your answer. It is a must, not an option. It is one of the most effective ways to boost engagement and prevent list fatigue. By identifying individuals with similarities, you are able to develop messages that are likely to be relevant to select portions of your audience. Before we get any further, I'd like to thank Morgan Stewart, Director of Strategic Services for ExactTarget and a segmentation expert, for weighing in on much of what I'm about to share.

BASIC SEGMENTATION 101: WHAT IS IT?

When marketers refer to a segment, they are talking about a portion of their database that has similar characteristics. Those characteristics are used to market in a relevant manner, which is different from mass marketing. Segmentation is an ongoing process that will help you build real relationships. The smaller you can make the segments, the more likely you are to deliver a relevant message.

In the old world of marketing, segmenting was difficult. The nature of television or paper-based marketing made it expensive and cumbersome to do real segmentation. How can a television know anything more than my demographics? Or how can a direct mail piece immediately measure my engagement? Both are time intensive and leave a lot for the marketer to fill in with his or her imagination.

With email, you're able to leverage all of your data to target smaller groups of people with the same characteristics, while tracking engagement from start to finish.

Many organizations aren't sure what segments will be beneficial to their business. To me, segmentation is the most fun aspect of marketing. It's like detective work. Who do you segment? Based on what attributes? Why? Was it Colonel Mustard with the rope in the billiard room or Miss Scarlet?

Not convinced? The alternative to segmenting your audience is to simply batch and blast messages to your entire subscriber list. Marketers who engage in batch and blast email marketing knowingly (or unknowingly) make several grave assumptions. Here is the reality:

- *Subscribers are NOT a homogeneous group.* Batch and blast tactics work on the premise that all subscribers are equally likely to respond to the same message. These tactics assume that there is no real difference between people that may cause them to respond differently to your messages. In reality, your subscribers are not all the same. They have different lifestyles. They have different needs. They have different experiences with your company. They have different attitudes toward your products and services. It's no wonder that organizations that segment their customer bases yield higher email campaign response rates—regardless of the attributes used for segmentation.
- *There will NOT always be more customers.* Batch and blast email tactics can work so long as the customer base is constantly replenished. Whether it's the total population in your target demographic or the total number of companies that are in the market, there are a finite number of prospects available to any company. There is also a limit to the number of people who will provide you with permission to communicate through email. Thus, driv-

ing revenue from email is no longer a matter of simply finding more willing subscribers. It is now a battle for email market share.

- *The well WILL run dry.* Batch and blast tactics assume that marketers can endlessly tap into their subscriber database to drive revenue. We know that sending irrelevant emails or sending email too frequently causes list fatigue. With each communication, subscribers subconsciously decide whether or not your message is worth opening today and in the future. If they decide that your communications are not worth their time, they respond by either opting-out of your emails or ignoring you. Once this decision is made, it is very difficult to rebuild trust and win them back. When you combine the reality of list fatigue with the fact that there is a finite audience, it isn't hard to see that the supply eventually runs out.

After you invest the time and money to get permission, it makes sense to invest in making sure you put your best foot forward. Doing so requires that you pick out those key bits of data that will allow you to communicate in an appropriate manner.

Marketing is not rocket science (maybe that's why I'm a marketer). The concepts are simple, and here is an example of that simplicity. There are basically three buckets that your constituent data belongs in:

1. *Demographic data:* These are common characteristics that are obvious to an observer. For example, where you live, how you make your living, and your marital status. Demographic data is a good starting point and can offer a marketer valuable trending insight. It's even more helpful as a supplement to additional data, such as behavior. The theory of demographic marketing is that people who are alike act alike, so patterns emerge. While demographic data can lend insight into general behavior across a group, it is not the best predictor of an individual's future behavior.

2. *Preference and opinion data:* Through surveys, polls, focus groups, and general conversation, people are often happy to tell you what they think. Here's the tricky part: Many people will

tell you what they think *you want* to hear or what *they want* to be true.

I remember a story that caught my attention a few years ago. As a group of women entered a speed dating arena, a writer asked the women what they perceived as the characteristics of an ideal spouse. Nearly all of the women included these attributes: sincere, honest, hard working, good personality. Looks didn't seem to matter.

Yet, at the end of the session, each of these women took the opportunity to date the great-looking, fun guy. They based a decision on something that originally hadn't mattered. It's the same thing when it comes to your constituents. Don't be surprised if some of them say one thing and do another. That's why behavioral information is the very best data to leverage.

3. *Behavioral data:* Past behavior is the greatest predictor of future behavior. Simple as that. Someone who buys coffee online is more likely to buy coffee online again as opposed to someone who *says* she'd like to buy coffee online. The proof is in the action, not in what people say. If your significant other told you that he or she was going to make dinner every night, you'd probably be thrilled. But if a month passed and you found yourself at the McDonald's drive-thru for the thirtieth time, you'd probably wonder what was going on. Saying that you'll do something is an *intention,* not an action. Again, that's why behavior is even more telling than what people say they will do or what they prefer.

WHAT BEHAVIOR SHOULD YOU LOOK FOR?

More than a hundred years ago, direct marketers came up with the solution known as Recency, Frequency, and Monetary value (RFM), which is a law of marketing, just as Newton's Law is a law of physics. Don't stray too far from the basics and you'll be able to learn from its principles.

Unless this is your first marketing book (and I'd be very honored if that's the case), you've probably learned about RFM before. Just about every marketing book on the planet will mention RFM. It's the lens that all of us should view our constituents through.

Recency simply means *how recently* the constituent exhibited a desired behavior. For example, if you were a grocery store owner, this would mean a shopping trip. If you were a nonprofit, this might mean the last time a constituent volunteered or donated something. Only you can determine what is the desired behavior for your organization.

When it comes to RFM, knowledge truly is power. The more you know about your constituents—especially when it comes to Recency—the more you can leverage that information to drive future desired actions. Recency is *the most powerful* single factor affecting customer repurchase. The person most likely to buy from you again is the customer who bought from you most recently. Recency implies retention, which is more important than Frequency. Why? Because when people stop engaging with you, they're hard to win back (we demonstrated that with a nice graph a few chapters back). As long as the person is still an active constituent, there's always the opportunity to increase Frequency or Monetary value.

Frequency is *the number of times* that a customer engages in the desired behaviors. This can be anything from site visits, to purchases, to referrals. Frequency implies a pattern, which you should assume can be maintained once it is established. It is an opportunity to monitor a pattern, encourage it, and notice if that pattern is broken or changes. It's no secret that frequent buyers respond better than infrequent buyers.

Monetary value involves categorizing all customers by the *amount that they spend in a given time period*. The high spenders often respond more regularly than the lower spenders. Given that most organizations place significant value on revenue, it's important to know who your big spenders are. When it comes to Monetary value, you'll again need to investigate what patterns and habits are the best for your business. For example, is a person who makes a big purchase once a year better or worse than someone who makes several smaller purchases throughout the year? Are there service fees associated with the multiple purchases? Is there less of an opportunity for up-selling with the one time spender?

What's great about Internet marketing—and more specifically, email marketing—is that you have the ability to use all kinds of data in combination to drive true one-to-one relationships.

RECOMMENDED SEGMENT: THE "BEST"

When segmenting for the first time, you should look no further than what you've already collected in your database. I'm guessing you can use this data to identify your best constituents and look for patterns among them. "Best" will depend on your business. It may be the biggest donors or most likely to volunteer. It might be the biggest spenders or the most frequent online purchasers. You must look at your database and ask yourself this question: "Which constituents are growing my business?" Then you must try your hardest to develop more of them.

Some very interesting findings can emerge from identifying the "best" population. Oftentimes, they are at the max of what they are willing to give to your organization. That means you should stop asking them to do more.

In a previous life, I was in the coupon business. One of the biggest problems with that business was the fact that it's usually your best customers who take advantage of the token discount coupon. The reality is that they're the customers who need the least incentive.

So for the best constituents, you might want to adjust your goal from increasing wallet share to simply retaining them. You want to keep a good thing going. This is where relationship marketing really becomes retention marketing. With this population, it's critical to make contact on a highly personal level. These are the folks you want to be close friends with. These are the people you want to love you. The constituents in the "best" group are the ones who will tell their friends and family about you. They'll forgive the occasional mistake and provide feedback that makes you stronger.

What does the "best" group want in return? Great service, appreciation, and respect. Make them feel extra special by making them part of the team. Everyone wants to be part of something, right? Emotional investment makes a huge difference. That's why we create advisory boards, clubs, memberships, and more. Call them what you like, just remember that your best constituents will provide behind-the-scenes insights ranging from development issues to service issues. These people deserve the inside scoop.

Also keep in mind that the very process of defining your "best" segment will help you identify the actions and characteristics that make them the top of your audience. In turn, it will help you determine ways to move others to this segment. Beyond keeping your "best" group happy, what's your other goal? Yeah, you're catching on. It's creating more of them!

Once you define the similar attributes that the "best" possess, you can look at your database for others who share all or some of the same characteristics. This is your "almost best" group. What gets really fun with this population is the marketing experimentation you can do to drive actions that move them to the next level.

In addition to the "almost best" category, there are others worthy of segmentation. Can you believe it? We get to spend money talking to people who aren't in the top deciles of the customer database. With traditional media, it's too expensive to continue to talk to these less desirable constituents. Consider the catalog business a good example. If you're a great customer for a specific catalog, you're going to get a lot of catalogs. The company is willing to make a significant investment in you so that you always have their marketing handy when you're ready to make a purchase decision. If you are not such a good customer—perhaps you bought once last year—you're going to receive fewer catalogs, simply due to cost. That little book of paper is so expensive, it can't be wasted on someone who seems unlikely to buy. It's a self-fulfilling prophecy because without the catalog, you couldn't buy if you wanted to.

Okay, so let's take away the cost restriction. Assume that the catalog merchant can afford to market to people whom it wouldn't ordinarily spend money on. The key to this segment still comes down to personalization and relevance. How do you move this group up the chain, toward the best customer segment? Not by pounding them with lots of offers, but by engaging them in a dialogue based on their attributes.

THE SUBSCRIBER BASE AS AN ASSET

Think of your subscriber base as an appreciating asset, like a bank or IRA account, instead of a resource that can be endlessly exploited. As long as you invest properly and draw against the account in moderation, the long-term value of the asset is maintained. More importantly, the asset will take care of you for a long time. However, if you liquidate the asset today, don't expect there to be much money left in the future.

I have encountered a number of retail companies that choose to send daily email promotions to their entire subscriber list. The logic is based on the simple fact that the more they send email, the more money they make. In the short run, these companies increase their overall sales. In the long run, they witness incredible list fatigue. Eventually sales begin to decline because their poor subscribers have simply had enough.

Yes, individuals should be treated individually—this is the objective of customer-centric marketing strategies. However, tailoring highly personalized messages to each individual in the customer base can be an overwhelming aspiration. Practically, marketers need to deliver the most relevant messages possible—with profitability in mind.

The 80/20 rule states that 80 percent of your revenue will come from 20 percent of your customer base. Time and again, this rule has proved itself in business. The thing that differentiates "great" marketers from "good" marketers is that they learn to use multiple layers of segmentation to change the dynamics of the 80/20 rule. They move beyond this first level of segmentation and refine segments so that each group generates more revenue, higher profit margins, and higher adoption.

Consider the following three levels of segmentation of a customer base (see Figure 6.1):

Level 1: Everything appears to be going well. The 80/20 rule is in tact as expected.

Level 2: Simply split the 80 percent of the customers in half. Looking at the bottom 40 percent of your customers, we identify a group that is having a negative impact on your bottom line.

Level 3: Take each of the three groups in Level 2 and split them in half again. There are now segments around which strategies should be developed. By dividing the customer base into fifths (or "quintiles"), and the top quintile in half (each representing a "decile"), the customers are in groups that may be manipulated in order to improve the overall profitability of the program.

These three groups require vastly different strategies:

Level 1: Profitable customers need to be thanked. The top decile is very profitable. While attempting to keep targeting these highly profitable customers with incentives to buy more, we may actually risk offending this segment and loosing their business. This group may not require any incentive. A simple "thank you" and recognition may go a long way.

Level 2: Losers may require "discipline." We know that the bottom quintile costs the company money. Simply stated, the organization is paying to have these customers. We could "fire" the bottom quantile and immediately save the company money or develop a

Figure 6.1
Segment Your Customer Base to the Most
Granular Level in Order to Maximize Profitability

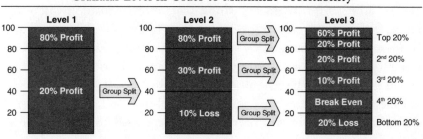

strategy that will bring them up to a profitable level. Either way, their profit-taking behavior cannot continue long term.

Level 3: Middle segments must move up the ladder. Moving segments up the ladder—from marginally profitable to highly profitable—requires understanding the motivations and expectations of each segment and then acting accordingly. This group will likely require additional information to help identify segments with similar value expectations. These expectations can then be addressed in ways that convince customers to invest more in their relationship with the organization.

BUILDING VALUE

Customer-centric strategies consider the segmentation of customers based on their current value to the organization, but it doesn't stop there. The future or potential value of the customer must be considered. Your current customer mix may not be as profitable as you would like. Your best customers today may not be your best customers tomorrow. Each segment should be addressed in a way that maximizes the long-term revenue and profit potential of the entire customer base.

A long-term segmentation strategy addresses the unique needs of each segment in order to increase the value of customers to the organization. This is accomplished by increasing your organization's value to customers. It is reciprocal—it is a relationship where each party gets something of value at the end of the day and feels good about it.

To increase overall value of the customer base, one must make decisions about which segments can become more valuable, which segments need to be grown, and which segments should be avoided. Remember, it is not realistic to expect that the value of *every* customer can be increased. We are not magicians. The objective is to increase the value of the overall customer base.

One approach is to consider the profitability and market share of different segments of your customers. Assume you are using age to

Figure 6.2
Establish Long-Term Profitability Goals for Each Segment

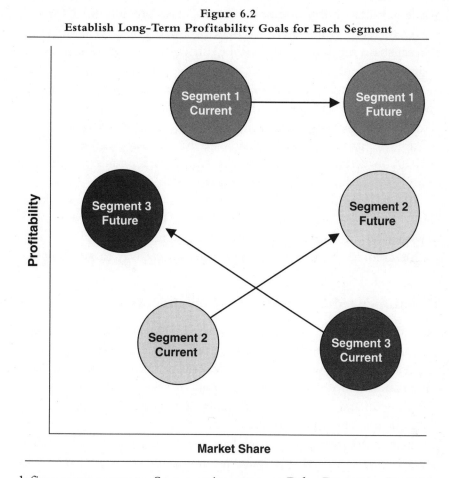

define your segments. Segment 1 represents Baby Boomers. Segment 2 represents Teens. Segment 3 represents Gen X (see Figure 6.2).

Looking at these segments, you identify that Baby Boomers are highly profitable but there's room to grow. The logical strategy for this segment is to increase your market share by stepping up your acquisition efforts.

Segment 2 (Teens) is not very profitable, and you don't have good penetration into this market. But teens are an attractive market since their buying power is going to increase over time. You must make a difficult decision: Does it make sense to grow this segment while simultaneously attempting to increase profitability? Or is it better to focus your efforts elsewhere? Increasing profitability and market share simultaneously will be difficult and may require significant investment.

Last, we have the Gen X segment, Segment 3. You already have a strong presence with this group, but they are not very profitable. This may be a group that you're paying to be your customers. That makes this group a strong candidate for further segmentation in which you determine exactly which Gen X individuals you want to "fire" due to the fact that they are unprofitable.

Always keep in mind that customer-centric strategies are long-term. Yes, you need to meet current goals, but you must do so in a way that optimizes future potential value. Creating a meaningful dialogue tailored to the right individuals is a great way to get there.

Recommended Segment: New Constituents

How do you talk to your new constituents? A well-known marketer hit me across the head with this one day when she said, "They have not seen your best stuff yet." She was referring to a company communication that we'd been doing for about three years. When someone came in as a new subscriber, guess what content we sent? Exactly the same content that everyone else received. In three years, we'd accumulated 36 past issues. Some of these issues were terrific; others were mediocre at best. Her point was: Why not give your new subscribers a taste of your best stuff? So we listened. We went through all of our content and picked five emails that we deemed the "best" and sent a portion of them to every new customer. That way, we put our best foot forward, and they had a good idea of what we stood for.

What do you want your new people to know about you? After all, this is your chance to make a great and lasting impression. Keep in mind your specific goals for your new customers. Are you looking for another sale? An up-sell? Cross-sell?

This is also a great time to get more information from your audience. A well planned welcome stream can be used to gauge what types of information is going to be of interest to the constituent. I like to provide a wide range of information at the beginning of the relationship and hone in on the things that get the constituent engaged with the program.

Recommended Segment: Lapsed Constituents

How does your organization treat someone who has followed a pattern that's suddenly broken? Perhaps a predictable customer stops coming in all together, or suddenly switches to another behavior such as buying online rather than in the store.

Earlier, we discussed RFM: Recency, Frequency, and Monetary value. I mentioned that Recency is the most important attribute because predictability of behavior is tied to the time frame in which the behavior occurred. The more recent the behavior, the higher the likelihood that the behavior will happen again. Do you think a customer who hasn't been into your store in the past five years is more likely to buy than a person who came into your store last year? Last year's purchaser is more likely. The relationship hasn't grown too far apart yet.

You want to constantly keep an eye on timing with respect to your segments. For example, if your "best" group typically exhibits a desired behavior every month, then you will want to immediately identify the individuals who *did not* do something as soon as the month ends. Waiting two months to identify them may be too long to make an impact. I'm not saying it's a cause for panic, but there should be some communication to help you understand the change or spark a response. Think of this communication like the defribrillator used in the emergency room. Sometimes a surprising jolt will get the patient back on course. Sometimes it won't. But to even have a chance for the jolt to work, it must be given immediately. It's the same thing with lapsed constituents. The less recent the change in behavior, the less likely you are to influence the outcome.

SEGMENTATION AND TARGETING METHODOLOGIES

Industry experts have proposed several different methodologies for segmentation and targeting. This section outlines a few and explores the common elements that can be used when applied to email marketing.

Peppers & Rogers Group: IDIC Methodology

This methodology consists of four steps:

1. *Identify* customers individually and addressably.
2. *Differentiate* customers or customer groups based on their needs and value.
3. *Interact* with customers in a way that benefits them and the company, continually gathering relevant information about them.
4. *Customize* the relationship over time by changing aspects of the company's behavior toward individual customers based on understanding the customer's needs and value.

DeBonis, Balinski, and Allen: Five-Step Process

As outlined in their book *Value-Based Marketing for Bottom-Line Success* (New York: McGraw-Hill, 2002), the five steps are:

1. *Discover—Understand the Customer* includes understanding the market, understanding customer expectations, discovering customer segments, assessing competitive position, selecting target segments.
2. *Commit—Commit to the Customer* includes defining segment strategies, developing offerings, creating an organization and processes that support the strategy, defining key performance indicators or metrics.
3. *Create—Create Customer Value* includes creating a culture committed to customer value, process planning, investing in required infrastructure, implementation.
4. *Assess—Obtain Customer Feedback* includes tracking won and lost business, seeking customer feedback, resolving customer complaints, assessing performance against customer ex-

pectations, performing analysis that can be used to improve processes.

5. *Improve—Measure and Improve Value* includes identifying gaps, challenging corporate understanding of customers, re-defining customer value commitments, improving customer value, anticipating change.

McDonald and Dunbar: Three-Stage, Seven-Step Process

In their book *Market Segmentation: How to Do It and How to Profit from It* (London: Macmillan Publishers, 1998), McDonald and Dunbar propose a three-stage, seven-step process for developing segments. (See Figure 6.3 for a diagram.)

Figure 6.3
McDonald and Dunbar's Process for Developing Segments

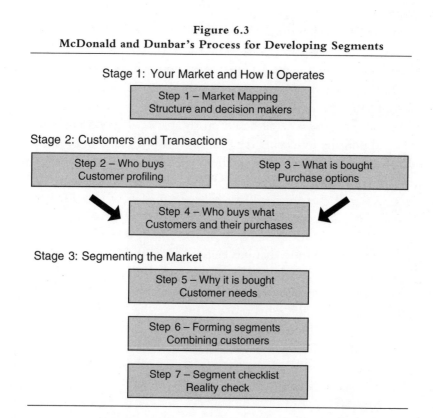

Stage 1: Your Market and How It Operates

Step 1 – Market Mapping
Structure and decision makers

Stage 2: Customers and Transactions

Step 2 – Who buys
Customer profiling

Step 3 – What is bought
Purchase options

Step 4 – Who buys what
Customers and their purchases

Stage 3: Segmenting the Market

Step 5 – Why it is bought
Customer needs

Step 6 – Forming segments
Combining customers

Step 7 – Segment checklist
Reality check

Each of these customer-centric models yields different insights into the process of segmenting and targeting customers and prospects. While there are definitely different points of emphasis, the proponents of these models agree on several critical components:

- The first and hardest step is committing to a long-term approach that is right for your company and your customers.
- Developing a strategy based on market conditions and actual customer information is a must.
- Implementation is crucial. Poor implementation will derail any strategy, no matter how good it is.
- Ongoing monitoring and adjustments need to be made to the strategy based on feedback from customers.

You are now ready to segment your database. Ready to have some fun? It's time for us to practice what we've covered so far.

If you have access to a database or a CRM system, then segmentation entails running a report on the various characteristics of your constituents. This doesn't have to be overly complicated, especially in the beginning. I like to export an excel spreadsheet from our CRM system and do some sorting based on the basics. If you're able to, go ahead and pull the following data for each record: date of most recent purchase, total purchases during the purchase cycle, and average purchase amount during the purchase cycle.

Because each customer will be scored on each of the three RFM variables, let's do a quick review:

- *Recency* is the time that has elapsed since the customer made his most recent purchase. A customer who made his most recent purchase last month will receive a higher Recency score than a customer who made his most recent purchase three years ago.
- *Frequency* is the total number of purchases that a customer has made within a designated period of time. A customer who made six purchases in the last three years would receive a higher Frequency score than a customer who made one purchase in the last three years.

- *Monetary value* is each customer's average purchase amount during a designated period of time. A customer who averages a $100 purchase amount would receive a higher score than a customer who averages a $20 purchase amount (Average purchase amount = Total dollars spent on purchases in last three years/total number of purchases in past three years).

For the sake of the exercise, let's assume that you're a candy store. We'll use a 1 to 3 scoring system for each of your customer segments, with 1 given to those who exhibited the least desirable action and 3 given to those who exhibited the most desirable action:

Recency Score Criteria

1 = Customers who purchased more than 12 months ago
2 = Customers who purchased more than three months ago, but fewer than 12 months ago
3 = Customers who made a purchase in the last three months

Frequency Score Criteria

1 = Customers who made a purchase in the past 12 months
2 = Customers who made between two and ten purchases in the past 12 months
3 = Customers who made more than ten purchases in the past 12 months

Monetary Value Score Criteria

1 = Customers with an average purchase amount up to $20
2 = Customers with an average purchase amount between $20 and $45
3 = Customers with an average purchase amount greater than $45

To distribute scores to your customer list, you can simply sort the appropriate column. Starting with Recency, you would sort that column by date of most recent purchase, with the most recent purchase date at the top descending to least recent purchase date at the bottom. A score of 3 should be given to the top 20 percent of customers, a score of 2 to the middle 60 percent of customers, and a score of 1 to the bottom 20 percent of the customers. Then you'll simply repeat this process for the Frequency and Monetary columns.

At the end of the exercise, you'll do a final sort on all of your data so that the customers receiving scores of 333 appear together to form a single segment. The customers receiving scores of 323 should appear together to form a single segment, the customers receiving scores of 322 should appear together, and so on.

Guess what? You've identified your "best" customer segments by completing this simple exercise (this is the group with the 333 score). You've also identified your worst customers and everything in between. The question is: How should you act on this enlightening information?

Move Segments up the Ladder with a Targeted Message

We want to maximize the value of each relationship and move more customers to the "best" segment, right? Why would you want to deliver the same message to every single customer on your list given what you now know about each person?

Let's start with the low hanging fruit, which are the people that have a variation of two 3s and one 2 (i.e., 332, 323, and 233):

- Keeping with the candy store example, for the group that has 3s for Recency and Frequency, but a 2 for Monetary value, we could deliver an email message offering a special 15 percent off coupon for a purchase of $60 or more. Sure, that's a lot of candy, but maybe it's right around Valentine's Day or Halloween.
- For the group that has 3s for Recency and Monetary value but not for Frequency, we could deliver an email message that includes a "Candy of the Week Club" that proves a special incentive if they join immediately.
- For the group that has 3s for Frequency and Monetary value, but not for Recency, we could deliver an email message that includes a free box of chocolates if the customer visits that month

(excess inventory at the end of its shelf life could make a great incentive here).

Okay, you get the point. We're using our earlier analysis to determine the appropriate message to provide incentive for the recipient to take steps to move up to the next customer segment. *Without* this kind of analysis, you're guessing as to whether or not your message is appropriate (or worse yet, delivering the same message to everyone and hoping for the best).

Trust me, segmentation is both easy and fun. There's no wrong answer and you can start small. If you're already segmenting, this is a great review to make sure you're handling segments appropriately and delivering a message that moves your constituents up the totem pole.

There's no reason to be afraid of your data. It's a tool that will help you segment in the most meaningful way possible. Play around with your database and get comfortable. Spend your own time or even hire an intern to do some database clean up that will help you get the best view possible.

Case Studies

Case Study 1: Segmentation Kicks Up Event Attendance and Retention Rate

A horse racetrack owner and operator shifted to a customer-centric strategy in order to drive event attendance and retention. Instead of sending the same email newsletter to all of its constituents, the company wanted to send targeted emails based on what was relevant and interesting to the individual subscriber. For example, it didn't make sense to invite each patron to every racetrack around the country. Instead, the racetrack owner wanted to send invites based on past attendance history (behavior) and location (demographics).

The company already had a thriving players club that provided a great start on the data that would be needed to perform heavy-duty segmentation. In addition, the company used its website and online surveys to collect information such as favorite horse and preferred wager type.

Geography, customer life cycle (new to the club or an existing member), club member level, and product interest were also leveraged to create 10+ segments. The end result was a completely relevant and personalized email that contained only the information and messaging that the recipient would identify with. For example, a customer new to the club and who had never wagered before received betting tips within his or her email. A "Gold Member," on the other hand, received special offers encouraging wagering on the racetrack owner's family of products. And if the recipient was a nonmember, then the email encouraged him or her to join the players club and included an incentive to start immediately.

Results: 3 Percent Increase in Attendance and 8 Percent Increase in Retention Rate

To better understand the action compelled by its new segmentation strategy, the racetrack owner monitored a "control" group without any segmentation. Results of the control group versus the segmented group proved that segmentation not only boosted customer email engagement, it translated into higher attendance and better retention rates. While there was no discernible lift with the control group, the segmented groups had a 3 percent increase in attendance and an 8 percent higher retention rate. Figuring in the thousands of people who frequent each of the owner's tracks, this number becomes a significant contribution to the bottom line.

Case Study 2: Reap Rewards by Making the "Best" Feel Special

A retailer of decorator fabrics and home goods needed an inexpensive, time-efficient way to kick-off its special weeklong sale events, in which all store inventory was marked an additional 50 percent off. The retailer had been diligent about collecting email addresses via a sign-up sheet located at the checkout counter in each store, which resulted in a list of 6,000 subscribers.

The retailer recognized that limiting the first day of the weeklong sale to only its "best" customers would add urgency (the best selection is obviously available the first day of a sale) and instill a feeling of value. And those who had exclusive invites to attend the "Private Shopping Day" were encouraged to invite others by forwarding the email, which kept exclusivity in tact (you had to be invited by the company or one of the "best" customers).

Results: Day One Revenue between 300 and 400 Percent of Usual Daily Revenue

The private shopping days generate between *300 and 400 percent* of the retailer's usual daily revenue. The kick-off emails inviting the "best" customers to the event keep loyalty and appreciation high by making the most valuable customers feel special. By holding back other segments of its subscriber base until later in the sale, the retailer drives more event revenue than ever before.

Case Study 3: Segmentation Is the Perfect Way to Reiterate a Message

A travel company recognized its high profit margins on travel insurance and therefore attempted to up-sell customers by convincing them to purchase during the booking process. Unfortunately, most travel-bound customers were not compelled by the insurance offer and chose not to purchase. That meant a tight window of opportunity to capture a sale considering that once the customer paid for his trip, he had only 10 days to purchase the insurance if so desired.

Rather than enlist agents to place follow-up calls selling the insurance during this 10-day period (the company found this wasn't economically viable), they decided to use rules-based segmentation in order to deliver a reminder to travel insurance candidates.

On a nightly basis, the company updated its database to reflect new bookings, altered bookings, customer changes, and other essential activities. These segmentation rules were then used to constantly score and categorize customers, including those in the "travel insurance candidate" group.

The company then developed a customized, trigger-based email offer to reach customers who had fully paid for their trip but not yet purchased trip insurance. The email included 33 profile attributes for ultimate customization, with each of those attributes automatically transferred to the company's email system. The attributes were then used to populate dynamic content within the email.

These insurance emails were sent in two waves. The first occurred eight days before the deadline for two segments, families and couples. The second wave occurred two days before the deadline as an act now/last chance offer. The response data was then captured within the email system and operational systems and sent back to the marketing database to ensure the quality of future data.

Results: Travel Insurance Conversion Rate of 5.6 Percent

Over 7,000 customers have been touched by the email program, which has resulted in over 430 new insurance package purchases. By redelivering the travel insurance message at a later time, when the customer wasn't distracted by other elements included in the booking process, the company was able to leverage segmentation, customization, and urgency to drive insurance purchases.

The company now benefits from a 5.6 percent conversion rate from the email program—a vast improvement from when the offer was made during the booking process alone.

What Are Other Marketers Thinking?
In their own words . . .

What Is the Ideal List Size for an Email Send?

By Morgan Stewart
Director, Strategic Services, ExactTarget

When Chris asked me what I thought the *ideal* list size should be, I answered, "One." Of course, I understand that there is a big difference between what is ideal and what's possible, but let me explain my reasoning.

As marketers, we want to grow our email subscriber database. But we should not send undifferentiated broadcast emails to our entire database.

I recently compiled a study of our organization's clients and found that list size was an incredibly strong predictor of both open and click-through response rates. Open and click-through rates were approximately 2.5 times higher for emails sent to fewer than 100 subscribers than for emails sent to 100,000 subscribers or more—indicating that smaller is better when it comes to targeting our messages.

There are two scenarios to consider:

1. *Subscriber initiated:* emails triggered based on the subscriber doing something and initiating contact.
2. *Sender initiated:* emails that are sent based on the sender's desire to leverage the subscriber database to initiate contact.

For subscriber initiated emails, the subscriber has started the dialogue through an event such as registration, cart abandonment, site search, or a telephone call. These emails respond to subscribers showing interest through their behavior. This is the best time to send a highly personalized message. Studies consistently show significantly higher response and conversion rates for these communications.

The challenge is anticipating the appropriate response and setting up the processes to react to these events. You should outline the scenarios, create the content ahead of time, and program the triggers to deliver the response message with appropriate personalization strings and dynamic content. For example, look at people who have searched for a product on your site and follow up with a limited-time offer for items in that product category.

For sender initiated emails, the single best way to boost email response is to segment your audience into smaller lists. The smaller the audience, the better you can target messages to your subscribers and make your email communications relevant. Consider the following before sending in order to increase response:

- *Which subscribers should receive this message?* Identify at least one group that should *not* receive the message. If you can't, you probably aren't protecting your subscribers from irrelevant messages. This will eventually erode your credibility and accelerate list fatigue.

    For example, don't send in-store promotions to people who don't live near a store. Don't send service offers to people who have already signed up for the service. Stop sending newsletters to people who only open promotions.
- *What information can we leverage to increase the relevance of this message?* If you have collected information on subscriber interests, make sure it's leveraged to drive dynamic content. Use demographic data to determine the right products, message, and offers to deliver. Use past response data to determine the types of information that interest the subscriber.

A successful marketing program is not rooted in campaign-level response, but rather long-term customer value. It is nearly impossible to convey a single message that is universally relevant to your customer base. Segment your audience into the smallest groups possible and leverage the data you have to drive relevant content.

CREATING CUSTOMER SEGMENTS

By Arthur Hughes
Vice President, KnowledgeBase Marketing
Author of *Strategic Database Marketing,* third edition (New York: McGraw Hill, 2006)

Customer segmentation is essential to successful direct marketing. Segments are groups of customers with similar interests in your products or services, which you have created based on their demographics and lifestyle. Your messages to customers in each segment should reflect these differing interests if you want to find a receptive audience. You would not send the same message to senior citizens that you would to college students. Empty nesters or families with young children will respond better if you target messages that are relevant to their needs, interests, and lifestyles.

An ideal segment is one which:

- Has definable characteristics in terms of behavior and demographics. For example, retired couples, business travelers age 30 to 60, students, families, and number of employees. Business customers should be segmented by SIC code, annual sales, and number of employees.
- Is large enough in terms of potential sales to justify a custom marketing strategy with appropriate rewards and budget.
- Has members who can be motivated by cost-effective rewards to modify their behavior in ways that are profitable for your company.
- Makes efficient use of available data to support segment definition and marketing efforts.
- Can be measured in performance, with control groups.
- Justifies an organization devoted to it. The managing organization can be a single person, or part of a person's

time, but there should be someone definite in your company who "owns" each segment.

Defining the segments requires insight, analytics, and anecdotes:

- *Insight* requires experienced marketing strategists who develop hypotheses about each possible segment, including the rewards necessary to modify member behavior.
- *Analytics* involves using statistical analysis, which supports or rejects each hypothesis: Does such a segment exist? How much are they spending now? What is their income? When do they purchase in our category? How much will it cost to change their behavior?
- *Anecdotes* are success or failure stories that illustrate what your company or other companies have done to modify the behavior of segments like this one. They offer a clue as to what is likely to work in terms of an actionable strategy. You start with an anecdote and develop a hypothesis that can be tested before any rollout.

Not every segment that you can think up will be a profitable one to pursue. Some segments may be too small in number. Others may have very low revenue potential. Others may be very infrequent in their propensity to spend in your category. Finally, others may not be responsive to any sort of communication you might send. The analytics are essential to test typical segments on real data to find out the correct methods for identifying the segments worth pursuing. Investment in communications to unprofitable segments should be minimal.

How to Create Segments

One of the most interesting ways to create segments is to ask your customers some provocative questions. From the answers, you can put customers into segments. What do you want to know? It seems to me there are some basic questions:

- Are these people interested in high quality products or in the cheapest price?
- Are they going to be loyal to you, or will they defect at the first opportunity?
- Will they respond to communications or ignore them?
- Do they spend enough in your category to make it worth your while to create a segment and put them into it?
- Can their behavior be modified by anything that you can do?

Dreaming up these questions can really tax your imagination—but it can be fun and worth the effort. One of the best sets of questions that I have seen has come from Sears. I bought a washer and dryer from them. After I made my choice, their website took me to a survey page where I was asked to answer some interesting questions. Chief among them were these two:

How Do I Feel about Brands?
- I typically buy top of the line name brand products.
- I buy name brand products at a moderate price.
- I am always looking for a bargain. I will try any brand if the price is right.

How Do I Feel about Technology?
- I buy products with the latest features and innovations.
- I buy products with mainstream features and *technology.*
- I am not interested in technology. Keep it simple for me.

The answers to these two questions can help you create up to nine meaningful segments. The questions clearly separate the early adopters from the wait-and-see types. They separate the price buyers from the value buyers. Knowing where people fit in these segments can help you craft messages that will get results, as opposed to messages that are ignored.

NEW MEMBER COMMUNICATION STREAMS

By David Baker
Vice President, Email Marketing and Analytical Solutions,
Agency.com

Congratulations! You've just acquired a new email subscriber! Now what do you do? How do you capitalize on the attention of these newly interested individuals and get them engaged with your brand and products? The answer for marketers is usually along the lines of, "We just start emailing them," or, "We hit them with marketing offers," or (raise your hand if this sounds familiar), "We blast them." Is there a rhyme, reason, or rationale to your new member messaging strategy? If not, there should be.

Here's why: New subscribers have just told you they are interested in hearing from you, but that interest can wane rapidly. In an October 2005 study, Informz showed that open and click rates of new subscribers drop noticeably after 30 days, and even more so after 60 days.

The bottom line: You have to get new subscribers into the fold quickly. How do you do that? For an increasing number of marketers, the answer is a new member communication stream. I have been discussing this issue with one of my senior strategists, Richard Rushing. We wondered why more marketers aren't putting more emphasis on this initial introduction. Richard summed up our thinking: Basically, a new member communication stream is a series of emails highlighting various aspects of a brand, program, or email list subscription, with the goal of sharing knowledge and building affinity (not just driving response). This type of communication stream has distinct benefits for us as marketers. It allows us to: quickly identify those who show interest by opening and/or clicking; test offers and response; identify potential laggards (defined as those who do not respond at all); systematically increase a subscriber's knowledge about us and our products; begin to manage subscribers' familiarity with and navigation of emails through the use of consistent layout, copy, look, and calls to action; build a relationship with subscribers while they are still in the "honeymoon" period; and set the stage for future interaction.

The Basics of a New Member Stream

This communication vehicle can take various forms, but there are several key elements that define the most successful new member streams:

- *Frequency:* A weekly email is usually optimal. Other emails for which a customer has subscribed must be taken into consideration. The last thing we want to do is flood a member in the first few weeks of membership.
- *Stream length:* Usually three to five emails will suffice. This should afford you the opportunity to highlight and educate on the program aspects you deem most important.
- *Relevance and expectations:* Tell your new members they are receiving these emails specifically because they are new to your list. Also set expectations in each email for what to expect within the next email.
- *Content areas:* What you talk about in these emails will depend on your business and the level of customer engagement you would like to attain. The most popular topics: reinforce the reasons for receiving the email, explain how to manage their account or use your website, and provide special offers for new members. This is a great testing opportunity, as you will want to find the optimal content areas.
- *Navigation to previous emails:* What if a member missed the third email in a stream of four? Not a problem. Just

include links within each email that allow the member to view the previous emails in the stream. You may choose to allow subscribers to view future versions as well, but you run the risk of deflating open and click rates in doing so.

- *Alignment with other channels:* If your website allows it, serve a targeted message that reinforces the content in the emails the new members are receiving. Regardless of how you choose to message to your new members and subscribers, it is absolutely essential to gain their attention, loyalty, and engagement quickly. Since most consumers have email subscriptions with multiple companies, you'll need to go the extra mile to cut through the clutter of the inbox. A well-thought-out, well-executed new member communication stream may be the key to getting started on the right foot.

SEGMENTATION: DO WHAT THE DATA TELLS YOU

by Scott Burkey
eMarketing Advisor, Definition 6, Atlanta

Both my printer and reading glasses get a good workout these days. I look at my lists, and I analyze my lists. I look at zip codes. I look at the age of the recipients. I look at purchase history, and I look at what links the users click on. I compare scores of email campaign metrics. Then I do what the data tells me to do (if I'm smart).

I know what the recipients want to receive in their inbox even before I send it to them. I'm far from psychic. I just use the tools that are readily available for email marketers. I also love the results I get when I do this right. I've got to segment, or I do more harm than good by sending the wrong email to the wrong person at the wrong time.

Email marketing metrics are key to segmentation. Who's clicking through? Who's converting? Who's a repeat buyer?

These concepts will help you determine whom to send what emails to. These are very key metrics that you should be studying. Watch the opens and click-throughs and conversions on emails that are sent to these recipients. They will prove that the segmentation efforts are worth the work.

Use dynamic content in the subject lines. My eye automatically picks up on my city, my first name, or a brand I like. This is another good example of segmentation as it relates to dynamic content. Subject lines are king.

For hospitality clients, I do a lot of segmentation based on location. However, one of the tactics that has worked well has been to watch users who go to a location away from home, perhaps during business travels. Then I can email them when a location is coming to their zip code or one close by. Of course, you need to be able to tie into a reservation system to do this, but it's a great tactic if you can pull it off.

Hotels present an enormous opportunity for segmentation when the email metrics are tied into the POS system and other internal applications that the client uses. This type of email sender can segment on a variety of different data points. Vacationers can often be enticed to go back to the same location in subsequent years if you catch them when they are making plans to go on vacation. You will want to customize the incentive that you offer depending on location, timing, and purchase history, but a well-timed, relevant email from a name they are familiar with may be just the ticket to get them to book a return visit. Regular business travelers are easily retained with proper segmentation, timing, and incentives. (Clean rooms don't hurt either.)

Again, relevance is the key. Lack of segmentation makes an email that the recipient requested look more like spam than a permission-based email. Active segmentation makes the email look more like an email from a good friend than a marketing effort. I like hearing from good friends. I open their emails.

The data tells me what I need to do with my next email, I just have to listen. You can do it, too. Use the tools. Talk to your colleagues who are doing it right. Know your audience and remember that it's an iterative process. You will have a lot of fun while you learn.

SEGMENTING FOR RELEVANCE

By Tara Lamberson
Vice President, Marketing, MindComet Corporation
Blog: http://blogs.mindcomet.com

A fundamental principle of targeted marketing is breaking up your audience into smaller, manageable groups that are likely to behave in a similar way. Email allows for concise segmentation ability as well as the opportunity to make the most of communicating with niche audience segments in a cost-effective manner.

Pertinent information collected for an individual should be used to the fullest in ongoing communication strategies. Aside from basic demographic data points such as name, age, location, income, and marital status, there are other opportunities to be unearthed by capturing recipient behavior with behavioral segmentation.

Segmenting your list by behavior gives you the ability to group individuals by content preference, allowing future communications to provide variable content with greater relevancy. The more relevant the content is to your audience, the higher your ability to influence the actions or outcome. One way to track this behavior is by monitoring click stream activity. Popular in web analytics, click stream activity will show the links users are clicking on for more information. These may be links to download documents, view a video, visit a website, listen to a podcast, or visit a blog or links to pages deeper within your site.

Another way to segment is by email activity. Consider segmenting by email opens, click-throughs, purchase decisions, or repeated behaviors. Conversion data is another viable way to use segmentation to better target your subscribers. By basing future message initiatives on previous conversions, you have the ability to reach out to subscribers who have already engaged with you and your product.

With a well-thought-out email strategy, the frequency of communication balance is just as important as relevancy of content. Most audiences can withstand a higher rate of frequency if the content is relevant. However, if you send out generic, irrelevant content on a highly frequent basis, you run the risk of over-saturating your target audience and potentially losing the subscribers to opt out.

Whether segmenting by behavior or demographics, marketers should continuously build strategies for gathering additional data about subscribers throughout the course of a communication strategy. After you've established a solid relationship of trust with your recipients, don't be afraid to ask for small pieces of information within the messages or consider creating an online survey. Surveying your list can be an easy and inexpensive way to learn about your subscriber list.

A good rule of thumb to follow is to plan on surveying your list two to four times a year, dependent on the industry. When architecting a survey with the intent of using the data to segment future communications, keep in mind the following:

- *Ask targeted questions.* Use surveys to learn more about your subscribers. By asking relevant, interesting questions about geographic location, company size, and concerns related to their industry, products, services, or overall brand experience, you will be better equipped to target your subscribers with the relevant information they are looking for.
- *Use surveys to determine level of interest.* If you have subscribers who have stopped responding to your

messages, send a short survey with an incentive for completion. If there is still no response, there is a good chance they are no longer interested, and it may be time to put future communication on hold.

- *Let your respondents know what to expect.* Tell recipients how many questions there are or how long it should take to complete. Also, let them know that there is a specific incentive waiting for them at the end.
- *If offering an incentive, make it relevant and special.* Offering an incentive that will be appreciated by your audience will provide better survey results than offering an incentive that will have serial survey-takers crawling out of the woodwork.
- *Get to the point.* While you have your subscribers' attention, it can be tempting to ask the world. But by maintaining your focus, you will get better results and minimize the risk of people dropping off half way through the survey process.
- *Consider rank systems versus open-ended questions.* Instead of asking your subscribers open-ended questions about the type of information they would like to receive, consider a way for the survey participants to rank industry issues that are important to them. This will allow you to see the most important areas to focus upon.
- *Review and test questions.* Make sure your questions make sense. Consider having someone else read the question to verify clarity.

If your email service provider does not include an integrated survey tool, consider using a link to an external survey site such as SurveyMonkey or WebSurveyor. The robust reporting tools are extraordinary and will give you the details you are looking for.

CHAPTER 6 REVIEW

- Recency, Frequency, and Monetary value (RFM) analysis is based on customer behavior. Use it to predict who will be most receptive to developing into a loyal, high Lifetime Value constituent.
- Recency is the most powerful predictor of customer response.
- The profits from RFM come in the form of higher response rates, greater LTV, and real dollar savings through efficiency.
- If a customer pattern is broken, you should act immediately in an attempt to discover what instigated the change or to get the behavior back on track.
- One of your marketing goals should be to identify the people who are taking your organization to the next level and develop more of these individuals.
- As such, I recommend these three segments for every organization: the "best" constituents, the "almost best" constituents, and "new" constituents.

CHAPTER 7

FINDING AND CREATING RELEVANT CONTENT

Content can be a multitude of things. It encompasses articles, offers, invitations, letters, and more. When we think about content in the context of email marketing, a common question is, "How much content is the right amount?" It's sort of like defining the best day to send email. There is no right answer. Depending on your business, an effective email might include a letter and three articles. Or maybe it's one longer article. One certainty is that marketers have a lack of time and resources when it comes to creating great, relevant content.

As we've already discussed, the ability to deliver a relevant message to the right person at the right time is highly dependent on data and segmentation. If you remember the 40, 40, 20 rule of database marketing, you know that 40 percent of your success is dependent on your database, 40 percent on your content, and 20 percent on the creative aspects of your marketing. Content plays a huge role in your overall success.

Also take into consideration the fact that you are likely competing with over 100 other emails in your audience's inbox. How many of these emails will actually be read? Ten? Fifteen? You must be one of those 15. And the only way to accomplish this is by delivering relevant content. Building a bigger list of opt-ins won't get you anywhere if you don't break into the top tier of your audience's inbox. A challenge, of course, is that relevance is subjective. It's subjective, and it's judged by the recipient, meaning no one cares if you and your marketing department think that the content is relevant. The true test is if your audience hates it or finds it irrelevant. Why do you think they do test screenings of major movies before rolling them out publicly? Sometimes, depending on feedback from the audience, they'll change a few scenes and maybe even the ending. There's a theme here: testing and adjusting. It's no different when it comes to email content.

WARNING: CONSUMERS WILL REVOLT AGAINST IRRELEVANT CONTENT!

This should come as no surprise to you. We already established the fact that your constituents don't like for you to waste their time. We also established the idea that the term *newsletter* may not accurately describe the type of communication you should be having with your audience. Here's another reason why: The idea of a newsletter is that if you include a few articles and stories, some of it will be relevant to every one of your subscribers. It's the same thing with a newspaper—maybe you read the Entertainment and Lifestyle section, while your wife reads Money and Current Events. The more variety, the better your chances of striking a relevant cord with each individual in the audience.

Let's take a time machine back to the pre-Gutenberg years, when there was no printing press. News traveled by word of mouth, right? The great thing about this type of communication was that you could guarantee it was received and likely to be relevant to the person receiving it. (I'd like to think that people spoke with a real purpose back then.)

On the other hand, oral communication presented a big consistency problem. Ever played the game telephone? You sit in a circle and whisper some saying or story to the person sitting next to you. Then this person tells the person beside him, and so on it goes, around the circle. At the end, the last person conveys what they heard ("Elephants have wings, and you sound like Elvis when you sing?")

and everyone gets a good laugh out of it when the first person tells them what the original saying was ("I once met a girl named Irene. She had dinner with the Queen"). How did that saying get so distorted along the way? Because people hear things differently. They interpret. They embellish for the sake of the story. And in the end, you are left with a singing Elvis instead of a Queen.

Another problem is reach, because news travels as far as the people delivering it. That's why oral content delivery has a significant scale limitation.

Now we're moving forward in our time machine and have arrived at the year Guttenberg makes the first printing press. Lo and behold, it's suddenly possible to create communications that can be widely distributed, while maintaining consistency. Eureka, problem solved!

Or maybe not. Execution was still a problem. The process was complex and distribution could be a real pain. Perhaps more significantly, since there was no human determining what was relevant to whom, batching evolved. Although it made the creation and distribution process more efficient, it was offset by the sacrifice of relevance.

Now we've jumped forward 600 years or so, and the thrill of the printing press has worn off ("Oh, come on, Bob. The printing press is *so* last year"). People are tired of irrelevance. They want control of what content they're exposed to. Yes, that's how the revolution against irrelevant content was born. Today, this revolt against what "they say" and the attitude of "what I want" manifests itself in the digital video recorder, satellite radio, the iPod, Internet homepages, and email.

You didn't know you'd be getting a history lesson when you started this chapter, did you? We can conclude that the world isn't flat. It's turning—consumer mentality is shifting—and you need to be on the right side of the shift, ready to deliver what your constituents want. Keep in mind that your audience has a finite attention capacity, and they will immediately decide if you are wasting their time. If so, expect them to revolt.

Now we're ready to get into more detail on the creation of data-driven content that results in a relevant message.

HOW DO I CREATE RELEVANT CONTENT?

Let's start with the most basic concept for driving relevance beyond segmentation. *Dynamic Content* refers to content that changes according to rules. The idea is that these rules are set up on the back end (i.e., a rule could be: Location = Indiana), and content to match this segment is easily created by the marketer. The email system automatically inserts that content into the email template for *only* the Indiana audience using the backend rule. For location targeting, you could have all fifty states defined by rules, and each version would use these rules to generate the appropriate content. Or you could split up the country by regions, with appropriate clothing based on those regions. The big idea is that in a *single* email, you can dynamically insert content based on information in your database (see Figure 7.1).

To recap, these dynamic content elements are inserted based on rules that the marketer defines within the email system that he or she is using. These rules can be as simple or as complex as the marketer desires. They can use "and" statements and "or" statements. For example, an "and" rule may be: Location = Indiana *and* Last purchase = July. An example of an "or" rule could be: Location = California *or* Location = New York.

Dynamic Content is a great place for experimentation. I've included some ideas to get you started on testing and driving stronger engagement. Again, every organization is different, and each example should be tested (testing is so important, it's coming up in a chapter of its own).

Dynamic Content Experimentation Ideas

- *Images:* You know how the saying goes: "A picture says a thousand words." Images are one of the most powerful elements to test when using dynamic content. I've seen some very successful image tests involving photos of people. Is the email recipient a man or a woman? Young or old? Part of a family or single? A condo owner or a home owner? Sending a message that includes an image that closely resembles your re-

Figure 7.1
Rules-Based Dynamic Content Drives Ultimate Relevance

cipient is a great way to drive a sense of belonging and relevance. After all, people associate with those whom they like, or those whom are like them.

Packaging is another good test. There is a very successful packaged goods manufacturer that delivers the appropriate package size based on whether the recipient is likely to consume jumbo size (i.e., someone with kids) or mini size cereal boxes (i.e., someone who travels a great deal). When the recipient views the email, he knows that marketer is talking to him as an individual by using appropriate imagery.

Localized images are also compelling. If you have several locations and are putting a picture of your store in the email, why not show the store that's closest to your recipient? I know a company that holds a simple in-store drawing every month. In every email created by this company, the winner of the local contest is featured. The key is that the winner is *shown* only to those recipients who associate with the specific store. Since these are neighborhood stores, there is a good chance that the recipients will actually know the winner. It's not only relevant . . . it's an implied endorsement from an individual who has won.

- *Offers and incentives:* Dynamic Content makes it easy to test incentives and offers so you can better understand what compels each individual to take action. Some individuals may respond better to specific dollar savings, while others may respond better to a percentage off. And yet others may go for the "free gift with a purchase" deal every time. Many organizations will use these elements to do A/B testing. They'll use the test to determine which offer they should deliver in the future. The problem with this approach is that you are basing an individual message on overall response. Why not segment the people who respond better to percentage offers and continue to send that message to them? As long as you can capture and pinpoint this behavior in your database, you can use dynamic content to deliver the most relevant offer and incentive in the future.
- *"From" side:* The effectiveness of localization also applies to the "from" name on your organization's emails. Consider the fact that the "from" line of your email may be the most important factor when a recipient decides whether or not to open your message. That's right—some individuals (myself included) have seen results that indicate the "from" name is even more important than the subject line.

Before sending an email, ask yourself, "Who owns the relationship with this audience?" Is it the President and CEO? The marketing department? A specific salesperson? You will likely find yourself answering with a human being. So why not deliver the message "from" that human being(s) rather than the institution at large?

Like most marketing, the "institution-to-many" relationship is a legacy caused by the execution pain of past tools. It's not that the marketer *wanted* to ignore the manager of the store, or the sales person, or even the appropriate customer service person, it's that it was too difficult to deliver a message from an individual.

I get so fired up about email because of its ability to leverage the *people* behind a brand. At the end of the day, we know it's all about the people in the organization, not the organization itself. People buy from people.

"From" side dynamic content is not limited to the "from" line of the email or email address. It also includes the content of the email itself.

The other day, I had lunch with a client who sells a very high-value service (it ranges from $10,000 to $20,000). Their current sales process works like this:

1. Television drives traffic to the phone or website.
2. Prospects register for more information.
3. Information is sent via a direct mail catalog or email based on a specific attribute.
4. Prospects are encouraged to visit with a local consultant.
5. Consultants convert the prospects to paying customers.

The client wanted to raise conversions considering that 30 percent of the prospects who visited with a local consultant became customers. Specifically, he wanted to know how email could help.

Our suggestion was a series of prospect nurturing emails that are "from" the consultant. That includes the consultant's name in the "from" line, email address line, content of the email, picture in the email, and signature at the end of the email. The prospect should open the email and believe it's been put together by the individual and not the marketing department. That's scaleable, one-to-one marketing at work.

I have another example with results that clearly spell out the success of this kind of marketing. In April 2004, a well-known travel company wanted to see what would happen if they switched from corporate selling to agent selling. They had always used agents to drive personal relationships, but they hadn't always called attention to these personal relationships when sending email. After testing an email from the company at large versus an email from the agent for a few months, here were their results:

- Deliverability rates were 5 percent better with the agent email.
- Open rates were 26 percent better with the agent email.
- Click rates were 79 percent better with the agent email.
- Unsubscribe rates were 250 percent better with the agent email.

Okay, you can pick yourself back up from the floor now. I've seen dozens of these personal "from" side success stories. Now are you convinced that it's worth testing?

BUILDING OR SOURCING RELEVANT CONTENT IS NOT NECESSARILY MORE WORK

While the concepts of *why* you want to deliver relevant content are probably clear, the how-to of creating or finding such content can still be an intimidating concept for many organizations. There are budget fears, resource fears, and time constraint fears. You may be thinking, "Great. Now this guy is telling me I have to deliver 752 different versions of this email. How am I going to get all of that content?" If you're still in this mentality, I encourage you to look at the above results one more time. You must understand that the gains that come from this kind of relevancy are absolutely worth your time. Okay, now take a deep breath. I have even better news for you: Relevancy does require more content, but it doesn't necessarily mean more work.

Here are some ways to keep the legwork associated with content creation minimal:

- *Reuse and recycle.* Dynamic Content such as "from" side can leverage two great concepts that most of us are familiar with: reuse and recycle. Think about it: You can create a content area for a representative that includes his or her photo, name, and contact info. You can store it. You can use it over and over again.

    Reuse and recycle also works with messages that you deliver to new customers. You can create it once and reuse it when your data indicates that it's appropriate to do so. In fact, messaging based on stage of the relationship—whether it's a lapsed relationship, a thank you, or a reminder—can all be created once and leveraged when appropriate using Dynamic Content.

- *Mine your website.* Happen to have a sitemap of your website? I bet you've accumulated more content than you'll ever know. Why not put those existing product descriptions and pictures, press releases, and mission statements to good use since they already exist in digital form?

- *Utilize third-party content.* In the old days, if you didn't create the content, it was nearly impossible to source it and use it in your communications. Fortunately, the Web has made information more readily available than ever before. Perhaps there's an industry expert who would be willing to license some content to you. Or a market research firm that's willing to partner with you and provide access to research reports and studies. There is a good chance that millions of people are covering the same topics that you're covering—and they're willing to share.

- *Develop relationships with bloggers.* Statistics show that the number of blogs doubles every six months. Currently, over 55 million blogs exist. These blogs are managed by people (bloggers) who want to share their thoughts and opinions on the topics that they care so deeply about. Chances are, some of these bloggers are creating content that's appropriate for your audience. One of the best things about these bloggers is that they are eager to spread their ideas and will see your organization as the vehicle to do so (many bloggers provide their content free of charge). It's important that you ask permission and give appropriate recognition to these individuals.

- *Check out association sites.* Do you belong to an association or trade group? Guess what? It's their job to know your industry as well or perhaps even better than you do. Associations are rich with research, news, and other relevant content that could be yours for the taking. For example, the Pizza Association of Nebraska might distribute a tip on cutting your pizza in a way that makes it last longer (this is a big struggle in the pizza industry—reducing waste caused by "per the slice" pizza). If you are a pizza equipment distributor, you may want to share this tip with your customers (accompanied by the latest and greatest slicer that just arrived). Think about associations that could help you.
- *Tap into professional copywriters.* Not all of us are great writers, or even decent ones. Some of us forget when to use "its" and "it's." The good news is that there are lots of people who know how to write clean, effective copy. Many of these copywriters are freelancers who would be happy to write your email content for a nominal fee. The turn-around should be fast, too, considering that you aren't contracting them to create a great American novel or anything. You should simply provide the frequency, length, segment variations, and provide some general information about your business in order to get a quote. You can also leverage several copywriters simultaneously to develop oodles of high quality content for a low investment.
- *Start an image library.* Several Websites offer free (or at least inexpensive), high-resolution images that can be appropriately sized for your emails. Go ahead and do a Google search on Image Libraries or check out sites like istockphot.com to find great images that can even be purchased directly from the photographer.

- *RSS & Http:Get.* Are you thinking that I might as well be speaking in another language? These are technologies that enable you to automatically populate your emails with content from other online sources. RSS stands for Really Simple Syndication, and HTTP: Get is a coding term. Both allow a marketer to pull content right from another web page without any creation or upload necessary.

Some of these suggestions might be a better fit for your organization than others. At the very least, I hope you're excited about Dynamic Content and its potential to help your email program.

Case Studies

Case Study 1: "From" Side Dynamic Content Requires the Right Tools

A leader in network administration was keeping in touch with 85,000 prospects and customers with a monthly email sent by the marketing team on behalf of the company's 65+ account executives. While the "from" side personalization and content of the email had a positive impact on the response side, managing the creation of the emails was labor intensive and difficult. Why? Because the marketing team was going through the process *manually*. Each time a mailing was due, they had to create all of the content from scratch, coordinate the sending of emails from each account executive (they did not have a central account), and track several separate results. Sending the emails *alone* took close to a day for one person to complete.

The company decided it was time to reuse and recycle, which meant finding tools that enabled them to create and store personalized content for each account executive. With the proper system in place, setup time went from days to minutes, freeing up execution time that could be used for strategizing.

Results: Time Is Money

The company significantly cut their email preparation and execution time, while still delivering consistent communications on behalf of its account executives. These emails are the company's most effective form of communication with its prospects and customers. With the ability to reuse and recycle, the company now has time to do more of what's working.

Case Study 2: Are 1,000 Versions of a Single Email Really Possible?

A leading supplier of consumer products for lawn and garden care recognized the importance of establishing itself as an educator by delivering *custom* lawn and garden care advice.

That's why the company uses its website and email sign-up pages to collect data on the registrant's grass type, location, gardening habits, and more to generate Dynamic Content emails that include the lawn and garden advice relevant to the subscriber. In addition to prompting customers to fertilize, plant, and perform other maintenance activities at the appropriate time for their geographic location and their lawn and garden type, the company also issues special email alerts with treatment advice regarding pests, drought, or other problems reported in a specific area.

A single mailing can end up with hundreds or even *thousands* of individualized recommendations from a single email template. These recommendations are based on the customer's zip code, grass and garden type, and continually changing variables such as weather and other local growing conditions. Rose gardeners receive different advice than vegetable gardeners, and residents of Beverly Hills receive different information than residents of Detroit.

For maximum effectiveness, all processes are automated and implemented with point-and-click procedures. So yes, 1,000+ versions of an email are really possible. You can start small (even a few versions are better than none) and grow from there.

Case Study 3: Using Web Content for Email Content

A law firm approached an agency for help with its email program. The agency noticed that the firm's website was full of great content that could easily be used in the email program. Rather than recreating that content, the agency advised integrating the law firm's website Content Management System (CMS) with its email system. With the integration complete, the process of delivering email messages that reflect website content and subscriber preferences captured on the site is broken into five simple steps:

1. A website visitor registers for information and selects preferences regarding practice areas. The visitor is automatically added to the appropriate subscriber list(s) based on his self-segmentation.
2. A marketing team member logs into the CMS system, where he can specify the practice area he wants to email and deem dates to retrieve content from the website.
3. Based on this initial information, the user can organize articles, seminars, and publications that are in line with the group's preferences and preview the email.
4. The user logs into the email system to choose the appropriate template (there are over 20, with one for each practice area) based on the designated content pulled from the CMS.
5. The appropriate list is selected and the email is sent.

Results: Optimized Web Content and Lighting-Speed Execution

By delivering highly relevant content that is of interest to each subscriber group, the law firm has seen an increase in open and click rates and unsubscribes are virtually non-existent. With content already in place, the law firm can quickly execute an email communication in five easy steps that take a matter of minutes.

WHAT ARE OTHER MARKETERS THINKING?
In their own words . . .

DELIVERING ON THE PROMISE

(Originally published by MediaPost)
By Bill McCloskey
CEO, Email Data Source Inc.
Blog: http://blogs.mediapost.com/email_insider/?cat=8

Deliverability: This is the main topic of discussion these days in the world of email marketing. But I wonder if we spend nearly the time we devote to white listing, ISP relationships, and Goodmail to actually thinking about what is getting delivered in the first place. There is a decided lack of creativity that goes into our electronic epistles, with rare exceptions.

I continue to marvel at the time and care companies such as Lexus devote to their outbound marketing efforts, but yet they seem the exception that proves the rule. Alcoholic beverage companies might come up with a holiday email that has interest once a year, but where is the ongoing humor that Tanqueray expends on its messages?

For all the thought that Scion puts into its messaging when it targets the gay community, thousands of others find it difficult to come up with unique messaging for any market sector.

Generic images: Text chosen not for its impact, but for its ability to slip through spam filters. Copy with all the subtlety of the ads in the back pages of comic books. Where is the email that impacts my life, makes me laugh out loud, furthers the brand equity I have with the product or service?

As an industry, we've embraced mediocrity, becoming more concerned with permission than persuasion. We've embraced the transactional but turned our backs on the transformational.

Email is the most intimate and powerful of marketing channels, and yet it is rarely used that way. A few weeks ago, I wrote about theater producer Ken Davenport, who sent out a thank-you note to those who filled the seats at his show on Saturday night and encouraged them to bring their friends to share the excitement the next week. There was a guy who understood the power of the medium and possessed the creativity and enthusiasm that more people in our industry need.

How about telling me a story that arcs over several days or weeks? How about engaging me in a dialogue on how to market to me—a real, two-way conversation, not just a survey. How about reintroducing rich media into the email mix, something that seems to be hard to find these days. How about giving me a real reason to care about your brand?

All too often, we instead get the car company that can't be bothered to put an email newsletter together, the guitar manufacturer that would prefer not hearing from its customers through email, the poor design, the broken links, the lack of a welcome letter, the lost opportunity, the missing graphics, and the same boring message delivered ad nauseam.

What we need is the creative shop that embraces email and transforms it, much like Crispin Porter + Bogusky have transformed television spots and Web ads. Some forward-thinking companies are doing it now: Unilever and Sara Lee to name a few. But for so many others, it is not deliverability to the inbox that they need to focus on; it is delivering on the experience I want when I opt in to be marketed to.

CREATING EMAILS THAT SELL

By Sheri Waldrop
Owner, Waldrop Marketing Communications
Blog: www.waldropmarketing.com

Creating great emails really isn't based on knowing the "right technique" or even having great writing skills. The difference

157

between emails that get opened and read and those that get deleted right away is how well they reflect *what the reader wants to learn about.*

This brings me to the first rule of creating emails that sell:

Rule 1: Know Thy Customer

Even the BEST email message, perfectly written, with an exciting offer, will fall flat if it goes to the wrong audience. You really *can't* sell snowshoes to people living in the tropics, hard as you might try. This is why broadcasting emails to everyone in the world brings in such abysmal response rates, with open rates measured in the hundredth of a percent, not to mention spam reports.

Instead, develop a *highly targeted* in-house email list. Once you know who will be reading your email, you can personalize.

Many people new to writing sales emails tend to oversimplify this process: "It's easy. My customers are anyone who needs car accessories and wants to buy them online." But dig a little deeper, and you'll find that your customers come in different sizes and shapes—and so should your emails to them.

Here are three possible audiences for car accessories:

1. Older individuals who are looking for a nice-looking seat cover to protect their expensive leather upholstery.
2. Middle-aged auto enthusiasts who love to restore classic cars but can't find parts locally.
3. Techno-savvy teens and young adults interested in checking out the latest rims or the biggest bass speakers.

You'll want to write your email to reach each of these audience segments individually, in their *own language.*

Rule 2: Know Why Customers Buy from You

Before writing your email, ask yourself, "Why do my customers buy from me instead of someone else? What problems do I solve for them, and what's the major benefit I offer them?" This is the basis of your UVP (unique value proposition), and it's the key to creating "killer sales copy."

Show the problem your customer faces, and how your company solves it. You'll see results that reflect this kind of targeting.

Rule 3: Create a Great Subject Line

Your subject line is the first thing that jaded, spam-wary customers see when they scan through their inbox. Remember, you have roughly *five to eight seconds* to engage your customers. After this, you have either won their attention and interest or created immense boredom (or even annoyance). It all starts with the headline.

And always remember to deliver on promises made in the subject line. If you promise information on current mortgage rates, then deliver this in the email body copy. If you promise a white paper, have a working link to download it. If you ask a question in the subject line, always answer it. This is essential to building trust with your customers.

Rule 4: Speak the Language of Your Customer in Your Email

Once you've created the subject line, continue your momentum with the main part of the email. Use a warm, friendly tone, as if you are talking directly to the person. "Are you tired of not finding the car part you want, and at a decent price? We understand, because at Auto Accessories Unlimited, we're car enthusiasts ourselves. We know what it's like to look for that special Chevy part because you want your car to look great."

Use the word "you" more often then "we" or "I." People don't really care how great you are; they care about whether you will meet their needs. By addressing them in the second person, you are letting them know that they are the important one.

Rule 5: Give Them a Reason to Buy

In your email, provide facts and specifics about what makes your product or service so good. You can keep it short and link to a landing page that offers more details, but at least address the highlights. Not sure what to say? Ask your sales force. They know why customers buy, and what questions they will have. Or ask others who have bought from you in the past. Why did they buy? What closed the sale? Use this information in your email.

Rule 6: Create a Strong Call to Action

Once you've given them a reason to buy, you need to ask customers to act—immediately. A call to action can be as simple as asking them to click on a link that goes to your website, or as complex as requesting that they enter information directly into a form in your email.

Don't let customers put off taking action. Offer a strong incentive, such as a discount or a "freebie" that is time-limited. Remind customers that the price will go up tomorrow if they don't act *now*. You don't want them to close out of your email without doing something. With most customers, "out of sight" means "out of mind."

What If You Can't (or Don't Want to) Write Your Own Emails?

If you are unable or too busy to write your own, you can have a copywriter write your emails for you. It's important to first check out any writer you consider regarding their experience, skill level, and success rate. Some suggested questions include:

- "How many email campaigns have you written in the past? For what types of clients/industries?" Ask to see recent examples of their work and check references.
- "What were the response rates to the emails?" This answer can vary greatly depending upon whom the email

was sent to. If the copywriter doesn't understand metrics or is unsure of response rates, they are most likely less experienced.

- "Do you assist with marketing strategy?" A good copywriter who has been around awhile can make suggestions on the graphics and layout, as well as the overall strategy, including coordination of the email with the landing page design and copy.

Whether you write your copy yourself or hire someone else to write for you, following the above suggestions will likely result in a much stronger email. Be sure to evaluate any email to see whether it's "following the rules" before sending it out. You'll be pleased with the response rates.

EMAIL USER EXPERIENCE

By Melinda Krueger
Principal, Krueger Direct/Interactive

URUE. You are the User *Experience.*

At the recent Word of Mouth Marketing (WOMMA) Conference, CEO Andy Sernovitz imparted this simple phrase that says so much. It made me consider how subscribers perceive their experience with a company's email program: Does it feel like a disjointed barrage of marketing messages, or is it a positive *experience*? Here are a few ways to move from the former to the latter:

- *Identity:* Can you create a name for your subscribers to help them feel recognized and valued? Let's face it, being an email subscriber sounds about as appealing as being a taxpayer. Make your subscribers feel like they're part of something special by developing an identity for Brand X VIPs, Brand X Insiders, Digital X Fans, or something that describes their importance to your organization.

- *Exclusivity:* A name for your opt-ins is just the start. Consider providing sneak previews, a behind-the-scenes story, or a VIP discount that is unavailable to nonsubscribers. Consumers enjoy feeling like insiders who get special treatment.
- *Personality:* Most email has a safe, generic tone and seems to come from a faceless corporation. A direct marketing rule-of-thumb is to always write a letter from one person to another and, when possible, to tell a personal story. Give your organization a human face and an interesting voice.
- *Gratitude:* In a country where "here you go" has replaced "thank you" as the phrase most often uttered at the close of a retail transaction, aren't we all starving for a little recognition? Tell your VIPs that you appreciate them—or better yet, show them with a wallpaper, screensaver, game, ring tone, e-card, or other downloadable digital freebie. As Andy Sernovitz says, "Do something frivolous that makes people happy."

Put Your Money Where Your Mouth Is

Email is for readers. That's why I'm always amazed that developing great copy receives so little attention and so little budget. I've worked with clients who devoted millions of dollars to developing a database and an email program but stopped short when it came to investing time or money in great copywriting. To me, it was like buying a Ferrari and using cheap gas. Sure, it will run, but will it give you optimal performance?

An accepted principle of direct marketing is that improving copy will have the biggest impact on response after list and offer. Here are a few things to consider that can improve your copy:

- *Background:* More is better when it comes to background material for your writer. Provide everything you can get your hands on: brand positioning, marketing materials, press releases, research reports, competitors' websites, industry publications, and so on. Don't filter what you think will be relevant to the task, thinking you'll save the writer's time. You never know what might spur an idea and writers like to steep in information while working on a project.

- *Interviews:* Provide opportunities for your writer to speak to people who are involved in your product or service. Yes, you hate to bother the CEO, but your readers may want to hear his or her childhood anecdote. Who designed and developed the product you're selling? What was his or her vision and what decisions/problems/ successes happened along the way? How about a satisfied customer? An interesting story is well worth the investment in in-person research.

- *Poetry:* What is the difference between a catalog marketer and a retail marketer's online store? The catalog marketer has learned that "poetic copy" works. Read the description for a pedestrian item like a wool sweater on Lands' End's website. Then look at a comparable product at a retailer that started out with bricks-and-mortar and has never mailed a catalog. At Lands' End, you'll see a description that tells a beautiful story about the product and makes you feel it will improve your quality of life. At the traditional retail site, you'll get the vital statistics: size, fabric, color, and so on. Which makes you want to buy?

- *Originality:* Much of what your readers want to know may not be readily available. This is when you need to invest in the creation of original content. Your writer will do all the hard work—you just have to choose the direction and provide the access. Don't just repurpose your marketing materials or rely on your website. Give the people what they want: the inside scoop, the inside story, and the view from the top.

Great copy not only makes for better reading, it can differentiate your email program from the competition's. Make an investment in high performance fuel to power your email machine.

FINDING OR CREATING RELEVANT CONTENT

By John Wall
Producer, M Show Productions
Blog: http://www.themshow.com

Anyone doing an email campaign struggles to find relevant content. With so much emphasis on technology, subject lines, click-through rates and landing pages, it sometimes feels like the content is an afterthought.

I've found that my email campaigns tend to fall into two major categories: simple notices ("Here is the link for the webinar you signed up for that is running tomorrow") or more elaborate messages that compel someone to take action.

For "notice" email, I've found that they can never be too short or too simple. A Jakob Nielson study that has stuck with me proved that bulleted lists of plain facts with hyperlinks are your ultimate goal, because readers want only the meat and links (read this legendary article by typing this into a web browser: http://www.useit.com/alertbox/9710a.html). Full paragraphs, blustering marketing copy, and elaborate descriptions do nothing but cause more people to jump off before getting to the moment of truth (conversion). The only way to screw up here is to drone on for too long or make the links difficult to find. My *tests* have proved that large fonts are a good thing and links should always be blue and underlined—no need to get crazy and try and set new standards.

For messages that are meant to inform or entice, you must choose between finding relevant content or creating your own. In my experience, the choice has always been simple: If there's any way you can get the budget and time to make your own content—do it. If you don't have the time or money, use someone else's and give him credit for it.

Our dear readers don't care who created the content, they are only looking to be entertained, promised a brighter future, or have their pain taken away. The problem with content generation is that it is usually 5 times more labor intensive as you think it will be when you first budget time for it.

Many trade magazines in my industry (software development tools) offer webinars for their advertising customers, often at rates from $10k to $50k and up depending on the size of the list being marketed to. I can easily re-create the infrastructure with a GoToMeeting account and Conference call line and put on a webinar for less than $5k. If you spread this over four or more webinars, you'd think this would be a thing to do in-house. But the problem is content generation—getting an analyst or industry notable to write an hour worth of relevant content closes the price gap and makes the turnkey solution seem like a bargain in some cases.

However, with such significant expense there is also the possibility of a huge payoff that goes beyond your email campaigns. If your content is so relevant that others want to use it, you now have a whole new distribution mechanism for your message. In a world where Google is watching every time a reader thinks you are relevant and decides to click through, you can't underestimate the strength of being a content provider.

So enough with the academic babble. How do you get relevant content? First, talk to your readers. They will tell you what's hot, and what they think is big. In fact, many of them will step up to do the content for you if you just ask.

Create a network of content providers for yourself. This is where blogs and RSS feeds can pay off huge for you. And if you have the resources, take the time to create your own content so that you can put it to work for you everywhere that it will fly on its own.

But then again, if you've got two hours to get that customer email out, get on the phone and call in a few favors and let your friends take the credit . . . you'll still get the clicks.

GROWING YOUR CONTENT ANTENNAE: 17 SOURCES FOR INSPIRATION

By Patsi Krakoff, Psy.D.
President, Krakoff Wakeman Associates, Inc.
Blog: http://www.coachezines.com

The first question to ask yourself when you publish a newsletter is, "What's its purpose?"

Are you writing a weekly or monthly newsletter to inform and educate? Are you writing a promotional message to get readers to buy a product or service?

An e-newsletter works by providing information that is relevant to a targeted audience. When readers subscribe to your e-newsletter, they are expecting to get valuable content. In turn, you become a perceived expert in your field. Sharing your expertise creates a relationship with readers. When you are perceived as a generous expert, you inspire trust. Readers will buy from you and your company once they decide they know you, like you, and trust you.

Ideally, an email newsletter should have only one intention. If your message's goal is to sell a product or service, you would be better off writing a separate email promotion that has the sole intention of selling. Online readers are in a hurry. They scan emails and quickly decide what to read or delete. Too many competing messages confuse readers, and they will do nothing (or read and delete).

The Blog Squad's own e-newsletter, *Savvy eBiz Tips,* includes a personal note, a main article tip, a special promotion, and an update on what's new on our blogs. The intention is to inform, create expertise and trust, and provide recommendations for complementary products and services that will help readers achieve their business goals. The proportion of information to promotional content is at least 80 to 20 percent. Promotion is not the primary intent of the e-newsletter.

We adhere to our stated mission for the newsletter: Practical information readers can apply right away to help build their business and attract clients. Clarity and consistency is the key if you are going to include more than one section in your e-zine.

Inspiration for Content: Growing Antennae

It has been a few years since I've sat down to write a newsletter and struggled to come up with content. I'm no genius; it has come about by developing what I call good "content-seeking awareness." I have two antennae sticking out of my head, scanning my environment for ideas:

1. What content would be interesting to my readers, what do they struggle with, where is their pain, and how can I help them?
2. What facet of my work and business would I like to showcase, what product or service do I want to promote, and how can I create a compelling offer that readers will love?

These two antennae—one directed to the readers, the other directed to my business—are triggered many times during the week. When it comes time to write the e-zine, I get out my notes and choose a topic that serves both purposes as closely as possible.

Mining for Content Ideas

Here's what to do if you struggle to find and create content for your e-newsletters:

- *Always keep the reader in mind.* It helps to clearly define and describe your ideal reader. He/she is probably similar to your ideal client, so that step should be easy.
- *Determine what your ideal reader wants to know.* You can probably estimate this pretty well, and you should also explore this with them. Ask. Ask in your newsletter, on your blog, through surveys, even on your website by creating an "ask" page whereby they can submit questions. You might also provide incentives to readers who submit questions.

Remember to use your *content antennae,* scanning for these two criteria:

1. What do readers want to know?
2. What can my business do for them?

Next, review this checklist of 17 questions and resources for content inspiration:

1. Where is your readers' pain?
2. What current event ties in with readers' problems?
3. What client situation can you use as a case study?
4. What unusual or unique story could benefit your readers?
5. How do you differ from your competitors?
6. What web or blog resources would your readers love to know about?
7. Who can you interview to provide your readers with information from other experts?
8. What personal experience or mistake can you turn into a valuable lesson for readers?
9. Set up Google Alerts to send you notification of web and news content in your field.
10. Set up blog feeds for all your keywords.

11. Use a service such as HitTail.com on your blog. It will give you specific keywords readers use to find you and suggest article topics using "long tail" search terms.

12. Use a keyword tracking tool such as Overture to find out what terms people use most frequently when searching on the Web. Then create content using those specific keywords.

13. Scan the online article directories for articles in your field. You can use OPC—other people's content—as long as you keep their name and URL intact.

14. Instead of using OPC, however, use articles as inspiration to write your own version on a topic.

15. Professional organizations, trade shows, and keynote speakers all provide targeted information in your field that your clients would love to know about.

16. Use quotations. There are many books as well as online quotation directories.

17. Use Amazon.com to track bestsellers and learn the hot topics that are popular in your field.

Whenever doing research on the Web, stay focused on your purpose: Find information your readers can use and tie it into how they can benefit from your products or services. Be careful not to get screen-sucked for hours. Always ask yourself, "What's in it for readers?" Then ask the "so what?" question to determine if information is merely interesting, or if it is useful.

Once you decide a topic, the fun begins. Write to deliver the most pertinent information in the most concise manner (short, sweet, and to the point). Create a compelling headline, use keywords, create an emotional connection with readers, and inspire a response to your call to action.

When you consistently deliver valuable content in a way that inspires or connects, you will see your subscriber list grow and higher response to your calls to action.

CHAPTER 7 REVIEW

- Deliver what *your constituents* want, rather than what you want to send them. Keep in mind that your audience has a finite attention capacity, and they will immediately decide if you are wasting their time. If so, expect them to revolt.
- Building or sourcing relevant content is not necessarily more work. There are several time-effective ways to gather or create more content. You can reuse and recycle content that already exists, mine the content from your website, seek third-party content from blogs, association websites, and more. Or, you can even hire a copywriter.
- *Dynamic Content* refers to content that changes according to rules. The idea is that these rules are set up on the backend (i.e., a rule could be: Location = Indiana) and content to match this segment is easily created by the marketer. The email system automatically inserts that content into the email template for *only* the Indiana audience, using the backend rule.
- Images, offers and incentives, and "from" side are all great Dynamic Content elements to test.
- Testing incentives and offers via Dynamic Content will help you better understand what compels each individual to take action.
- Before sending an email, you should ask yourself, "Who owns the relationship with this audience?" Is it the president and CEO? The marketing department? A specific salesperson? Deliver the message from the specific human being rather than the institution at large.
- If you remember the 40, 40, 20 rule of database marketing, you know that 40 percent of your success is dependent on your database, 40 percent on your content, and 20 percent on the creative aspects of your marketing. Content plays a huge role in your overall success.

CHAPTER 8

THE ROLE OF EMAIL IN VIRAL AND WORD-OF-MOUTH MARKETING

Many people see or hear the term *viral marketing* and automatically cringe. You're probably brainstorming prevention methods—maybe a vaccine, plenty of fluids, and lots of rest will do the trick?

The truth is that both word-of-mouth marketing (WOM) and viral marketing can have positive effects on your business. Trust me, you *want* viral marketing. Yes, it's contagious, but in a good way. It's one of the most powerful means for encouraging individuals to pass your message on. Consider the fact that your audience is twice as likely to react to a message coming from a trusted source, such as a friend. One day as I sat here writing this, I saw an article come through from MediaPost concluding that mothers feel disconnected from the way most marketers portray them, and 67 percent of them would rather talk to a peer than hear from a celebrity. That means a surprise visit from your neighbor with brown teeth (who also happens to be a mother) could be more likely to convince you to switch to Colgate toothpaste than Brooke Shields. That's a big deal.

Many people wonder if viral marketing and WOM marketing are the same as *buzz marketing*. In my opinion, buzz marketing is about making an impression and getting people to talk about you. (Note: buzz can be both negative and positive.)

I would describe WOM and viral marketing as ways to compel your constituents to take a positive action that compels their peers to take action as well.

Make sense? You want your constituents to refer friends and family members to you, who in turn refer more of their friends and family to you. There's a saying that goes: "Just because everyone else jumped off a bridge, would you do it, too?" Your constituents are jumping off a bridge and plunging into your product or service. You want all of their personal networks to nod and jump with them.

Viral marketing also includes a few strategies that are not necessarily components of WOM marketing.

According to Wilson Web, the six principles of a viral marketing strategy are:

1. Gives away products or services
2. Provides for effortless transfer to others
3. Scales easily from small to very large
4. Exploits common motivations and behaviors
5. Utilizes existing communication networks
6. Takes advantage of others' resources

Not all strategies apply to a single activity, but viral marketing should include at least one or more of these characteristics. Both WOM and viral marketing are all about leveraging existing relationships to develop other relationships.

At this point, you're probably wondering what WOM and viral marketing have to do with email. I thought you'd never ask.

First, think about why people actually do what you want them to do. It may simply be because they want to help. It may be because you've earned enough trust, or because they're flattered that you've asked. Or, you may make such a compelling case for the action, there's no downside to it. In any event, the key first step in getting others to do something is to ask them. If this were a personal relationship book, we'd go into an example like, "How could your spouse possibly know that you have a sore neck and want a massage if you never ask?" Or maybe that's a trick question because we should know our spouse so well, we should be able to recognize when he or she is craning in discomfort and moaning in pain. That's why I'm writing an email marketing book, not a personal relationships book. In this book, there is no ESP or intuitive reaction. You must ask. If you don't ask, then what you want to happen isn't likely to happen.

What are some of the components of a successful WOM marketing program? First, you must communicate your desire to your constituents. Of course, email is the perfect way to ask since you can ask personally, in a relevant way, and track engagement.

Next, you should think about the risk factors associated with what you are asking. The lower the risk, the more likely the constituent will do what you want. For example, my friend might tell me that I really need to change laundry detergent. Today! And I might think she's crazy for bringing it up so suddenly and so adamantly. Doesn't she know that I've already pledged my allegiance to the drugstore brand? Who cares that there isn't any discernable difference between my brand or her brand? If my friend can't articulate the compelling reasons for a switch, I'm going to think that she's asking for reasons outside of her genuine concern over my detergent. That means I'm going to disregard her advice and stick with the drugstore brand. However, if she forwarded me an email that included secrets to a better laundry experience and a coupon for a discount on my first two purchases, she may get me interested. And if the next time I see her, she lets me know that several people have complimented her on the pleasant scent of her clothing, I may very well be convinced that I should go ahead and switch. It's low risk for everyone and has a high probability of success. It makes it easy for her to endorse the brand, and the coupon incentive adds urgency.

Earlier, I said that you must ask your constituents to do what you want them to do. If you don't, then what you want to happen isn't *likely* to happen. In some cases, it might happen. If your organization or product or service or salesperson is so wonderful and amazing, your constituent can't help but talk about it, you have a recipe for natural WOM marketing. Most often, it happens organically when cool new experiences hit the scene, such as the iPod or *Desperate Housewives*. I'm not going to share any ideas on building an iPod or writing an

Emmy-winning show, in case you were hoping. For the sake of this book, we'll focus on WOM and viral marketing that isn't organic.

Sure, without organic magic, there's some work involved. But again, you'll be happy to know that there isn't much heavy lifting. What you really need to grasp first and foremost are the key components to successful WOM marketing, which I'll tackle in more detail using a personal example.

The reason I wrote this book is not because I walked to work one day, thinking, "Hey, what if I wrote a book?" I never had any intention of writing a book. This book happened because the publisher contacted me. How did the publisher know about me? Because I've been keeping an email marketing blog for the past few years, which gives me credibility on the subject of email marketing.

Okay, I know you're thinking, "Big deal. Lots of people have blogs, Chris. My 10-year-old daughter has one about cats."

I understand your rationale. Several people do have blogs. The differentiator in my case is that my blog happens to have won some awards. How did I win? By compelling people to vote for me in an online poll. That's right—I asked them to vote. Gasp! Now you're thinking, "What kind of self-centered marketer *asks* people to vote for him?" A marketer who wants to win an award, that's what kind. Sure, I could've just sat back and hoped that enough people who read my blog would vote. But I knew the response would be greater if I acted, so I emailed all of my friends and family members and loyal readers, asking them to vote and to pass along my request to anyone else who might be willing to vote. It's a low-risk request. Simply click on a link in the email and check the box next to my name. Forward to whomever you'd like. See the components of successful WOM and viral marketing here? I asked for a favor. I approached an audience who I had a relationship with and made it clear I'd like to tap into their individual relationships. I made sure it was low risk.

The result, of course, is that I won the award, and I got to write this book. And yes, they are results, not the end game. Word-of-mouth and viral tactics work best when they start a journey rather than conclude a journey.

Another quick personal example I'll share is the referral incentive used by ExactTarget. Referral leads are often the least expensive type of lead in any organization. For the most part, referrals are pretty well qualified. The simple fact is that people are not going to refer their peers or friends unless they think there is an opportunity for both parties. There is a higher close ratio for referral leads (due to the trust factor), and they tend to engage in a shorter sales cycle.

The incentive ExactTarget uses is a monthly drawing for a nice prize. Each referral earns the person an entry into the drawing. Any referral that turns into new business is an automatic prize. The keys to success are the same as the other examples: We ask our clients and prospects to refer others via our email program. We mitigate risk by making sure that the people whom we ask are happy with us, which makes the incentive an extra thank you. Our goals are clear. Our communication is clear. We get around 50 of these referral leads per month, with the average conversion rate into actual business opportunities around 60 percent. Not bad for a program that's basically running itself, right?

Forward to a friend (FTAF) is another viral component that can drive success. Many email marketers put FTAF buttons on the bottom of their emails. Unfortunately, those buttons are about as effective as the "Sign up for our newsletter" slot at the bottom of your homepage.

I encourage you to approach WOM and viral marketing with a small sense of entitlement (if you've earned it). If you've kept your promises, provided good service, great products, and whatever else is instrumental to good relationships in your business, you've earned trust. A company I know asks its constituents these simple questions every once in a while:

1. Are you happy with us? (Yes/No)
2. Would you refer us to your friends? (Yes/No)
3. Have you referred us to your friends? (Yes/No)

I don't care what sophisticated data analytics people say about the effectiveness of yes or no questions. That's compelling information that doesn't take long to gather. (And obviously, the people who take time to answer these questions get a follow-up treatment.) What a great, yet subtle message to use when communicating your goals to your constituents.

I'll wrap things up by hitting on a very simple and easy way to drive personal referrals. Your organization is likely to send hundreds of outbound emails *daily* through Outlook and Gmail. Each time an outbound email is sent, you have an opportunity to put a subtle message out there. Some of your employees may have the company logo on the bottom of their emails; others might use a 6 point pink Verdana signature that you have to get out a magnifying glass to read. Why not standardize this email footer for your entire organization? It's a terrific way to leverage the entire relationship network of your organization. Think about the success of Hotmail, who made it easy to invite others to start a Hotmail account by including a Hotmail message and sign-up link at the bottom of every Hotmail email. That strategy resulted in 12 million subscribers in 1.5 years.

There may even be opportunities to equip advocates outside of your organization. For example, my wife is a homemaker by job description, yet she's never home. She deals with school committees, 12 different sports teams, a large family, and volunteers at our local hospital. Guess how many emails she sends each month due to these activities? Just over 500. Many of these emails go to multiple recipients. Can you guess what footer is on the bottom of every one of those AOL emails? Bingo. Her email contains a nonoffensive footer about my company, blog, and email marketing. (And yes, we have actually closed business as a result of the footer on my wife's email.)

If you've caught on to the way my mind works, you'll guess that I'm already thinking about doing the same thing with my mother, sisters, and kids. (And when my kids can drive, their cars will have my company's name emblazoned on the side. For anyone to get a ride from them, they'll have to commit to telling 10 people about Mr. Baggott's great company.) In all seriousness, why not leverage the people who are invested in your success? Think about your own personal network and family. Wouldn't they want you to be successful? Engage them in carrying the message.

Case Study

"Too Good to Be True" Job and Referral Incentive Goes Viral

A revolutionary new search engine based in Indianapolis faced a rare challenge: Convincing people that a dream job and an incredible referral incentive were 100 percent true.

The search engine is unique in that it utilizes real, live humans (called "guides") to assist its visitors with finding the information they are looking for on the Internet. The job description for these guides? Work whenever, from wherever, help people, share your knowledge, dig into the Internet . . . oh, and get paid for it, too.

Wow. It does sound too good to be true. And as an added bonus, anyone referring others who chose to sign up for the job would receive an ongoing portion of their referrals' earnings. Of course, people expected a "catch"—something hidden in the fine print that required an upfront payment on their part (none) or a drawback that confirmed that the job was, in fact, too good to be true.

The marketing team's initial email follow-ups to candidates were met with questions and resistance. In testing several different job descriptions and details, they found that it was important to deliver the information in pieces rather than all at once. Too many good things put forth in the same email made the candidates skeptical of legitimacy.

After testing 10+ descriptions and follow-ups, a winner was identified, and conversion rates went through the roof (10 percent commitment rate went up to over 30 percent).

To establish the trust factor between the guide and the company before the guide began inviting others, a brief training period took place. Guides who passed training and reached a certain level of job performance had the go-ahead to invite others to try the job. For consistency reasons, the guide was equipped with an email that included a bulleted description of the job offer and could easily be sent to friends and family members.

The Result: Average of 10 Referrals per Person and 14,000+ Committed Guides

In 10 weeks, the search engine went from a few hundred guides to 14,000+ guides. On average, each guide sent the message to 10 people, explaining the explosion of growth. The company learned that testing and adjusting the positioning of the offer, building trust, and providing an easy means for distribution to an individual's network are critical to the success of viral marketing.

WHAT ARE OTHER MARKETERS THINKING?
In their own words . . .

COULD YOUR EMAIL GO VIRAL?

By Ron McDaniel
Speaker and Author, Buzzoodle
Blog: http://blog.buzzoodle.com

Viral marketing is not always something you plan. Viral marketing is when a message starts spreading from person to person rapidly and uncontrollably. This could be a message you craft to be funny or extremely informative. Or it could be something that just happens by accident and spreads quickly.

One important note about emails and viral marketing is that the viral and interesting part of the message does not have to be in the email itself. Your email could simply be a way to point people to something of interest, and they will forward it to a friend. Or the opposite could happen. Your email may not go viral, but it might trigger other forms of viral messages that take off.

My Best Five Minutes of Marketing

The latter happened to us a few weeks after we launched a new company named Buzzoodle. I am a fan of Seth Godin's work, and just before going home from lunch, I decided to send him an email letting him know about our company. I'd never communicated with him before, and I really did not expect a reply. But I figured there was no down side.

The email was two to three sentences long with a link to the Buzzoodle website. When I came back from lunch, the tech group said the server was either down or there was a DNS attack on the server. After further investigation, it turned out Seth had added a comment on his blog about the email message and thousands of people were hitting the site within the first hour. (Seth has one of the top-rated blogs on marketing.)

Within a week, we had clients in 17 countries and over a year later, I still get hits from the posts on his blog. That one email has paid huge dividends without ever being forwarded.

It was the best five minutes of marketing I ever did, and it did not seem that special when I sent it out. It was about finding an advocate—and a popular one at that.

How to Use Email for Viral Marketing

Email can be used in several different ways to create a buzz. Here are some ideas:

- *Get people to visit a website.* If you create a funny or interesting thing on the Internet, email is the most effective way to get people to tell other people where it is. For example, you could post a video on YouTube, and in a few hours, it could have thousands of visitors as a result of a few email messages.

- *Get people to pass on the message.* If you have a message that really interests people, they are likely to want to share it with friends. In your email, let people know that it is not an exclusive offer, and they can forward the message. If you are sending out a crazy sale or truly remarkable offer, encourage them to send it along. If your message is funny or information that is very valuable to people, it will also be forwarded, probably with or without permission.

- *Distribute an eBook or other media.* Notice the word "mail" in email. Email is also a way to deliver something. Consider creating a document, including it in your email, and allowing people to deliver it to all their friends via a forward. A health care agency or insurance company may want to create an "Annual Family Health Checklist" and send it to all of their clients. In the email, let recipients know that they can forward the valuable worksheet to anyone they care to. Just be sure that the checklist is properly branded and has a clear way to contact you.

Remember that email is often a permanent message. Be careful you do not say something negative or critical that could also go viral and damage your reputation or the reputation of your company. It is simply too easy to forward it on.

Email is a powerful tool for creating buzz and getting your message out. Your message is not always going to go viral and triple your sales, but don't let that stop you. If you are careful with your message, respect people's privacy, and keep reminding them that you exist, you are going to have a better relationship with your customers. You increase the odds that one of your messages will end up generating incredible interest and be seen by millions.

Viral Email Marketing: Top Ten Best Practices

By Tara Lamberson
Vice President, Marketing, MindComet Corporation
Blog: http://blogs.mindcomet.com

Throughout MindComet's experiences with viral marketing campaigns, email has been a core component to promote the initial launch of the campaign and the continued driver for enhancing exposure and interaction. Lessons have been learned and strategies improved along the way, resulting in our top 10 best practices for successful viral email marketing campaigns:

1. *Message clearly and keep it simple.* Many campaigns that fail to generate significant viral buzz are a result of complicated, drawn out and overthought messages. Complex messages may be difficult to understand across audiences and create delays in the decision-making process that prevent the forward-to-a-friend action from ever being taken. For this reason, keeping your message simple, short, and clear may provide the best return and the highest viral conversion rates.

2. *Make a suggestion and provide the tools.* You have a hilarious video, funny pictures, slogans, or catchy news ready to hit the viral highway . . . but have you optimized your email marketing to ignite exposure? Too often, email marketers set up viral campaigns and fail to ask recipients to share the buzz. Let recipients know that you want them to send it to their friends. Provide them with the tools to increase exposure, such as the ability to send to their IM list, to post badges on their blog, or to post your viral piece on their MySpace page.

3. *Monitor and analyze results.* Continuously track the success of your viral campaign, set measurement points, and compare this to your original goals. If you find out early enough that your viral campaign is not taking off as it should, consider revising slightly and adding tools that broaden your exposure to online video outlets, blogs, forums, and other online arenas that will encourage consumer generated media. The metrics you track will ultimately allow you to see the offers driving the best return on investment (ROI).

4. *Cap incentive-based offers.* Viral marketing works best when a tangible value-added offer is included. You will want to consider capping the incentive with a specific quantity to avoid spam-like spreading of your message. For example, offer a 15 percent discount on the referrer's next purchase if they forward the message to five friends. Incentives without a cap, such as five dollars off for every five friends referred, may cause serious customer service and privacy-related nightmares for your company, resulting in increased traffic that overloads servers and higher demand than supply for free giveaway offers.

5. *A referral is not an opt-in.* When your subscribers refer their friends, the referral should not be considered opted in. Be sure to include an easy way for referrals to opt in, such as a checkbox to receive future mailings. Immediately follow this message with a double opt-in. Even if you do not have plans to launch an ongoing communication campaign, you may want to do so in the future.

6. *Personalize the referral email and subject line.* Response rates have the potential to increase radically when users can see that the message is coming from a friend, not a company. Consider personalizing the subject line to show that it is coming from a recognizable source. Your

subject line may read: "Jane Smith Thought You Would be Interested in 15 percent Off at ZZZ.com." By doing this, you have identified that the message has been sent by a friend, and that there is a special offer.

7. *Avoid message overload.* As you monitor the results of the campaign, ensure you are not overcommunicating, which may result in lower open rates and ultimately affect the ROI of the initiative. Revisit open and click-through rates to determine the responses you are receiving. Over time, recipients may become tired of communications, causing a drop-off in email activity. The open and click-through rates may be good indicators you are sending too much, too often.

8. *Establish clear business goals in advance.* Be sure to determine the overall goal of your viral email campaign in advance and define how you will measure the success. Whether it was designed to raise brand awareness, increase sales, increase sign-ups for a particular service, or promote a new product launch, clear goals and measurements will help eliminate any discrepancies with reporting further down the road. Remember, viral campaigns may not always produce immediate results and may take months to disseminate to consumers.

9. *Only risk what you are willing to have associated with your brand.* Viral campaigns aren't for every brand. Remember, you are dealing with a consumer market, allowing them to take your message, send it to friends, and post it throughout the Web. This often leaves room for free interpretation that may not always have a positive spin. Carefully consider some of these nuances and have a plan for proactive brand reputation management.

10. *Content should be worthy of sharing.* As simple as it may seem, your content should be "forward-worthy." If you have any reservations as to whether your

message will be passed along, consider A/B testing to determine which message is shared more frequently.

CHAPTER 8 REVIEW

- Buzz marketing is about making an impression and getting people to talk about you. (Note: buzz can be both negative and positive.)
- Word-of-mouth and viral marketing are ways to compel your constituents to take a positive action that compels their peers to take action as well.
- Viral marketing is also likely to include one or several of these strategies: gives away products or services, provides for effortless transfer to others, scales easily from small to very large, exploits common motivations and behaviors, utilizes existing communication networks, and takes advantage of others' resources.
- To encourage viral marketing, you must ask, keep risk factors low, and provide an incentive for both the constituent and the person that he or she is referring. Email is the perfect medium to test various offers and incentives to find out what compels your constituents to act.
- Forward-to-a-friend is a viral component that can drive success, but it extends beyond slapping a button onto the bottom of your email. Your content itself must be conducive to viral marketing.
- To leverage viral and WOM tactics, take a look at your close personal network. Husbands, wives, parents, and children all care about your success and will likely be more than willing to help.
- Remember, referrals are typically the least expensive leads for any organization. That's why WOM marketing and viral marketing are worth your time.

CHAPTER 9

ANALYTICS THAT MATTER

In my introduction, I mentioned the adage, "I know half of my advertising is wasted. . . . I just don't know which half." Oops. I said that we weren't ever going to say that again. I promise we're really finished at this point. Because with email marketing, you are free of this uncertain mentality. You are no longer restricted by intuition and ambiguity, which have plagued marketers since the beginning of the mass marketing movement.

By paying attention to analytics, you now have the power to know exactly what's happening, why it is happening, and apply a return on investment to every single email marketing activity.

Wow, that's powerful. It's better than a crystal ball, isn't it? Instead of predicting, you can witness actual behavior, measure effectiveness, and make future decisions based on that learning. Go ahead and let it soak in for a minute.

It's very different from the direct mail and catalog world, isn't it? Remember, in those mediums, we have to worry about delivery, whether it was opened and read, which pages people browsed but didn't buy, whether the catalog was passed on to others . . . we wait and we wonder. I feel the pain of businesses like Restoration Hardware, because every time I get one of their beautiful catalogs, I eagerly turn to those pages with sofas. I give each of them a loving look. Then I get distracted by something else and eventually throw away that wonderful work of art. Do you see how broken this model is? Unless the recipient actually makes a purchase, the catalog or direct mail piece might as well have fallen into a black hole.

Now compare that to email marketing. Can you measure delivery? Can you see what products I'm most interested in? Can you see that I've visited a special offer on hot tubs seven times but not yet pulled the trigger? Can you ask me why I haven't made the purchase? The answers are yes, yes, yes, yes.

If there's something I can't stand, it's when an organization makes a decision based on "gut feeling" rather than data. It happens all of the time. The marketing department meets. They look at six different colors for their brochure. The boss says, "I've always liked green," and all of a sudden, your brochure, your website, and your email are all a nice emerald hue. Why? Because your boss "liked it." Ugh.

Or what about focus groups? Has your marketing team ever conducted one of those? Essentially, a bunch of "average users" gather around a table, eat free cookies, and chose your marketing materials. I hope you're cringing now, too. I hope you're cringing at the thought of feelings and focus groups and applauding the reality of analytical marketing. After all, analytical marketing is *measured* marketing. And if it can be measured, it can be improved. Awesome.

WHAT SHOULD YOU MEASURE?

In Chapter 4, we focused on analytics with respect to subscriber engagement. In this chapter, we'll get into greater detail on those analytics. First, let's come back to the fact that, sometimes, it's hard to know if what you're measuring indicates good or bad results.

The most important lesson in measurement is to accept that *you are only competing against yourself.* Industry averages shouldn't mean squat to you. How your competitors fare is useless insider information.

When measuring the success of your email marketing program, the only comparison you need to make is against yourself. Over time, are you getting better, or are you getting worse? You have the data at your fingertips, so now you just need to get a read on it. You really have an advantage here, because the speed at which you can receive feedback and implement changes has never been faster. This creates an endless circle of improvement, which is what testing is all about. I know you're excited to learn more on that topic, so stick around because it's in the next chapter. But for now, let me say that you should think *only* about incremental improvement for *your* organization.

Back in the "old days," when measuring really was rocket science, it was easy to spend cycles obsessing over what your competitors were up to. Did they have some big tactic that might hurt you? Did they have more "exposure?" I would be naive to think that any of us can ignore our competitors, because monitoring is an important function that impacts your organization's growth. Yet, here is the trap: Your competitor seems to be doing better than you, for whatever reason. You notice that they are running big full-page ads in the trade publications, so you conclude that you should also run big ads in the trade publications. But you have a problem, because you still can't measure your own marketing very well . . . and now you're trying to measure the marketing of a competitor. You might as well be flying a plane without wings. Free yourself from the competition for now. Focus on your own activities. Concentrate on improving one step at a time.

Now that you understand that you should consider analytics with respect to only *your* organization, you're ready to learn more about what you can measure. (Note: these are in no particular order.)

Deliverability Rate

Your deliverability rate indicates whether or not you're getting to the subscribers you intend to reach. If you sent to 100 people and 50 messages were undeliverable, you had a deliverable rate of 50 percent (ouch). Obviously, deliverability is critical to your success. If you get blocked or wind up in the subscriber's junk folder, all of your effort is a waste of time. In Chapter 13, we'll talk about the reasons why filtering issues and deliverability problems might emerge. At this point, you should make a commitment to measure your overall deliverability rate. You also need to measure deliverability across several ISPs and domains. Without going through this exercise, you have no idea if you have a problem with one particular ISP, such as Gmail, or if you have issues across the board. If you are a B-to-B marketer, you may have a bigger challenge on your hands since a higher proportion of your email database may be company domains rather than the bigger ISPs (i.e., john@companyx.com as opposed to john@gmail.com).

There are a few ways to monitor your deliverability. The simplest and most effective way is by creating a seed list. A seed list is simply a list of test email addresses that enables you to see the results of your deliverability firsthand. A good practice is to sign up under several email addresses, at as many ISPs as possible, including the majors (Gmail, AOL, Yahoo, Comcast, Earthlink, Hotmail, MSN, etc.) and the minors. If a specific organization is a big part of your mailing list, you should also look into whether or not you are able to get a test email address there (a friend inside the organization may be willing to help).

Using this list, you can send yourself a test of the email before sending externally. If the message appears in the inbox without any issues, you can assume that it will be the same case when you send to subscribers with the same domain (i.e., @gmail.com).

A more efficient way to approach seed lists and a deliverability test is to utilize the services offered by many deliverability companies. Instead of limiting your test to the number of email accounts you find the time to open, these services enable access to tens of thousands of seed addresses, across every domain imaginable. It's less work on your end and a much better initial read on deliverability. Along those lines, these services provide excellent reporting and analysis that can quickly pinpoint specific problems, which help your organization fix the issue.

Most email service providers should also provide *domain monitoring* as part of their standard analytics package. With domain monitoring, you can look for aberrations in your overall results (opens, clicks, etc.) by domain. If you see that your average open rate is 45 percent, but your AOL open rate is significantly lower, you might have a deliverability problem with AOL.

The bottom line is that every email counts. Sure, email is inexpensive, but it adds up over time. If you can afford to waste 20 percent of your emails, then you probably don't have the right objectives in the first place. Monitor your deliverability and work to push this number up.

Open Rate

$$\text{Open rate} = \frac{\text{Unique opens}}{\left(\text{Sent} - \text{bounced}\right)}$$

We've already covered the fact that email opens are really nothing more than impressions. Just because some of your audience opens your email doesn't mean that they have actually read it.

While open rates don't tell the entire or final story on email success, they are still important to measure. As I've said before, you are measuring *incremental changes* in your program. If you notice your open rates going up, that's generally a good thing. If you see your open rates declining, it may be cause for concern and further investigation.

Before you go into a panic attack when you see email open rates declining over time, I encourage you to keep in mind that many ISPs and Outlook have image rendering turned off as the default. Unless the individual user changes the default, email sent to that subscriber will not register an open. (As review, it ties back to the fact that a tiny image inserted in an email actually renders an open.) Additionally, handheld devices such as BlackBerries and Treos don't render images, meaning that they don't register opens. In fact, it's been estimated that 50 percent of all email is delivered to subscribers that are unable to render images. That kind of percentage throws the entire metric into question.

Figure 9.1 depicts the findings from a study of ExactTarget client emails sent during the fourth quarter 2004 through the first quarter 2006. As you can see, the open rates steadily decline. However, there is promise in the fact that click-through rates and the unsubscribe rates held steady. ExactTarget concluded that this likely

Figure 9.1
Declining Open Rates May Indicate a Trend in Image
Suppression Rather Than Declining Engagement

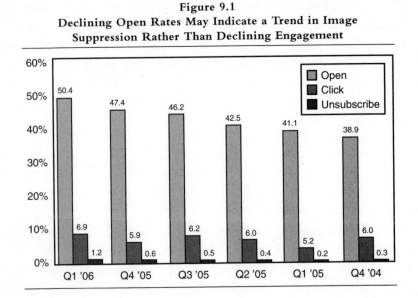

indicates an overall trend in image suppression rather than a decline in email engagement.

All things considered, I still believe that you should monitor and care about your email open rates. And the important thing to remember is that you must benchmark against *yourself*.

Click-Through Rate

$$\text{Click-through rate} = \frac{\text{Unique clicks}}{(\text{Sent} - \text{bounced})}$$

Your click-through rate is much more important than your open rate. A "click" happens any time a recipient engages with a hyperlink included in your email. These links may take the subscriber to your website, landing page, or even a downloadable document or video. Each of these indicates a positive step that your subscriber took in order to engage with your message. Of all top-level metrics (those that measure initial success), high click-through rates are exactly what you want to accomplish as a first step. I repeat: *As a first step.*

Many email marketers use a combined metric called a "click-to-open ratio" to measure success. They compare the ratio (or percentage) of how many emails are opened to how many click-throughs registered. The higher the ratio, the more successful the marketers' efforts . . . right? Well, not really. Because of the open rate issue we discussed earlier (the fact that there is a trend in decreasing open rates that may represent an image problem, not an actual open problem), you may be getting a "false positive." Because your click-to-open ratio goes up, you assume you're improving. The reality is that you might be treading water. Or, you could even be less successful than before. Another problem with click-to-open ratios is that they can reward marketers for poor deliverability. A far better way to measure success is by click-through rate. It will tell you if engagement is taking place. That click is the indication that your audience is taking the next step.

Unsubscribe Rate

$$\text{Unsubscribe rate} = \frac{\text{Unsubcribes}}{\left(\text{Sent} - \text{bounced}\right)}$$

Your unsubscribe rate is an indication of whether you're keeping up with the expectations and value promised to your constituents. Obviously, you want this number to be between low and nonexistent. You probably know that by law, every commercial email in the United States (and most of the world) must have an "unsubscribe" link found within the email and an easy way for the subscriber to opt-out of receiving future messages.

If the number of individuals unsubscribing from your email program is going up, you will want to reevaluate the relevance of the message and the audience it was delivered to. You should also pay attention to the individuals who are unsubscribing—is it your most valuable customer base? Is it all males? Also, you'll want to see if these unsubscribes tend to come from one type of email communication. You're trying to pinpoint trends and reasons in order to act accordingly.

Some marketers are of the mentality that unsubscribes don't matter. "They don't want to hear from me, so why should I care about them?" Wrong mentality. This is the most efficient measure of dissatisfaction you will ever get. People may say that they love your exclusive email offers (because they don't want to offend you), but they may unsubscribe due to inbox clutter. Most of the time, irrelevance or lack of value is to blame. A phone call to that constituent may help you figure out what's going on (obviously email is inappropriate. And if your phone calls go ignored, this constituent may not want to hear from you at all).

I've seen a lot of good email marketers use a preference center landing page for their unsubscribes. Instead of losing the email relationship altogether, the preference page offers other communications that may be more often or less frequent. The preference center is also a place where you can ask a couple of departing questions to better pinpoint dissatisfaction. But don't even think about requiring answers to your questions. It's a guaranteed way to tick someone off even more. And don't try to hide the "unsubscribe from all" option. If someone wants to leave your entire mail program, it's best not to stand in the way.

On the other hand, many of your constituents will not unsubscribe. But they'll still ignore you (as I pointed out earlier, I still receive airline emails so I can point out what not to do). If your open rates and click-through rates suddenly plummet, but unsubscribes remain constant, you may want to survey your audience to see if they've "mentally unsubscribed." In other words, an unsubscribe might not always manifest itself in the direct results you're getting.

Spam Complaints

Sometimes subscribers are afraid to use the unsubscribe link. Maybe they assume that by clicking on it, the joke will be on them, and it will cause hundreds of new spam messages to flood their inbox. Or maybe they don't trust the unsubscribe link because there was insufficient permission for the marketer to mail to them in the first place. It's a bad situation for marketers, because if your constituents don't feel comfortable complaining directly to you, they'll find someone else who is ready and willing to listen. That's right, they'll push that little red button that every marketer dreads: "This is spam." Getting reported as spam enough times can take a big toll on your deliverability rates (to the point that you're unable to deliver any email to your audience at that ISP). Even worse, your subscriber might complain to one of the third-party blacklist organizations. These organizations make their money by providing their clients—usually ISPs—with a list of known spammers. Earlier, I mentioned that the term *viral marketing* may sound unpleasant, but it's actually good for your organization. In this case, the spam list is just what it sounds like—bad, bad, very bad. You don't want to be on that list.

Your email service provider or software vendor needs to provide your spam complaints as an element of its general reporting. Nothing can cut off your email marketing efforts faster or more painfully than getting blacklisted due to spam complaints.

Multichannel Analytics

So far, we've touched on metrics directly related to the email itself. Guess what? There are several important metrics outside of your email. While a click-through is an indication of *initial* success, you must determine whether the desired action was actually accomplished. Did 772,000 people click to download your new white paper, but only 50 finished registration. Uh-oh. Red alert. Your form may have been too long, or your website could have been experiencing problems during the peak click time frame. Without knowledge of the conversion metric, you'd be giving your boss a big, silly grin and saying, "Yes, we had over 700,000 people download the white paper. We're doing great." Correction: 772,000 people took a step toward the download, which is great. Fifty actually received access to it, which probably isn't so great.

That's why it's so important for you to measure both performance of the email and the website or landing page. Again, you have a goal for your constituents to do something. If the interest (click-throughs) appears high, but the conversion is low, you need to figure out why.

Perhaps the call to action in the email was misleading. Perhaps the audience had too many choices on the landing page and veered off the path. Without conversion analytics, you would never have a reason to determine the cause of a completed step, or the obstacle that prevented it.

The great news is that email marketing and web analytics can be fully integrated now. Many email software companies offer simple web conversion tracking, but it's even better to find a vendor that can integrate with one of the major web analytics providers. These tools can be as expensive and complicated as you need them to be, or they can be really simple and inexpensive. You don't need to buy both systems from the same vendor unless you want to. Most email and web analytics vendors have software called "Application Programming Interfaces" (APIs) that enable them to easily communicate to each other without a lot of work or complexity on your part.

To provide an idea of how combined email and web analytics work, I've included a depiction of the packaged analytics program offered by ExactTarget and WebTrends (Figure 9.2). (Again, most major vendors offer an API that makes this integration very easy.)

Combined analytics provide the marketer with two huge advantages:

1. You can determine the big picture effectiveness of your email. Did you actually accomplish the immediate goal for the communication? If not, the metrics provided will help determine where the process broke down.

2. You are able to capture additional data on an individual subscriber's behavior—a huge advantage. You can find out exactly what that person does on your site and incorporate your findings into future communications (i.e., "Chris, we noticed you looked at hot tubs 11 times today. We're ready and willing to help, so we encourage you to fill out our quick survey and let us know what we can do"). Think back to the Restoration Hardware catalog example I used earlier. How much more likely are they to succeed when they know I'm

Figure 9.2
Email and Web Analytics Provide the Complete Behavioral Picture

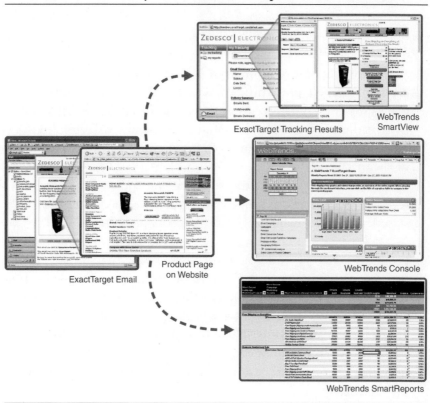

ExactTarget Tracking Results

WebTrends SmartView

ExactTarget Email

Product Page on Website

WebTrends Console

WebTrends SmartReports

interested in sofas? Exactly. Knowledge is power. Measurement provides knowledge that drives conversions and the bottom line.

Revenue and Return on Investment

Revenue and return on investment play an instrumental role in your company's bottom line. So of course you want to measure as much as you can with respect to what your email program accomplishes.

Case Studies

Case Study 1: Tangible Advantages of Web and Email Integration

A leading manufacturer of large LED message centers had traditionally relied on a mix of brand-building advertising and batch-and-blast email to sustain their sales. And while the company had an active client list of approximately 10,000 individual salespeople, the company only had email addresses for 450 of them.

The manufacturer partnered with an agency in order to leverage email technology to reach out to a greater number of sign dealers and create "active dealer" opportunities.

They embarked on an integrated marketing communications program aimed at building a permission-based email list; then utilized their email system to drive ongoing email communications with their new dealer network.

The program started with six print ads placed in three publications over two months. The ads were measurable due to a call to action to visit a unique landing page specific to the ad. (See how this company has leveraged offline media to generate online conversions?)

The landing page gave the salespeople the opportunity to opt-in to the email list in order to receive a white paper by email, which also included links to products and dealer support tools, such as free traffic analysis and brochures.

Results: Better Future Targeting due to Behavioral Data

In seven weeks, the email opt-in list doubled to nearly 1,000 qualified subscribers. Using an integrated email and web analytics platform, the company was able to track exactly what traffic was generated by the various elements of the program. Armed with detailed conversion data, profile data, and behavioral data, the company was able to better target future communications depending on each salesperson's interest. And the company didn't stop at white paper downloads. By using the download site as a means to begin collecting behavioral data on their products, the program generated opportunities projected to be worth $1.2 million.

Case Study 2: What to Do if Your Website Converts Peanuts

A two-store specialty bicycle retailer did only a tiny percentage of its $6 million in annual sales on its website. Due to extensive navigation options, the site served mostly informational purposes rather than purchasing purposes. In addition, many of the retailer's equipment suppliers insisted on having customers pick up bikes and other items in-store to ensure that they were properly assembled. The retailer knew there was a huge opportunity to drive site traffic that translated into revenue, but the question was: How would they do it?

The timing of the dilemma was perfect. When the store-owner learned that the jerseys worn by Lance Armstrong and other U.S. racers during the Tour de France had been re-designed due to a sponsorship change, he knew it was the answer to boosting online sales.

He immediately called Nike and confirmed that he would be able to place an order. He then created an email message informing the 10,000 customers who had opted-in to his email program that the jerseys were available while supplies lasted. Within three days, the email was out the door and driving customers to the website, where they could easily preorder the re-designed jersey.

Results: $10,000 in Online Sales—In One Week Alone

In one week alone, the campaign generated $10,000 in online sales, which *surpassed* the amount of online sales taken in the first six months of the year.

The email also limited risk because with preorders, the owner knew exactly how much inventory to order.

WHAT ARE OTHER MARKETERS THINKING?

In their own words . . .

BEYOND OPENS AND CLICKS: USING ANALYTICS TO DRIVE EMAIL ENGAGEMENT AND SALES

By Joel Book
Director of eMarketing Strategy, ExactTarget

Not that long ago, it wasn't all that uncommon to see email marketers glued to their office chairs, staring at their monitors and watching the numbers change before their eyes as subscribers opened and clicked an email sent just minutes earlier. Those "heady" days of using only opens and clicks to measure email effectiveness are gone.

Today, e-marketing effectiveness is measured by how many web visitors are converted to buyers, how many one-time buyers become repeat buyers, and eventually, how many of those buyers become your best customers and advocates. This process of customer acquisition, retention, and growth is the very definition of *customer engagement.*

Properly planned and executed, an effective customer engagement strategy increases profit by keeping customers connected to the brand longer. And the argument for customer retention is compelling. Frederick Reichheld, author of the book, *The Loyalty Effect,* observed that a 5 percent reduction in customer defection can boost profit by 25 percent or more depending on the customer's tenure with the company. For example, newly acquired customers are less profitable because the cost of sale has not been fully recovered. The longer customers are retained, the greater their contribution to profit.

But effective customer engagement strategies require *customer insight* that reveals not only what the customer has purchased, but also the customer's product interest and purchase intent. In the hands of a strategic marketing professional, these analytics are the difference between being an e-marketing contender or an e-marketing pretender.

Successful customer engagement strategies are anchored by two categories of analytics:

1. *Customer analytics:* These analytics provide the information needed to measure current behavior such as product purchase and predict future behavior based on website click stream behavior or survey response. Examples of customer analytics and the source through which this insight is gathered include:

Customer Analytics	Data Source
Website behavior (click stream)	Search behavior (keywords)
Interests (declared)	Campaign response (view/click)
Interests (inferred)	Attitudinal (survey)
Purchases (transactions)	Demographics (registration)
Tenure	Marketing database

Strategic e-marketers will use customer analytics to:
—Determine which segment logically fits the customer.
—Calculate the customer's current value (NPV) and Lifetime Value (LTV).
—Determine the next best offer to make . . . and when to make it.
—Predict the customer's propensity to respond to the offer.
—Personalize email content to fit the customer's needs and interests.
—Calculate the customer's satisfaction or defection risk.
2. *Marketing analytics:* These analytics provide the information marketers need in order to measure and optimize interactive marketing programs and track sales

performance by channel. Examples of marketing analytics and the source through which this insight is gathered include:

Marketing Analytics	Metrics
Website visitors	By tactic (SEO/SEM, print ads, banner ads, PR)
Conversion	By type (email opt-in, event registration)
Buyers	By channel, offer, region, time
Repeat buyers	By channel, offer, region, time
ROI	By campaign/tactic, channel, medium
Nonpurchase transactions	By type (customer service, downloads, events)

These analytics are used to:

—Measure revenue and profitability by campaign.
—Determine customer engagement effectiveness (i.e., repeat visits, transactions).
—Measure segment and channel profitability.
—Refine budget allocation to maximize marketing performance.
—Measure and refine email opt-in performance.
—Pinpoint under-performing channels (or segments) and take corrective action.
—Optimize tactics for driving new and repeat website visitors.

A Roadmap for Success

Companies planning to put an e-marketing strategy in place to drive sales and build profitable customer relationships should consider the following top 10 lessons learned from organizations that have done this successfully:

1. Think it through. Define your organization's strategy for customer development and management. Align the strategy to the organization's business objectives. Create an *eMarketing Blueprint* for developing and executing the strategy.
2. Establish *Engagement Business Rules* that serve as guidelines for "treating" customers correctly based on their needs, interests, purchase behavior, and attitudes related to product use.
3. Create a *Customer Management Plan* that supports customized communications, sales, and service contacts based on customer demographics, predicted product/service purchase, customer value, and lifecycle stage.
4. Develop a "closed-loop" *Marketing Process* for planning, executing, and measuring multichannel marketing communications programs.
5. Establish a *Customer Marketing Team* to manage marketing program planning, execution, and measurement. Staff this group with people experienced in customer-focused marketing.
6. Integrate data on current and prospective customers in a *central* marketing database. Eliminate the usage of multiple customer databases used to support communications, sales, and service. Create a "single view" of your customer.
7. Develop an enterprise customer data acquisition strategy for developing and maintaining customer insight. Implement a *Customer Profile Review* to regularly verify and update customer needs.
8. Employ the use of integrated marketing technologies including website hosting, web analytics, email marketing, campaign management and CRM. Use these technologies to automate and support the "customer conversation" throughout the relationship lifecycle.

9. Define metrics for measurement and analysis of marketing program performance. Use these "key performance indicators" to monitor program results and refine marketing strategy.
10. Align marketing, sales, and customer service processes by integrating marketing communication, sales, and customer service systems to provide a single view of the customer throughout the enterprise.

The Rules of Marketing Have Changed

Have you changed, too? Performance is no longer measured by email opens and clicks, but by increases in revenue, customer retention, and customer value. In short, companies are achieving success by using analytics to first understand the customer's interests and intent; then using this insight to deliver precision-targeted offers and information that are relevant and timely.

Having the best product is no longer an ironclad guarantee for business success. Progressive companies have discovered that the key to long-term success is the ability to attract, retain, and grow customers. Doing this well requires the ability to "know" your customers and use this insight across the enterprise to personalize and leverage every interaction. And analytics are the fuel that drive e-marketing decision making and action.

CHAPTER 9 REVIEW

- Analytical marketing is *measured* marketing. If it can be measured, it can be improved.
- The most important lesson in measurement is to accept that you are only competing against yourself. Industry averages shouldn't mean squat to you. You should care most about benchmarking your own analytics over time.
- What should you measure? Plenty of things: deliverability rate, unsubscribe rate, open rate, click-through rate, spam complaints, multichannel analytics, revenue, and ROI.

- If you see open rates steadily declining over time, don't go into a panic attack. Keep in mind that many ISPs and Outlook have image rendering turned off as the default. A trend in image suppression may indicate image filtering rather than a decline in engagement with the email.
- Achieving high click-through rates is typically a good thing. Getting reported as spam is always a bad thing. If it happens enough times, it can take a real toll on your deliverability rates.
- Combined web and email analytics can provide you with two huge advantages: You can determine the big picture effectiveness of your email, and you can capture additional data on an individual subscriber's behavior (remember, current behavior is the best predictor of future behavior).
- Which is the most important metric? It depends on your business. But at the end of the day, we are trying to build relationships that make our organization money. You want to focus on what's impacting your bottom line.

CHAPTER 10

TESTING AGAINST YOUR GOALS

In the last chapter, we discussed analytics. The ability to measure success opens up a whole new world of improved marketing. Measuring makes it possible to find out which elements of your messages are more likely to work before you commit your entire database.

But even with the power of measurability and testing at their fingertips, the majority of email marketers don't test. If you're already testing, you have a huge advantage over marketers who are still relying on what "looks" or "feels" right. You've recognized the fact that the data from a test will tell you what *is* right. The success gap is widening in email marketing, and a line can be drawn between people who are testing and those who are not.

Another line can be drawn between A/B type testing and the advanced (yet simple) techniques of multivariate testing.

A/B testing means that you are simply testing one sample against another. A/B tests can be run using subject lines, layout, copy—just about any single variable you can think of with respect to your email. It's easy to do. It yields results. The drawback is that you can only test one variable at a time. When you first start testing, you might want to test a lot of variables.

Here is a simple example of A/B testing: Chris wants to send an email to his subscribers to tell them about his upcoming book. The subject lines are (A) Buy the new book by Chris Baggott and (B) I really would like your feedback on my new book.

One of these subject lines is probably better than the other. But which one? In traditional marketing, you simply guess the top performer. Half the room picks A, and half the room picks B. Then the boss says, "I've never really liked Chris Baggott," so he'd rather not put his name in the subject line. Wow, what great rationale.

In our new world of marketing, we get to decide a winner by consulting the real results. First, we pull two random samples (the same size or near the same) from the entire group of recipients. One segment will receive subject line A, one will receive subject line B. (It's important that the rest of the emails are identical, and that they are sent at the same time. If more than one variable differentiates the test, you won't know which variable caused one version to perform better than the other.) The winner is then mailed to the remainder of the audience.

Multivariate testing is just as easy to understand. Farmers have been doing it for generations. The idea is to simultaneously test several variables and measure the net result. Multivariate testing offers some significant advantages over A/B testing. First, it gets the answers back faster than if you were testing one element over a long period of time. It's less expensive and time consuming. And you get better information because you aren't just testing one element against another, you're testing how all the factors influence all other factors. What really matters is the combination of elements that works best. That's the very reason why farmers use multivariate testing rather than A/B testing. They grid their entire farm and test all variables in the same season.

Before the Dynamic Content era, multivariate testing was practically impossible. It was too labor intensive, and it took too long to get the results back. Suppose you are in the catalog business, getting ready to put together your spring book. How do you test? Ship small samples of multiple versions a few months before the real book is going to be mailed? Oh, but unfortunately it's a seasonal book. In fact, it's a wintertime holiday catalog. Do you really want to ship it in the spring? As you can tell, something as simple as timing made old world testing too difficult (and impractical). With email marketing, it's easy to execute any kind of test. Even better, the results are usually clear within a few days.

The opportunity (or threat) that comes with ease of use is the reality of a level playing field. In almost every other aspect of marketing, those with the deepest financial pockets have the advantage.

That isn't the case with data-driven email marketing. The tools are easy for anyone to use; they are inexpensive and easily integrated with the other tools necessary to manage successful one-to-one marketing. If the goal is to build relationships, the argument could be made that smaller companies have an advantage. Why? Many times, small company must rely on relationship building exercises rather than branding exercises because they can't afford to spend money on something that isn't going to generate immediate results. I've actually seen several examples of small companies leveraging email in a personalized manner, and big companies simply replicating their mass marketing tactics in a different medium.

WHAT SHOULD YOU TEST?

Good question. In fact, such a good question that I decided to ask Morgan Stewart, director of strategic services at ExactTarget and a testing mastermind, to provide his insight on this question and a few others.

Where Should Someone Who Is Just Beginning to Test Start?

We already hit on this in an earlier chapter, but first, we always need to test to ensure that our email gets delivered. Beyond that, there are three major areas to consider:

1. Do subscribers open the email or not?
2. Do subscribers click through?
3. Do subscribers actually do what we want them to do? (Completing a purchase, completing a survey, calling a specified phone number, etc.)

Notice that each element is usually dependant on the preceeding step. For example, if your emails have a low open rate, then the click-through rate will likely suffer as a result. When focusing on getting the email opened, "from" lines and subject lines are critical.

The "from" line is generally something you test once and stick with your winner. Subject lines should be tested as often as possible. Do recipients respond to a catchy subject line, or are they more responsive to a simple promotion?

Do You Think Frequency Is Worth Testing?

Absolutely. Frequency is an important test that's often overlooked. If you email too often, your audience may start to ignore your message. If you email too infrequently, you'll miss opportunities to get your message out. That's why it's important for each organization to run its own test to find the frequency balance that maximizes sustainable return on investment (ROI).

What Other Tests Should Both Testing Pros and Beginners Consider?

The email offers and call to action should be tested regularly. But it doesn't stop there. Here's a list of additional items to consider testing:

- Which segments respond to your emails?
- Which offer drives the greatest conversions?
- What is the right balance of graphics and text?
- Are you better served sending content with a lot of links or a single focus?

The list can go on to cover elements such as:

- Personalization
- Landing pages
- Day/time sent
- Length of copy
- Intro text content
- Intro text style
- Body text content
- Body text style

- Closing text content
- Closing text style
- Bullets or numbering
- View above the fold
- Images
- Pricing
- Unsubscribe wording
- Taglines
- Response buttons/links
- Colors
- Coupons/discounts
- Sense of urgency
- Press mentions
- Store locations
- Conversion—online, phone, or both
- Animations
- Charts
- Strikeouts
- Signatures
- Testimonials
- Celebrities
- Polls/surveys
- Multimedia
- Refer a friend

What Is the Most Important Thing to Keep in Mind When Testing?

Just keep testing. It is a discipline you must commit to if you want to see your email's success soar. You can't rest on the results from a test a year or two ago, because the rules are always changing. Anything can be improved and everything is up for grabs. If someone has an idea on how to improve the program, try it. If the idea fails to improve the program, scrap it and move on. No big deal. The organizations that embrace testing as an integral part of their programs simply outperform those that don't.

Now we understand what elements we can test. For those who have not tested before, I want to add some urgency here. You must start with something. It doesn't have to be complex. It can be the subject line test at the beginning of the chapter if you want to help me sell my book. Again, we all agree that relevance drives success, so look for areas to test around the theme of relevance.

If you're selling something, you'll probably want to do a simple variable test to ensure that your offer is the best offer possible (e.g., do people react better to dollars off or a percentage off?). As a reminder, you should keep all other variables consistent when engaging in A/B testing. Unlike multivariate testing, all other things must be equal for the email results to tell you a winner. Timing is a variable just like any other. If you do want to test the best day to send, you should be sending the exact same email with the same subject line, just at different times.

GETTING STARTED WITH YOUR TEST

The first step in testing is getting organized. You'll want to log your results so that you have ongoing record, notes, and analysis of your tests. I suggest setting up a simple spreadsheet grid like the one pictured below:

Test	Email ID	Element Tested	Result Click Rate (%)
Version A	45678	25% off today only	47
Version B	54679	$10 off today	32

In this case, it's a simple matter of version A testing a "percent discount" versus version B testing a "dollars off" offer. The measure of initial success was the click-through rate. The email ID allows me to look up the actual email in my ESP software to review the elements and maintain consistency next time. I say "next time," because I'll use the winner as my control version the next time around and test a new version against it. Without record of your tests, you'll mentally lose track at some point.

Determine Which Elements You Want to Test

There are many examples of things to test in this chapter. What makes sense for you? If there are things you are debating internally, get started by testing those things. Create a friendly competition to see which ideas perform best in the real world.

Determine Which Segments You Will Test

Determine the overall audience for which the results will apply and then determine the size of that audience. If you've come this far, you realize that not all of your subscribers are equal. If you are going to send different emails to different segments, then you need to identify those segments and test different versions within those segments.

Sampling

Sampling refers to the size of your test list. Sample size is important because if your test lists are too small, then your results might not be statistically significant (they won't accurately indicate what is going to happen with your larger list). A sample size that is too large wastes an opportunity to send the winner to more people. The goal is to find the smallest sample size that will provide relevant results. There are complex formulas that can be used to estimate sample size, but I don't think it's necessary if you follow a few simple guidelines:

- Test with approximately 10 percent of your list since this leaves 90 percent of your list to receive the winner.
- You should have at least 250 people in each test group, which can be less than ideal if you're testing several versions. But if your list is less than 10,000 total, then this will provide usable results, while still giving you the opportunity to send the winner to the majority of your list.
- There is no reason to go with more than 20,000 in each test group. If you don't see statistically significant results with these large test groups, then there isn't a meaningful difference.

It's also important that you pull a *random sample* from your segmented list. To do so, you start with the segment you want to mail to (so you are not mailing to the entire database). Then you randomly select the number of subscribers required for each test sample from this list. Most email tools will make this easy for the marketer to simply ask for a random group of x number of names from a given list.

Multivariate Testing

If you aren't testing at all, need a quick answer, or want to upgrade your email to another level, multivariate testing is absolutely the way to go. You can still do A/B testing if you so choose—perhaps run a multivariate test every few months and use A/B testing on every other email.

Although multivariate testing may seem a little more complex at first glance, it is still very easy to execute. You are essentially following the same steps that you use for A/B testing, but you will have more segments and variables. I'll use ExactTarget as an example here.

Like many companies that deliver an ongoing communication, we ran into a situation where a high number of our recipients were no longer actively engaging with our email. The marketing team decided it was time to reengage our readers. This wasn't going to be an easy task, but developing a more responsive e-communication base would be worth the effort. We were in the process of migrating to a new and improved communication, so the timing was perfect to introduce subscribers to the email while asking them to define new preference options.

To ensure that we were getting the most out of our reengagement campaign efforts, we first performed a multivariate test. If we were going to take on a task of this magnitude, why not make sure we were sending the most effective campaign possible? There were numerous elements of the proposed email that could have a potential impact on its performance.

We decided to conduct tests on four elements, or factors, including the subject line (Figure 10.1). By testing these four factors, we aimed to create and deploy the most high-performing email possible:

Figure 10.1
Creative Examples from Reengagement Email Test

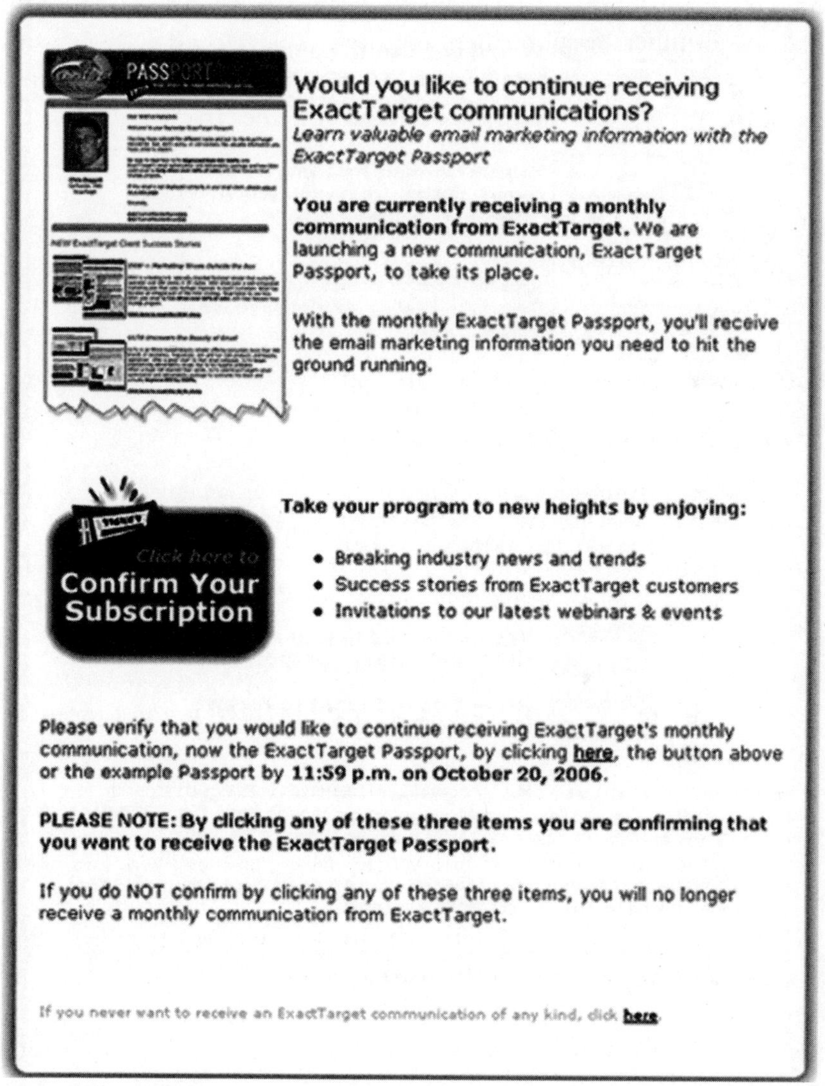

Figure 10.1 *Continued*

Would you like to continue receiving ExactTarget communications?
Learn valuable email marketing information with the ExactTarget Passport

You are currently receiving a monthly communication from ExactTarget. We are launching a new communication, ExactTarget Passport, to take its place.

With the monthly ExactTarget Passport, you'll receive the email marketing information you need to hit the ground running.

Take your program to new heights by enjoying:

- Breaking industry news and trends
- Success stories from ExactTarget customers
- Invitations to our latest webinars and events

 YES -- I would like to receive the ExactTarget Passport.

 NO -- I do not want to receive the ExactTarget Passport.

Please verify that you would like to continue receiving ExactTarget's monthly communication, now the ExactTarget Passport, by clicking **here**, the YES button above or the example Passport by **11:59 p.m. on October 20, 2006.**

PLEASE NOTE: By clicking any of these three items you are confirming that you want to receive the ExactTarget Passport.

If you do NOT confirm by clicking any of these three items, you will no longer receive a monthly communication from ExactTarget.

If you never want to receive an ExactTarget communication of any kind, click **here**.

Figure 10.1 *Continued*

Figure 10.1 *Continued*

Would you like to continue receiving ExactTarget communications?
Learn valuable email marketing information with the ExactTarget Passport

You are currently receiving a monthly communication from ExactTarget. We are launching a new communication, ExactTarget Passport, to take its place.

With the monthly ExactTarget Passport, you'll receive the email marketing information you need to hit the ground running.

Click here to Confirm Your Subscription

Take your program to new heights by enjoying:

- Breaking industry news and trends
- Success stories from ExactTarget customers
- Invitations to our latest webinars & events

Please verify that you would like to continue receiving ExactTarget's monthly communication, now the ExactTarget Passport, by clicking here or the button above by **11:59 p.m. on October 20, 2006.**

PLEASE NOTE: By clicking either of these items you are confirming that you want to receive the ExactTarget Passport.

If you do NOT confirm by clicking either of these items, you will no longer receive a monthly communication from ExactTarget.

If you never want to receive an ExactTarget communication of any kind, click **here**.

1. The subject line was our first opportunity to make a good impression and engage recipients. We settled on the following two subject lines: "ExactTarget: Please Confirm Your Email Subscription" and "Don't Miss Out On Your ExactTarget Newsletter." It was important that both subject lines contained our company name.
2. Next, we tested the impact of having a strong and direct headline, "Would you like to continue receiving ExactTarget com-

munications?" at the top of the email versus a softer and personalized introduction, "Dear First Name." Would individuals interact differently based on the first thing they read?

3. We also chose to test whether a sample image of the newsletter would alter people's behavior and increase click-throughs.
4. Finally, we tested the number of buttons provided in the email. Would a single confirmation button covert better than a yes/no option?

To test all variables, eight versions of the email were created and each version was sent using each of the two subject lines. It is important to note that all other elements of the emails—copy, color schemes, creative style—remained consistent throughout all of the emails. This ensured that the differences we observed in the test were the result of the factors we tested. The following table outlines the eight versions that were created as part of the test:

Version	Headline	Sample Image	Opt-In Buttons
1	Direct	Yes	Opt-in only
2	Direct	Yes	Yes/no
3	Direct	No	Opt-in only
4	Direct	No	Yes/no
5	Personal	Yes	Opt-in only
6	Personal	Yes	Yes/no
7	Personal	No	Opt-in only
8	Personal	No	Yes/no

In total, 4,000 subscribers were randomly selected for the test. These subscribers were then randomly assigned to one of sixteen different test groups (four factors with two options each = $2 \times 2 \times 2 \times 2$ or $2^4 = 16$) of 250 subscribers with each test group receiving a unique combination of test factors—subject line, headline, sample image, and opt-in button treatment. As such, half of the test population saw one of the two variations for each factor in the test.

For example, 2,000 test subscribers saw an email with a sample screenshot while the other 2,000 test subscribers received an email without the sample screenshot. By conducting a multivariate test and splitting the test group into 16 test cells of 250 subscribers each, we were able to see how different combinations of factors affected the overall response. What was the overall effect of the different combinations?

Before calculating the results, we allowed 24 hours to pass to ensure that the email had a sufficient amount of time to perform. After our deadline passed, the results were then evaluated to determine which combination of factors resulted in the highest percentage of people requesting that we continue their subscription to our email program.

After investing considerable effort in the campaign, our marketing team was understandably eager to see the final test results. They were also very interested in learning if all the effort was worth it (Figure 10.2).

The differences were substantial. The worst performing combination of factors resulted in only 4 percent of the subscribers confirming their new subscription. The best performing combination performed 630 percent better, with more than 24 percent of the subscribers confirming their subscription. Moreover, the multivariate aspect of this test proved to be very important. Both the worst and best performing versions of the email contained the strong and direct headline, "Would you like to continue receiving ExactTarget communications?" and had the yes/no opt-in button treatment.

However, the top performer had the subject line "ExactTarget: Please Confirm Your Email Subscription" and *did not* have the sample newsletter image.

Based on the testing results, the final email creative was comprised of the headline, "Would you like to continue receiving ExactTarget communications?" and both a yes and no button. The subject line of the email was "ExactTarget: Please Confirm Your Email Subscription," and it did not contain a sample image of the newsletter.

Figure 10.2
Surprise Winner from Reengagement Email Test

Would you like to continue receiving ExactTarget communications?
Learn valuable email marketing information with the ExactTarget Passport

You are currently receiving a monthly communication from ExactTarget. We are launching a new communication, ExactTarget Passport, to take its place.

With the monthly ExactTarget Passport, you'll receive the email marketing information you need to hit the ground running.

Take your program to new heights by enjoying:

- Breaking industry news and trends
- Success stories from ExactTarget customers
- Invitations to our latest webinars and events

YES -- I would like to receive the ExactTarget Passport.

NO -- I do not want to receive the ExactTarget Passport.

Please verify that you would like to continue receiving ExactTarget's monthly communication, now the ExactTarget Passport, by clicking **here** or the YES button above by **11:59 p.m. on October 20, 2006.**

PLEASE NOTE: By clicking either of these items you are confirming that you want to receive the ExactTarget Passport.

If you do NOT confirm by clicking either of these items, you will no longer receive a monthly communication from ExactTarget.

If you never want to receive an ExactTarget communication of any kind, click **here**.

Once we determined the optimal version of the email, we sent that version to the remainder of the people on our list. The results of that email were consistent with the results of our test, with 24 percent of the recipients electing to continue their subscription. Clearly, this testing effort was time very well spent.

WHAT ARE OTHER MARKETERS THINKING?

In their own words . . .

TESTING AGAINST YOUR GOALS

By John Wall
Producer, M Show Productions
Blog: http://www.themshow.com

For marketers, email is a gift from the gods. It removes virtually all of the friction from customer communication and the campaign, squishing cycles that used to be months down to hours.

The greatest benefit of such rapid cycles is that you are now free to test everything. I still remember the first time I heard Chris Baggott speak on email testing: He said, "Every campaign must have a champion and a challenger."

The variables that can be tested are infinite, but there is one best practice: The earlier in the process you can improve results, the greater the possibility of significant benefits. For example, if you could increase conversions on your landing page by 20 percent, that may not be as beneficial as a 10 percent increase in deliverability if your list is large enough and you have a large number of click-throughs.

While you want to tweak the process from the front, you should measure your results from the end. Worry about closed business first and work your way up to conversions and then opens (although you will probably do this all concurrently if your sales cycle is beyond one month). Increasing opens by 200 percent means little if the lift never equates to a signed purchase order.

The only hard part about testing is that there is no "right" answer. The target is always moving. The things that delight customers go in and out of fashion, and all you are doing by testing is trying to catch and ride that wave.

I've seen champions fall and come back years later (even plain text may have a shot at the title again soon. Remember the lift you got on those very first HTML messages with color graphics?), and there is one thing I've noticed: Rarely can the people within a company judge what is going to be successful outside of it. Many champion campaigns have been called "The Ugly One" or some other disparaging moniker, but the great marketers are able to see beyond the walls of their own ivory tower.

CHAPTER 10 REVIEW

- Testing gives us the ability to see every aspect of our marketing as it unfolds. With that kind of insight, we can fine-tune our marketing and constantly focus on improvement.
- A/B testing means that you are simply testing one sample against another. A/B tests can be completed using subject lines, layout, copy, and more.
- With an A/B test, you want to make sure you test one variable at a time. All other elements (including time of send) should remain the same.
- While A/B testing is an effective means of fine-tuning your email program, multivariate testing offers some significant advantages. You'll know the "winning combination" sooner, and it's less expensive and time consuming.
- For either A/B or multivariate testing, I recommend these steps to get started: get organized, decide what you want to test, decide which segments you will test against, and create your test groups by selecting random samples.
- Ultimately, testing gives us the chance to act like *real* marketers driving *real* actions. We get to play in a giant sandbox full of data, creative, and strategies in attempt to build the biggest castle for our organizations.

CHAPTER 11

USING SURVEYS, FORMS, AND OTHER FEEDBACK TOOLS

Successful email marketing begins and ends with our favorite d-word: data. Segmentation and personalization both require quality data that can be leveraged as actionable, individual-level attributes. While many organizations maintain a long list of desirable data points, most of these attributes remain unpopulated throughout the life of the subscriber. Just like books sitting in a bookcase collecting dust and never getting read, those data attributes sit in a database collecting cobwebs, too. Marketers have a tendency to create a wish list (if only I knew eye color. Then I could deliver the proper message to everyone) and either never get around to collecting the data or never use it.

Historically (here I go on another history lesson), I understand it's been hard to gather and leverage data. After walking barefoot and uphill for seven miles, rescuing a cow from the side of the road, and finally arriving at work, you probably didn't have the energy to collect customer data.

Lucky for us, we live in a world full of conveniences, technology, and solutions that mitigate the pain we once felt. Today, it's easy to collect data. It's also easy to leverage that data. There is no excuse for *not* collecting and leveraging data. The more perplexing question is: What data will drive your business?

A small number of actionable attributes (in the 10 to 15 range) are the power behind many of the best programs. While there may be hundreds of data points leveraged to compute end values, the day-to-day program is based on the maintenance of a small set of critical attributes that are updated regularly. So what's going to drive your business? And once you decide on that, how will you get more people to offer up that information?

In the Analytics chapter, we discussed collecting behavioral data based on your constituents' actions. Often, the most widely used method of data collection is by way of a very complex tactic. It's called "asking." In fact, you can ask for information directly from your email subscribers. The request can be made during registration, at the point of purchase, or via a survey. Ideas on data that you might want to ask for:

- *Contact information:* Email address, name, physical address, phone numbers
- *Basic demographics:* Gender, age, occupation
- *Preferences:* Program interests, best time to contact, frequency
- *Attitudinal information:* Survey responses that reflect viewpoints, opinions

It can be tempting to collect as much information as possible directly from the subscriber since it takes less effort. It can also be tempting to collect all of the data you need right away (remember my birth certificate and driver's license example in an earlier chapter?). This can be counterproductive because each data point presents an element of friction between the survey form and the submit button. Your constituents place a value on their personal information and consistently evaluate whether the service they expect to receive in exchange for that information is worth the trade. If too much information is required, people may be inclined to lie or simply abandon the registration or purchase process.

Remember, our goal is a *relationship*. Marketers need to earn the right to more information, and that trust is only built over time.

Four points need to be stressed here:

1. *Assure your constituents that their privacy will be protected.* Just saying, "Rest assured, we like our customers and will always protect their privacy," is reassuring. Having a clear and unequivocal privacy policy explaining your security measures will help build this trust.

2. *Explain why the data is important for both of you.* If you have trouble coming up with reasons as to why the data is important, you probably don't need the data. This is a good doublecheck to make sure you're asking for data you'll use. And you need to be able to support your efforts by making it clear what's in it for your constituents. (A better experience? More value?)

3. *Ask low risk questions.* If you ask someone a question, they must make a decision: Will I answer? Will I answer honestly? Or will I not answer at all?

   In the beginning of the relationship with your constituents, you'll want to ask very low risk questions. I'm familiar with a lawn care company that starts the dialogue with a question such as: "Are you a green thumb or thumbs down when it comes to your lawn?" It's simple, fun, and provides a huge chunk of data for this organization to properly get started on a relationship. Another company in the swimming pool supply and care business asks if the constituent has an in-ground pool or an above-ground pool. Future questions might be about the presence of a spa or a zip code to determine pool season for this specific subscriber.

4. *Use that data.* If you ask the question and receive the data— use it. It's that simple. You build trust by earning it. You earn trust by continually increasing the value of your relationship with your constituents. If you prove that there is a benefit when your constituents answer a question, they will answer more questions. Think about the lawn care company and pool company examples I used above. Let's expand on those:

   a. The lawn care company is able to completely change the tone of the communication sent to each of these segments. "Green Thumbs" receive more advanced info to fit in with their level of knowledge and the "Thumbs Down" don't get content that may be over their heads. Is that kind of message beneficial to the recipients? You bet.

b. In the pool example, zip code enables the company to talk about the right pool care at the right time. Constituents living in Atlanta should receive advice and tips for spring at a different time than people in Minneapolis. Is that beneficial? Of course.

As you build trust by delivering relevant, data-driven messages, you'll have some new opportunities to gain additional insight that could really boost your program. Remember a few chapters back when we talked about our "best" constituent group? These are the constituents who are your true fans. What makes them the "best" (other than buying a lot)? What value do they perceive from this relationship? How do they use your service or product? Why not use an email survey to collect this kind of information from them? After all, if they are a highly engaged group as it is, they are likely to provide feedback.

Just like in a real relationship, earning trust is your chance to dig deeper into the psyche of your constituents. If you're like me, in your early dating experiences, you started with questions about basic demographics: "Where are you from? Do you have any siblings? What school did you go to?" Eventually, as trust was established, I asked questions like, "Why did you pick that school? Do you like your job?"

The other aspect of a relationship is that *dialogue* never stops. It's an ongoing conversation. Is it possible to know all you need to know about someone? I don't think so. Many might argue that there are diminishing returns on data. As I mentioned at the beginning of this chapter, there can be hundreds of potential data attributes for a specific constituent. However, it's typically 10 to 15 that really make the big difference.

I'll stand by that statement with the caveat that you can never take things for granted. People change, needs change, and your competitors change. You have to stay on top of what your constituents need, think, and want—and you can only do so with careful attention and dialogue.

So you're wondering how and where should you ask data collection questions. Here are my thoughts:

- *On the phone or in person:* Often, this is the initial point of contact, and the spot where permission is gained to continue the relationship. What's great about CRM systems is that marketers are able to build upon data that might have already been gathered by others. The key here is to make sure that your salespeople or customer service folks know what data you need and why. A simple meeting between two departments can make all the difference between thousands of data elements being collected in a few weeks, or none getting collected. Think about the three key things you need to know about the person to get the relationship started on the right foot. Have other departments understand these data points and how they will ultimately help the constituent.
- *On the Web:* Many times, the first point of contact with a constituent will be on the Web rather than the phone. Again, your website or landing pages are not the place to ask every question you can dream up. Most Web forms fail because they ask too many questions (or worse, questions that the marketer already knows the answer to).

  Some organizations have a page-long form but require only one or two fields. This may or may not be fine (your results and testing will show you). I'll warn that a first glance means a lot, and if the form looks long and you have tiny asterisks indicating that something is required, your visitor may not realize that he or she has a choice as to how much time the form takes. In general, I also would advise treading lightly with regard to required questions. Perhaps one field (email address) really is necessary. But if there are too many required fields, your visitors might be discouraged to provide any information at all. Or worse, they may even lie. Either one is not a great way to begin a trusting relationship. Again, ask only the bare minimum to get to the next step in the relationship.

- *Via an email survey:* You knew I was going to get here, right? Throughout this entire book, I've talked about the magic of email marketing and its power to engage your constituents in a dialogue. The previous two methods are great ways to get a relationship started, but they can't sustain a relationship or help it grow. Email is perfect for this. You have data, you know what data is valuable, and you know what data is missing from different constituents. Almost every email you send should give the recipient a chance to answer a question or two.

  There are several ways that surveys can add value to your communications. Transactional emails are a great vehicle for questions because they are likely to be read. Take advantage of that to learn something else about the constituent. Here's a tip about transactional email: They don't have to be emails confirming a purchase. I've seen successful follow-up emails for almost any kind of interaction.

  There's a company in the event business that follows up every event with an email that contains a thank you and a quick survey asking about my satisfaction level. The survey is never any longer than five questions, and I always answer. In the next chapter, we'll talk about triggers, which are the perfect opportunity for follow-up emails such as this one. If a survey is completed, you can immediately send a thank you email. You can also send different versions depending on the survey answers (i.e., a simple "thank you for your participation" to the happy folks, and a "sorry, here's $50 off your next visit" to the unhappy folks).

Remember, the goal of any data collection tool is to sustain a dialogue. There are two components absolutely necessary for a dialogue to take place. The first is listening. The second is responding. There are many ways to listen and respond to your constituents.

So What's the Issue with Surveys?

Go back to any real life relationship you've had in the past. I'm guessing it started with a question. Why? Because you wanted to prove that you were interested in learning about the other person. One of the easiest ways to establish a relationship is to get the other person talking about him or herself. Thus, it's no secret that forms and surveys can drive off the charts engagement.

The secret of the survey is to do it well. In college, the school I attended offered a class called, "How to lie with statistics." The point of the program was to show how easy it was to do the following:

- Conduct a survey and gather the "right" stats to prove anything the author of the survey wanted to prove. When motivations are taken into consideration, it becomes apparent how easy it is to build a biased case.
- Lie to yourself with a poorly formatted survey. If you have a survey that is poorly formatted, you might interpret the information incorrectly. For example, the question "Is price important to you?" might compel you to lower your prices when customer service is actually a bigger motivator for your customers.

How Can You Develop an Effective Survey?

An effective and compelling survey does not take much more time to prepare than a poorly structured survey. Let's start with the basics:

- *Pay attention to sponsorship.* The person behind the survey is one of the most important factors determining success. You're working on a relationship, meaning your constituents should know who's on the other side of your questions. In email marketing, the "from" side should be the one making the appeal.
- *Invest in preparation.* Invest the time and resources needed to structure the survey correctly. You should be able to answer this question before you start: What are the goals and how will the

data be used? I know this is review, but it's important to the success of your survey.

- *Ensure that the data doesn't exist elsewhere.* You wouldn't want to deliver the same constituent the same exact email message five times in a row, would you? And you probably wouldn't want to ask the same 10 questions five times in a row. Before getting too far down the path on your survey, you should see if the data could be found elsewhere. It may exist internally or externally. Asking the same thing over and over again shows that you aren't listening, or that you may even be lazy. Don't make your constituents do your work for you. Two of the most common causes of repeat questions are lack of segmentation and blanket surveys. It's a recipe for repeat. It's critically important that you segment and ask only the questions you don't know the answer to. That means custom surveys, not a blanket survey.

- *Play it safe with your questions.* Earlier we talked about making your initial questions as non-threatening as possible. Here's a reminder that you need to earn the right to get to the various steps in a relationship. If you ask questions that require too much thought or seem a little too personal, your constituents are more likely to ignore you. A good way to test is by asking a friend or family member to play the role of your audience and take your survey. If he or she feels uncomfortable answering, your constituents are likely to feel that way, too.

- *Add some fun.* A safe survey doesn't necessarily mean a boring survey. After all, people are attracted to other people who are fun, entertaining, and interesting. Put a new twist on the boring old survey by adding something funny or engaging. And use personable language in all of your questions to put your constituents at ease.

- *Make it easy.* We've already talked about friction and the fact that a long survey or a survey with difficult questions contains a lot of friction. An easy survey is one that doesn't take much time and makes the benefits of responding obvious. The more steps a survey entails, the harder it is to complete. In other words, if a relationship becomes too much work for the other person, he or she will walk away.

- *Use the data you collect.* I can't say this enough. Your constituents are going to give you information for one very selfish reason: to make their experience better. They want to help you help them (sort of like in the movie *Jerry Maguire*). Ignoring what they tell you or asking pointless questions tells your constituents that you don't care about your relationship with them. In fact, it can be downright insulting.

- *Give incentives careful consideration.* There are many incentives that can work to encourage survey participation. It may be contest entries, discounts, or even coupons. You should test the incentive to see if it results in a higher participation rate without sacrificing quality of the data. In many cases, simply explaining why you're conducting the survey and the value for participants provide far more benefit than an incentive. On the other hand, the more friction in the survey, the more likely you'll need to bribe your constituents to participate. For example, I'm a Platinum member with Starwood Hotels. I'll do anything for those points. And generally, I think Starwood does a great job with their email marketing. But I've never taken one of their surveys. Why? Because they make it too hard and never offer a compelling incentive. Even worse, they tell me how long the pain of filling out the survey will last (10 minutes). I'm not going to spend a sixth of an hour on a survey that puts me into a drawing for a prize that I don't feel like I'll have any chance of winning. On the other hand, for 1000 points, I'd be willing to spend 10 minutes or even more considering that it's equivalent to a free night. My point is that incentives may or may not be worth it to both parties. The only way you will know is by testing.

- *Keep it short 'n sweet.* I'll repeat one of the best customer satisfaction surveys I've ever seen:
  —Are you happy with us?
  —Would you recommend us to a friend?
  —Have you recommended us?

I don't have the insight into this particular survey to know how effective it was, but I love the spirit of it. Oftentimes, easily getting 70 percent of the answer is preferable from a cost, complexity, and response standpoint versus the pain of going for the full 100 percent of the answer. Poking a little fun at the Starwood example, their surveys ask questions like, "Were the towels nice or too scratchy?" Or, "Was the phone answered promptly when you called the front desk?" Well, I never called the front desk, so how should I reply to a "yes" or "no" question there? My point is that you're probably asking untargeted questions if a survey takes 10 minutes.

- *Repeat this:* "I am in several relationships." I'm sorry if this is starting to sound like a relationship self-help book. But if you continually remind yourself that you are in a relationship with each of your constituents, you will soon start to view them as people rather than a vast audience. And if you manage the relationship properly, you're going to have future opportunities to ask questions.

- *Test.* Of course, I made the above Starwood statement glibly, as someone who has never participated in their surveys. Perhaps they have tested the heck out of their surveys and have discovered that the prize drawing incentive is enough to drive participation and the questions do in fact have tremendous value for both the Starwood organization and for their guests. The point is: I don't know how their surveys perform. Testing is the only way to know what's going to work with just about any component of a marketing initiative or program. Remember, you should assume nothing and test everything. Don't even take the word of experts or specialists without seeing confirmed test results. Data doesn't lie.

Wondering what characteristics a good survey question has? I'm glad. Questions are the bread and butter of your survey and require careful thought.

Checklist for a Good Survey Question

- *Has a clear benefit:* If you can't articulate the benefit of the question to you and your constituents, you shouldn't ask the question.

- *Is one-dimensional:* A common problem with survey questions is putting multiple dimensions into a single question. For example, if a question asks, "On a scale of one to five, how would you rank the shipping and handling of your item?" I may be unsure how to respond. Let's assume that the shipping was fine because the item arrived on time, but the product was broken so the handling wasn't great. Questions with multiple dimensions hinder the participant from providing a telling response due to lack of focus.

- *Allows multiple responses:* Why make someone choose if they have multiple reasons for liking your business? Rather than limiting constituents to one response, listen to all that they have to say. In some cases, a ranking system may be appropriate. (More on that later. You will need to keep in mind how this changes the time needed to answer a question.)

- *Eliminates ambiguity:* Make sure that you provide a clear answer choice for the participant. For example, "What do you like best about vacationing in Florida?"
  —The weather
  —The sunshine
  Don't laugh. This happens all the time.

- *Embraces variability:* This means that you want to ask questions that different people will answer differently. Think about it: If everyone is going to answer the same way, why bother asking the question in the first place? "Do you love your kids?" Who's going to say "no" to that?

- *Includes an obvious transition:* One question should flow into the next question. Follow a theme. Make your questions related so that the participant is aware of continuity and isn't derailed from the value of the exercise. You can hit another subject or area next time.

- *Excludes assumptions and jargon:* Another common mistake with respect to survey questions is assuming that the participant has a level of knowledge that may not exist. "Do you support Net Neutrality?" Well, all I have to say to that is: "Huh?" The last thing you want to do is make your constituents feel inadequate.

If you must use unknown terms or industry jargon that your constituents may not be familiar with (which I'm not sure why you would), a simple tactic is to link each term to a definition.

- *Doesn't imply an answer:* Back to my point on how easy it is to lie with a survey—adjectives can lead the participant down a certain response path. For example, "What is your preference for a vacation?"

—Warm, sunny beaches?

—Cold, snowy mountains?

If you're sending this survey out to a bunch of Midwesterners during the middle of February, you're likely to get 100 percent response to warm beaches.

Along those lines, adjectives may imply different things to different people. What constitutes warm in my opinion (70 degrees) may be completely different from another person who thinks that 90 degrees is borderline warm. This is a really common area where even experienced survey creators can get into trouble. If you want honest, meaningful answers, you should be as specific as possible.

- *Doesn't branch into another question:* Questions that are dependent on the previous answer are referred to as "branching questions." My recommendation is to keep it simple and avoid them *in email* unless you are conducting very deep research. You can always use a follow-up email to branch into new questions via segmentation.

- *Limits ranking:* My earlier point on ranking was that it may help gauge importance of multiple responses. I do warn you that it requires a lot of thinking on the part of the participant and adds friction. If you feel that you must include ranking as a way to get the best survey responses, I recommend no more than five ranked responses. Again, you should test.

Don't Forget the Heads Up and Thank You

If you really want to humanize your survey efforts, consider a courteous heads up email letting your constituents know when your survey is coming and why. It's also appropriate to follow up with a "thank-you" or reminder depending on whether or not the constituent replied. An appropriate follow-up to a nonresponder might be, "Why aren't you responding?" Think back to my Starwood example. I've never answered any of their surveys. So why not send a message asking what would make me respond? Now that's a survey I'd respond to.

Privacy

Let me end with a note about privacy. You should *always* make your privacy policy clear to your constituents. Constantly assure them that their data is protected, and that it will never be shared with other organizations. Your constituents will appreciate the fact that you have their best interest in mind. Why make them guess your privacy policy when you can simply tell them?

Case Studies

Case Study 1: The Power of Asking

A franchise with over 25 coffee stores faced the challenge of ensuring equal satisfaction throughout its various locations and communicating with thousands of customers in an affordable manner. Prior to implementing email marketing, the franchise had not found a cost-effective way to gather customer feedback. Their only direct marketing efforts were via expensive printed cards and coupons sent to a customer on his or her birthday. The process was expensive and labor-intensive. Between printing, assembly, and postage, each birthday package cost around two to three dollars.

After realizing the positive impact that email could have upon their marketing efforts, the franchise compiled a database of loyal customers by asking for email address on customer frequency cards. Then they designed an email featuring the same posters and graphics found within many of their stores. The email included a four question survey asking customers what they liked about the franchise's stores, what they didn't like, which store they frequented, and how they would rank their local store given a set of criteria. Although they didn't advertise any sort of reward for filling out a survey, the franchise sent a follow-up that included a thank-you note and an in-store coupon.

Results: Survey Response Rate of 36 Percent and Cost Savings of $20,000

The survey went out to nearly 8,500 loyal customers, with response rates reaching 36 percent in a matter of days. The franchise was able to gather 20 times the number of responses they had collected from previous offline campaigns. They learned exactly what their customers wanted and compiled a Red Flag Report based on the rankings given to each local store. The report fostered a healthy sense of competition between the stores and confirmed which locations were meeting corporate standards. Conducting the same campaign in direct mail/print would have cost the company $20,000 more than what was spent on email.

Case Study 2: A New Twist on the Old Survey

A well-known restaurant franchise put a fun twist on a survey to its patrons by driving in-store traffic rather than data collection via the survey imbedded in its monthly newsletter.

The survey contained a quiz that encouraged subscribers to visit the restaurant's website for clues to the quiz questions. Those who answered the survey correctly receive a coupon good for in-store use.

Results: Survey Response Rates near 20 Percent and Increased In-Store Traffic

The franchise enjoyed response rates near 20 percent, which was greater than any offline survey it had attempted in the past. Due to coding each coupon, the marketing team was able to track the revenue generated by the quiz email and concluded that the survey gave them the in-store boost they had set out to accomplish.

Case Study 3: How a Nursing Society Used Surveys to Achieve Financial Health

A nursing honor society with over 400 chapters and 340,000 members faced a revenue challenge similar to what many other nonprofits face. Sixty-two percent of the society's revenues came from membership dues, and it had operated on a zero budget for more than five years. That meant an increase in dues was critical to the financial health of the organization.

In order to pass fiscal authority to the board of directors, 800 member delegates needed to approve a bylaw change. However, historically proposed changes presented to the delegates did not pass, and awareness of the need for fiscal change was extremely low. Adding to the challenge was the society's small budget of $25,000 for the entire awareness program.

The cost-effectiveness and interactivity of an email survey proved the ideal way to monitor perception on the critical issue at hand. A total of four email surveys were sent throughout the campaign, enabling the organization to maintain a pulse on the members' perception and understanding of the bylaw changes. The immediate feedback available through surveys provided the ability for the organization to tailor each follow-up message accordingly.

Results: Approval of Bylaw Change Resulting in $1.25 Million Increase in Dues

The final survey showed that 60 percent of delegates felt highly confident making a decision about the bylaw change—a dramatic increase from the 0 percent awareness that existed prior to the campaign. In addition, the bylaw change granting fiscal authority to the board of directors passed with an astonishing 99 percent approval rate and drove $1.25 million back to the organization annually.

CHAPTER 11 REVIEW

- In a relationship, dialogue never stops. It's impossible to know all you need to know about someone, which is why you should strive for more information on an ongoing basis.
- At the same time, a small number of actionable attributes (in the 10 to 15 range) are the power behind many of the best programs. While hundreds of data points may be leveraged to compute end values, the day-to-day program is based on the maintenance of a small set of critical attributes that get updated regularly.
- The best way to receive information directly from your constituents is by asking.
- When collecting data on the phone, it's important to make sure that your salespeople or customer service folks know what data you need and why. Data collection is often a team effort, meaning that a meeting between two departments could make the difference between thousands of data elements being collected or none being collected.
- Most Web forms fail because they ask too many questions (or worse, questions that the marketer already knows the answer to). Risk and friction must be low in order to encourage individuals to answer. And any collected data *must* be used. Not using data will erode trust and perhaps prevent further participation when questions are asked.
- Email is the perfect way to fill in data points once you know what data is valuable, and what data is missing from different constituents. Almost every email you send should give the recipient a chance to answer a question or two.

CHAPTER 12

TRIGGERS, TRANSACTIONS, AND INTEGRATION

What, exactly, is a triggered email? Often referred to as "event-driven email," these are emails that are automatically sent to a subscriber when an *event* happens.

Earlier in the book, we talked about listening as a key component of any dialogue. Typically, an organization will have several systems in place that help them listen to each constituent. The dialogue usually starts with real conversation, either in person or over the phone. Marketers then listen for web visits, form submissions, downloads, and purchases since they indicate the stage of the relationship.

With that said, a *transaction* occurs when a constituent tells you something. Any time your constituent engages with you on any level, he or she is telling you something. Each of these actions is an "event."

The second element to the relationship dialogue is the appropriate response. What's cool about marketing (and real life) is that with experience, you can learn what's appropriate to say under almost any circumstances. Over time, most of us have learned how to respond appropriately for 80 percent or so of our interactions. Triggered email gives us the same ability. How do you talk to a new constituent? How about someone who hasn't made a regular purchase in three weeks? What are the five things you want someone to know about you and your organization?

There's been a lot of talk about email triggered from an abandoned shopping cart that includes an incentive for the product you didn't quite buy. I've not seen this in real life, so I can't say if it works or not. What I can say is that there are hundreds of events to listen to and learn from. When you learn what behavior influences your constituents to action, then you're able to look at who else might exhibit similar behavior and use email as extra encouragement.

The amazing thing about triggered email is that it solves a huge execution problem. Setting up and sending several targeted emails takes time and effort. If you automate the process, all you have left to focus on is the actual marketing. Imagine that. By "actual marketing," I'm referring to the testing, content tweaking, and creative effort that goes with driving the right responses. The idea of triggered email is not to set up the process, design your emails, and then ignore them. Automating these communications takes the pain of execution off your shoulders so you can focus on the marketing aspects of these communications.

Transactional emails are the perfect place to start. It should be standard practice to send a follow-up email any time there is a transaction. What's a transaction in your organization? Here are some ideas:

- A purchase
- Attendance at an event or webinar
- White paper or other download
- Registration or email opt-in
- Customer service call or email interaction
- Shopping but not purchasing
- Web visit after registration
- A break in pattern
- Use of product X, which is complementary to product Y
- A completed survey

I've probably left out some of the most obvious transactions for your organization. The point is that you should say something to your constituents based on all of these interactions. And they can be set up to automatically trigger when an individual transaction occurs.

Here are some opportunities for triggered, automated transactional emails:

- *Satisfaction surveys:* This always leaps to my mind first. A constituent took advantage of something you offered. (This could be attending an event, buying something, or making a donation.) That means they are freshly familiar with you and your organization. It's the perfect time to trigger an automated thank-you and ask a few questions, such as, "How was the experience?" Or, "Would you do this again?" Remember, transactional emails are going to be among the most read emails in your subscribers' inbox. You should use them to learn more, and you can leverage triggers to make them easy and timely.

- *Pre-event reminders:* If a satisfaction survey is considered a post-event triggered email, what about the opportunity for pre-event communications? I've seen pre-event communications work successfully in everything from 10k races, to webinars, to concerts. If I bought tickets to an event, why wouldn't I open an email reminding me to attend it? And even better, what if that reminder included an up-sell such as a T-shirt so that I wouldn't have to stand in line at the event? Or what about a special discount on my next ticket purchase if I encourage five friends to accompany me to the event? In catalog marketing, it can work well to use email to announce that a catalog will be coming by mail. A follow-up after a catalog mailing is a great idea, too.

- *Geography-based messages:* Are there geographic aspects to your organization? Touring music acts are masters of geography. Rather than sending an email to the whole country that includes every city where the band will play, it makes sense to trigger specific emails when the band comes to "my" town. Another take on geography has to do with weather and climate. I've already mentioned the lawn care company a few times. Here's another great thing they do: trigger emails based on weather. It makes sense, right? Spring arrives in different parts of the country on different dates. The company is able to trigger the geographical emails using an integrated, live weather feed. The rules that trigger the email are something to the effect of: "When the temperature is greater than 53 degrees for three out of five days, it's spring." That means that people in Atlanta are getting their spring communications at the appropriate time, and folks in Minnesota are getting theirs perhaps a month later.

- *Lifecycle emails:* We started this book talking about Lifetime Value. As you look at your constituents, where are they in their lifecycle? How do you talk to people at the beginning of a relationship? What is the path you want them to follow? The potential exists to have triggered email in place for every step of the relationship.
- *Preference emails:* What do your constituents tell you they want? You should ask them what type of content they're looking for and then provide it. Such content can be created for only email or for the Web at large. With the advent of Really Simple Syndication (RSS), it's possible to pull content and trigger emails from sources available almost anywhere. And like the name says, it's really simple.

Hopefully you get the idea that triggered email is a good thing. It drives relevance, controls frequency, and (when done correctly), it's highly engaging.

THE EXPERTS WEIGH IN

For the rest of the chapter, we'll consult with two integration experts regarding what to consider when managing trigger-based email. First, we'll talk to Amol Dalvi, an integration consultant. Then we'll talk to Doug Karr, a product manager at ExactTarget, for his take on what to look for in an email system that offers integration capabilities. Here is what Amol Dalvi has to say in response to some typical integration questions.

What's a High-Level Way to Think about Integration?

Every time I receive a sharp looking email from Banana Republic or Home Depot, I'm reminded that email marketing has a very sexy side to it. But underneath all that snappy looking creative messaging, it's all about the data.

This data typically resides in one or multiple systems, which serve as home to the valuable, relevant, personalized information about your leads, prospects, and customers. Typically, such systems are homegrown and come with their own TLA (three letter acronym). They could be off-the-shelf CRM systems (Siebel, Salesforce.com, Saleslogix, etc.), or WebAnalytics (Google Analytics, WebTrends, WebSideStory).

The real question is: How do you get the data from these marketing systems into your email marketing provider's database? That's where you can consider setting up a direct connection between the two systems, which happens via integration.

What Happens during Integration?

Integration basically allows data from one device or system to be read or manipulated by another. Essentially, your developers can write a software program that runs on your servers and invokes actions in your email system.

For example, actions like uploading lists and triggering emails can automatically happen behind the scenes. Imagine sitting at your desk, working in your CRM system, and identifying a list of 5,000 contacts to send a reminder about a webinar. All you do to start the process is click a button. Then behind the scenes, using the Application Programming Interfaces (API), your CRM system sends the list of contacts to your email system. Then you click another button and a reminder email is sent from your email system to that list of contacts. Voila!

Why Would an Organization Want to Integrate?

There are four major reasons to integrate:

1. *Sync the database of record.* When setting up your email marketing program, you make a choice—either your vendor or your marketing system is the database of record (DoR). However, no matter how well you planned it, changes to the data always flow into the non-DoR (especially subscription, unsubscribe, or bounce information). Integration can help you sync that data, even in real-time.

2. *Provide email marketing from within other systems.* You probably have at least half a dozen IDs and passwords between your machine login, your marketing systems logins, and your personal logins. Wouldn't it be nice if you could define your recipient criteria and kick off an email to only those who meet it—just by clicking one button? Integration makes that sort of simplification possible.

3. *Automate.* You are always moving data from your marketing systems to your vendor's database. That means you may be manually exporting email addresses and attribute data and importing into your email system. Or, you may be exporting tracking data (opens, clicks) and importing in to your marketing systems. It's a lot of back-and-forth, which can be automated via integration as nightly or weekly data feeds.

4. *Syndicate content.* Content already resides in your database or on your website (it may even be categorized by audience). With integration, you're able to pull that custom content in from your servers or website at email send time and include it in the appropriate message.

Can You Get a Little More Technical with How Integration Works?

Yes, integration does require getting into some tech talk. Most vendors have application programming interfaces (APIs) to programmatically handle what a marketing person would do in the email system's user interface—create, deliver, and track emails. These APIs are what make integration possible. Programmers make API calls to connect the marketing systems to vendor databases directly (and vice versa). So, yes, your IT staff must be involved with integration. However, it is normally lightweight work, even for mid-level developers.

What Are Some Examples of Emails that Utilize Integration Capabilities?

A common scenario is sending a birthday email. Let's assume I've captured subscriber email addresses and birth date. Every day, I should be able to generate a list of people with a birthday equal to the current day and trigger a birthday email to them.

While you may not want to send birthday emails to your subscribers, the point is that you can use specific criteria to segment out a group of subscribers and trigger an email to them. The same segmentation can be applied to various scenarios. Some examples are: concert-goers who need reminders on directions, or newspaper subscribers who are up for renewal.

Each scenario is a perfect fit for API-based activity because the daily routine of segmenting and sending an email can be automated. A process can be set up that runs on a nightly basis, invokes a segmentation or group refresh API call, ensures the group refresh has completed, and then triggers an email send using another API call. Once set up, this process can run by itself, hands-off. Some checking or monitoring of the process is required, but the process can scale as you acquire a larger subscriber base, and greater demands are put on your marketing efforts.

How Can Integration Fully Leverage Confirmation Emails?

As already described, confirmation emails are a great way to stay in touch with your subscribers while the interaction with your company is fresh in their minds. A confirmation email also serves as a unique opportunity to up-sell or cross-sell based on message content. For example, if someone purchased a pair of running shoes, you could include a coupon for $10 off their next purchase. Or, if someone bought a new stereo, he or she might be in need of additional speakers.

Confirmation emails offer a huge opportunity for relevancy. They are one-off emails, meaning they are very specific to both the subscriber and the transaction completed. The same subscriber could purchase something else two days later, and as a result, relevant content will change. One way to achieve this relevancy "on-the-fly" is to force the email system to reach out to your servers at send time. This will allow you to dictate to the email system's send engine what content to include at send time.

Some email systems offer *content syndication,* which allows you to embed a specific command in the confirmation email. At send time, as the confirmation email is about to leave the email systems servers, these servers reach out to your servers and include any content your server returns. You can tailor this content to the specific transaction, thus providing the most relevant content in every confirmation email.

On the back end, this program should accept a unique identifier such as an email address or transaction ID that will enable you to identify who has done what. It also has business logic that uses the value passed in to decide what is relevant to that transaction and return the appropriate content to your email system. As you can tell, there is some upfront work involved in setting up this kind of a program. You would need to have a technical team involved to make sure your servers are accessible over the internet, and that they can handle the load placed on them. Most importantly, the marketer needs to create the custom business logic that drives the program behind the scenes. Again, once a program such as this one is set up, it's a fairly hands-off process and has the potential to generate additional revenue.

We mentioned the role that an API plays in successful triggering and automation. The truth is that it is a critical component of pain-free integration, which is why I'll turn to Doug Karr to share his thoughts on selecting an API.

What Should a Marketer Consider When Contemplating the Integration of Different Systems?

When shopping for a vendor with a comprehensive API, the fact that development resources and expenses are usually an afterthought can make the selection process challenging. Marketers typically drive the purchase of an email service provider (ESP), with IT along for the ride. If you commit to an ESP with a poor API, you're going to drive your IT folks crazy, and your integration will likely fail. Find the right ESP, and your integration will work, and your IT folks will be happy to assist.

Here are 10 questions you must ask regarding an API:

1. Identify what features of their user interface (UI) are available via the API. Ask what features the API has that the UI doesn't (and vice versa).
2. Ask how many calls are made to their API daily. If they answer, "Millions every month, and we have a dedicated pool of servers available," that's a good sign. Quantity is incredibly important since you want to identify whether the API is an afterthought or actually part of the company's strategy.
3. Ask for the API documentation. It should be robust, spelling out every feature and variable available in the API.
4. Ask whether or not they have a Developer Community available for sharing code and ideas with other developers. Developer Communities are key to launching your development and integration efforts quickly and efficiently. Rather than just leveraging "the API guy" at the company, you're also leveraging all of the customers that have already had trials and found solutions during integration.
5. Ask what their API uptime and error rate are, and when maintenance hours take place. Strategies to work around them are just as important. For example, do they have an internal process that will reattempt API calls in the event the record is unavailable due to another process? Uptime should be upwards of 99.9 percent; however, what matters more is how it will affect your operation and productivity.

6. Ask what type of API they have. Typically there are REST APIs and Web Service APIs. They may be developing both.

7. Ask what platforms they have successfully integrated with and request contacts so that you can find out from those customers how difficult it was to integrate and how well the API runs.

8. Ask what limitations the vendor has with respect to number of calls per hour, per day, per week, or other time period. If you aren't with a scalable vendor, your growth will be limited.

9. Ask what professional API organizations the company is involved in, and who their mentors are for further development of their API.

10. Ask if they have dedicated integration resources within their company. Do they have solutions engineers, integration consultants, and an entire partner integration framework team?

Keep in mind that integration essentially takes your applications and processes and "marries" them to your ESP. You don't want to marry someone without getting to know him or her as much as you can, right? That's why it's worth the time to get to know an ESP's integration capabilities.

What Else Should You Ask When Considering a Vendor for Integration?

Beyond the API, you should also check-in with respect to the following:

- *Content syndication:* Does the ESP have a means of integrating content from their website to your email? This type of functionality makes it possible to integrate content such as bar codes, maps, data tables, RSS feeds, and more.
- *Web forms:* Do they offer "out of the box" solutions for integrating web forms without the need for an API?
- *Partner integrations:* What other vendors has the ESP partnered with to seamlessly integrate their solution with others?

- *Scripting engines:* Does the ESP offer customers the ability to write scripts within their emails to dynamically generate content? This enables customers to create robust, dynamically generated, and targeted emails both through the user interface and through the API.

Case Studies

Case Study 1: How Does Automation Work?

A company targeting millions of individuals dealing with a specific medical condition (lactose intolerance) developed a powerful e-commerce site that could integrate with its CRM solution. While the data collection means was effective, the company quickly tired of shuffling data back and forth between its CRM system and email system.

In order to effectively move customers through the lifecycle, the company needed to remove several manual steps. After consulting with an online business solutions company, the decision was made to integrate existing systems rather than build a new system from the ground up. Using an API to automate several steps in the email process, the company hoped to make its back-of-a-paper-napkin sketch a reality.

The two companies collaborated on designing the following branch tree based on the recorded date variable:

- *Leads:* Individuals who expressed interest in the product but didn't purchase. Leads had a CRM field date variable of "Brochure Request Date." (Leads automatically moved to the customer bucket when the opportunity was marked "Closed/Sold" in the CRM system.)
- *Customers:* Individuals who purchased a product already. Customers had a CRM field date variable of "Purchase Date."

Given these customer and prospect buckets, an email communication timeline was designed to address the concerns of the company's audience relative to their specific point in the lifecycle. Emails were triggered by how many days passed since an individual's start date. For instance, if a new lead requested a brochure on January 1, she received an automatic email thank-you. One day later, the e-brochure arrived. After eight days, if the lead had still not purchased the product, she received an email with customer testimonials. Product comparison and medical emails followed on assigned days, and so on.

For customers, the company constructed emails with messages running parallel to the person's progress through the program. Once a customer finished the 38-day period, he also received an invitation to provide a testimonial and to refer friends.

With the integrated system in place, the company is now able to automatically pull the correct customer and lead data from Salesforce.com each night, build the appropriate email lists, load them into its email solution, and trigger the correct email—without any intervention from the marketing team.

Results: 30 Automated Emails and 47 Percent Increase in Sales

With over 30 unique emails that are sent *daily* to constantly changing lists, the automation process is a huge time saver. The entire email process executes during the night, leaving the company time to focus on growing the business rather than dealing with execution.

The company has also seen sales increase by 47 percent since starting its automated email program. The company knows that customer satisfaction has increased significantly since they are able to communicate precisely depending on customer lifecycle.

Case Study 2: What Goes on behind the Integration Scenes?

A credit counseling service needed to deliver highly personalized, dynamic messages with up to 10 fields containing customer profile information. Using an open API, the company was able to easily leverage data residing in its CRM system to deliver 64 unique, operational emails that were created without ever needing to log into their email system.

From requests for loans sent on behalf of clients, to payment reminders, to follow-up collections, integration enabled the company to send between 16 and 64 different variations of emails a day using this "magical mail merge" process.

Behind the scenes, the process begins when the company pulls a list of email recipients and profile attributes from its CRM system. A file containing this data and indicating which email should be sent is then written out to a server and converted from a .csv file to an xml file. This xml file hits an API and loads into the company's email system as a subscriber list, complete with all information. The email is automatically sent, and open rates, click-throughs, and all other metrics are captured in the email tracking system. This data is converted back to the CRM system, where it is available for 10 days at an aggregate and individual level.

Results: Pain-Free Emails That Save Money

At an estimated $0.40 per letter, these emails save the company between $2,000 and $3,000 per month in printing costs. Due to such significant cost savings, the counseling service will soon use the system for email statements.

Case Study 3: What Happens When You Eliminate Execution Pain?

A niche music marketing company that provides tour dates, concert reviews, articles, and links for thousands of improvisational bands needed a cost effective means to reach the masses of fans counting on them to provide timely information.

Although the company was using an internal system to develop hundreds of dynamic, specialized, and targeted emails specific to each subscriber's area, they needed a partnership that would guarantee successful delivery of these communications.

By integrating their subscriber database with their email vendor, the company is able to send 10 to 15 specialized email communications *a day* to different parts of the country. This is made possible via a custom geo-targeting script developed internally, which segments the company's master list and schedules automatic delivery through the email vendor.

Results: Hands-Off Delivery and Highly Targeted Emails

During one month alone, integration enabled the company to painlessly schedule 180 campaigns and deliver over 600,000 customized emails. The campaigns are delivered to only those who are interested in the featured content rather than blasted to the entire database. With integration in place, the company is able to focus on developing more attributes and content to promote the musicians and concerts that its subscribers care about.

CHAPTER 12 REVIEW

- When a constituent engages with you on any level, he or she is telling you something. Each of these actions can be referred to as an "event" or a "transaction."
- Triggered emails are the perfect way to leverage the power of an event-driven message. Automating the process means solving the execution pain and making time to focus on testing, content, and creative.
- Satisfaction surveys, pre-event reminders, geography-based messages, lifecycle emails, and preference emails are all perfect opportunities for automation.
- Typically, automation and triggering entail "integration," which is a means to seamlessly move your data from system to system. A direct connection enables synching your database of record, providing email marketing from within your other systems, automating, and even syndicating content.

- Remember, integration essentially takes your applications and processes and "marries" them to your email service provider. You don't want to jump the gun without doing your research. It's worth the time to get to know an ESP's integration capabilities.
- The beauty of automated emails is that once set up, the process is fairly hands-off. That said, you should continue to test your messages, segments, and other email elements. "Hands-off" is intended with respect to the process, not the actual email marketing messages.

CHAPTER 13

ARE YOU
A SPAMMER?

You know what they say: Admitting that you have a problem is the first step to recovery. I understand that a spammer isn't necessarily something that you aspire to become (if so, you probably shouldn't be reading this book). But somehow, despite best intentions, we can get sidetracked. We take our eye off our constituents' needs and send them irrelevant junk via email. And the next thing we know, our spam complaints are through the roof, and we can't even send an email to our own mother because our IP address has been blocked everywhere.

By definition, spamming is the abuse of electronic messaging systems in order to send unsolicited, undesired, bulk messages. Therefore, a spammer is a person or organization that engages in such abuse.

In Chapter 3, I mentioned that spam may fall into the category of "permission spam," which encompasses both explicit opt-in and implied opt-in. Although a relationship does exist in the case of permission spam, it doesn't prevent these emails from qualifying as junk.

Because I have already covered some of the high-level characteristics of spam and the issues associated with getting a reputation as a spammer, I'm going to turn the stage over to ExactTarget deliverability specialists who can take us through deliverability consequences of spam in much greater detail.

EMAIL + ONLINE REPUTATION = MAXIMIZED DELIVERABILITY: DECIPHERING THE REPUTATION EQUATION

By Chip House
Former Vice President of Privacy and Deliverability
By R.J. Talyor
Deliverability Specialist

Your company has likely spent endless hours and dollars on creating and maintaining a solid reputation. Just as you watch and protect your company's branding, marketing collateral, and advertising reputation, all marketers sending email must also monitor their email reputation. So as a first step, are you monitoring?

Many marketers have unknowingly tarnished their standing with Internet Service Providers (ISPs) with years of mass-blast email campaigns, abuse of opt-in, and disregard of technical and creative factors. While the neighborhood postman rarely refuses to deliver a direct marketing piece to a physical mailbox, email marketers face a different delivery challenge: the cyber-postmen—or the ISPs—who check online reputation. Without a sufficient amount of "postage," or reputation, your email won't get delivered.

ISPs use a complex algorithm to calculate a score that equates to your company's deliverability reputation. And this reputation score determines whether your email will be delivered to the inbox, the bulk folder—or not delivered at all. In several ways, you could consider your online email reputation a simple mathematical equation. Our goal is to define each of the factors that add up to this reputation equation, and to expose the "formulas" for doing so. The answer to the reputation equation is maximized deliverability.

Arithmetic: Let's Start with the Basics

What Is an Online Reputation, and What Factors Build It?

Reputation can be defined as the general opinion of a community toward an entity. In regard to email, reputation is the general opinion of the ISPs, the anti-spam community, and subscribers toward a sender's IP address, sending domain, or both. The "opinion" is a reputation score created by an ISP (or third-party reputation provider). If the sender's "score" falls within the ISP's thresholds, a sender's messages will be delivered to the inbox; if not, the sender's emails may arrive in the bulk folder, be quarantined, or get bounced back to the sender.

The main factors in this equation include:

+ Legal compliance and unsubscribe request management
+ ISP whitelisting and feedback loops
+ Low spam complaints
+ Avoidance of spamtrap hits
+ Sender authentication
+ Technical components
+ Reputation aggregators' data
+ Accreditation services

While each ISP and third-party reputation provider calculates a sender's reputation score by giving different weights to these factors, according to Michelle Eichner, vice president of client services at Pivotal Veracity, "All the major ISPs are using reputation at this point." Therefore, it's more important than ever to ensure that your email marketing efforts are within the guidelines of reputation of best practices. Before going any further into this equation, it's important to know exactly why reputation is becoming the most trusted method of email filtering.

The Unsolved Equation: The Authentication "Hole" in SMTP

Most email systems that send email over the Internet use Simple Mail Transfer Protocol (SMTP), to send messages from one server to another. Unfortunately, SMTP was created without checks in place to ensure that the sender is authentic. Therefore, spammers exploit this weakness by sending emails from recognized brand domains in hopes of tricking recipients into opening or clicking on their fraudulent emails. The more clicks, the more money they make. Other illegal spammers can make money by stealing and selling your personal information or using your credit card number. Spamming that attempts to impersonate another sender is called "spoofing," and spamming that attempts to steal personal information is called "phishing."

The screenshot in Figure 13.1 is an example of a spoofed email that is "phishing" for personal information. Though it appears to be sent from a recognizable brand (eBay), the actual sender is a phisher attempting to trick a recipient into divulging account information.

Messages such as this expertly spoofed example necessitate email reputation as a more reliable method to protect ISP customers from spamming. Because a legitimate company's domain is spoofed in this example, ISPs monitor both sending IP address and domain—especially when deciding whether to deliver messages to the inbox.

Incomplete Answers: How Current Email Filters Work (and Why They Don't Solve the Problem)

ISPs originally blocked messages based on only one factor, whether it was content, list quality, volume, IP address, or domain or URL blocking. Each type of filter served its purpose, but had limitations that spammers have exploited. A brief description of each filter follows:

Figure 13.1
Phishers Spoof Big Brands in an Attempt to Trick Recipients into
Divulging Account Information

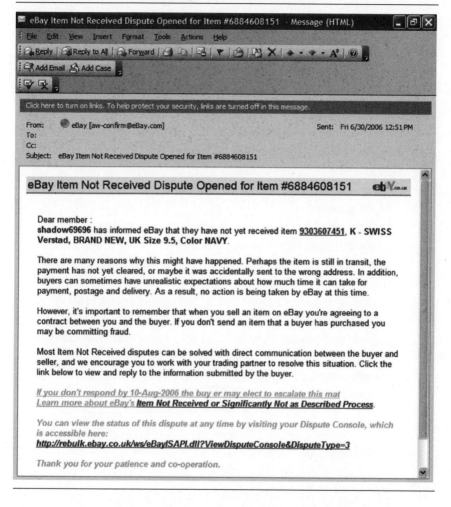

- *Content filtering:* Many companies and anti-spam software systems use content filtering as a method to reduce spam volume. These systems, including SpamAssassin and others, focus on the email subject line and body content to determine whether or not to deliver an email. Using point scoring, these systems focus on the email subject line and body to identify words, content, or text formatting indicative of spam. Common examples include words such as "free" or "save," the use of ALL CAPITAL LETTERS, and the inclusion of bright colors or very large fonts. Because these are commonly used words, content filters can result in many false positive spam identifications.

- *List quality filtering:* Many spam lists contain a large number of bogus addresses, so spammers are known to have high bounce rates at ISPs. To combat this problem, many ISPs have added list quality filters to detect when a large percentage of email addresses are bogus. If the volume of bounces exceeds a certain quantity, all of the other emails from this IP address or sending domain may be disallowed.
- *Volume filtering:* Since many spammers send bulk emails without regard to their accuracy or volume, many ISPs filter using volume-based filtering. Volume filters focus on the number of simultaneous connections that are opened at any one time with an ISP, or the rate of email being sent via those connections. Based on the number of connections opened with a server, the server may deny all messages from being delivered when the sender is suspected of sending extraordinary volumes of spam.
- *IP address filtering:* An IP address defines a specific "node" on a mail server from which email is sent. Many organizations employ IP address filtering in an attempt to determine the IP addresses that send spam. All emails from these IP addresses are then disallowed into their system. The technique of adding suspected IP addresses to a filtering list is called "blacklisting." There are numerous active blacklists in use today—some operated by private companies and individuals, and some operated by anti-spam organizations. A growing number of organizations are filtering incoming mail this way.
- *Domain and URL filtering:* ISPs and anti-spam software are beginning to focus not only on the IP address of

unwanted email, but also the email domains that send them and the URLs that are included in the messages. For example, a URL filter called a SURBL (spam URL Realtime Blacklist) focuses on the links in spam as an indicator of future unsolicited messages.

While each filtering method continues to be a factor used in ISPs' delivery decisions, one factor alone does not provide an accurate enough picture of the sender for an ISP to block on just one criterion. Imagine an ISP using only a content-based filter that blocked all messages with the words "free" in it. Because many emails offer complimentary goods and services, ISPs blocking emails based on inclusion of one word may result in many false-positive bounces. Instead of blocking on one criterion such as content, ISPs and the anti-spam community rely on a multifaceted reputation score tied to the sender's IP address and domain.

According to Laura Atkins, founding partner of the anti-spam consultancy and software firm Word to the Wise, ISPs lose customers if they let too much spam through their system. For example, if a parent finds that a child has received a spam email with inappropriate content, that customer is likely to change to another ISP that will protect her family from pornographic spam. "From an ISP's perspective," Atkins explains, "it's critical to monitor reputation of the senders for customer retention and support costs."

Due to spam problems that affect their bottom line, ISPs have moved away from individual filters (like those listed earlier) to holistic filtering based on the following factors.

Deliverability Factor: Legal Compliance and Unsubscribe Request Management

In order to curb spamming, country-specific legal measures have been enacted across the globe. While legal compliance varies by country, audience (Business-to-Business or

Business-to-Consumer) and purpose of communication, the best policy is to ensure explicit opt-in is in place before you send email. Below, you'll find summaries of relevant country or region-specific spam laws for your email communications.

Note: We recommend that you contact your own legal counsel to best interpret how these laws may apply to your organization.

United States CAN-SPAM Act, Enacted: January 1, 2004

- All commercial messages must include a functioning unsubscribe mechanism.
- All unsubscribe requests must be honored within 10 days of initial request.
- All commercial messages must include the physical mailing address of the sender.
- Unsolicited commercial messages must include a notice of advertisement in the body of the email.
- Criminal charges included for fraudulent sender or deceptive subject lines.

European Union E-Privacy Directive, Enacted: December 11, 2003

- No direct emails are allowed which "conceal or disguise the identity of the sender and which do not include a valid address to which recipients can send a request to cease such messages."
- No marketing emails to natural persons (e.g., consumers) "unless the prior consent of the addressee has been obtained (opt-in system)." An exception is where the email address was obtained through a prior sales transaction with the owner, called, "soft opt-in," in which case you can send marketing emails to that address, provided:
  —You must be sending the message ("Data may only be used by the same company that has established the relationship with the customer").

—The products or services you are marketing are similar to those originally bought by the addressee.
—You give the recipient the opportunity to opt-out in each message.
—You "make clear from the first time of collecting the data, that they may be used for direct marketing and should offer the right to object."

Canada PIPEDA, Enacted: January 1, 2004

The Personal Information Protection and Electronic Documents Act addresses email and privacy:

- Consent is needed to collect, use, or disclose personal email addresses.
- Consent is required to send e-marketing materials even if the company has an existing relationship with a customer.

Australia SPAM ACT 2003, Enacted April 10, 2004

- Subscriber must have given consent to receive the messages.
- Email message must contain a way for the subscriber to identify who the sender is and how they can contact the sender of the message.
- Email message must include a way for subscribers to remove themselves from the list.

Deliverability Factor: ISP Whitelisting and Feedback Loops

ISP whitelisting and complaint feedback loops (FBL) are essential tools used to solve the reputation equation. Whitelists are typically created and maintained by ISPs or third parties, and are lists of IP addresses or domains that are allowed to send mail to a domain. An FBL is a reporting mechanism by which ISPs provide data, including unsubscribes and spam complaints, back to a sender.

While not all ISPs offer whitelisting and/or feedback loops, those that do typically require senders to have explicit opt-in permission from subscribers. The anti-spam community and ISPs use spam complaint rates and spamtrap hits in order to judge a sender's reputation. Senders receiving high rates of spam complaints, or those who mail to spamtrap addresses (even once) can fall off of an ISP's whitelist. Therefore, obtaining subscribers' explicit permission is the only way to ensure that your email campaigns achieve highest deliverability rates from the start. Here is a review of the definitions for the various levels of permission:

- *No permission (opt-out):* Provides an unsubscribe link or checkbox. While such practices are legal per CAN-SPAM and some international anti-spam laws, opt-out (or unsolicited) email typically leads to spam complaints that negatively affect a sender's reputation. ISPs are often hostile to mailing lists whose addresses were obtained via this process.
- *Implicit permission:* Does not require subscribers to take an action, and opt-in information may be in a privacy policy.
- *Explicit permission:* Requires a subscriber to take an action to opt in. Typical implementations include an unchecked box on a web collect or registration form, use of a radio button selection or other method requiring "action" on behalf of the subscriber. The best explicit permission includes both the content and frequency that a subscriber should expect by opting in. Explicit permission has a number of variations, ranging in stringency from simple opt-in to double opt-in.
- *Simple opt-in:* Occurs when a user chooses to receive an email by checking an unchecked box. Example:

  ☐ **Yes, please send me monthly, exclusive email offers and specials.** (We will not provide your information to any third party without your consent. For more information, read our Privacy Policy.)

- *Confirmed opt-in:* Occurs when a user receives a confirmation email after choosing to receive an email in a simple opt-in.
- *Double opt-in (closed-loop opt-in):* Occurs when a user must click on a link within a confirmation email to verify an opt-in.

Deliverability Factor: Spam Complaints

ISPs and the anti-spam community view spam complaints as their top source for identifying spammers. Most commonly used email clients now have a "Report spam" button easily accessed by subscribers. When a subscriber receives a message and identifies it as "spam," he or she can press the spam complaint button and log it with their ISP. These spam complaints can be logged at the ISP level or also relayed back to the original sender by way of feedback loops. Eichner at Pivotal Veracity views these spam complaints as "votes" that email recipients can use to vote "for" or "against" a sender's reputation.

Because ISPs do not collect intent of a spam complaint, subscribers marking a spam complaint as a way of unsubscribing aggregate with the true spam complaints. Due to this common practice of unsubscribing via spam complaints (in AOL, for example), ISPs have set their spam complaint threshold to allow for some level of false positive spam complaints. However, high spam complaints by originally opt-in subscribers can be a result of sending irrelevant messaging, or sending too frequently. After reviewing what "engagement" is with respect to your email campaigns (e.g., opens or clicks in the past 90 days), a reengagement strategy aimed toward those subscribers without opens and/or clicks will ensure that your audience is less likely to complain that your message is spam.

Deliverability Factor: Spamtraps

Becoming an effective email marketer requires constant list cleansing and hygiene. Most lists shrink by 30 percent each year due to subscribers changing email addresses (according to

Return Path). In addition, ISPs sometimes recycle old email addresses as spamtraps aimed at catching commercial emailers with old, rented, or purchased lists. Spamtraps typically come in two varieties:

1. An email address published in a location hidden from view such that an automated email address harvester (used by spammers) can find the email address, but no sender would be encouraged to send messages to the email address for any legitimate purpose. These are also called "honeypots." Since no email is solicited by the owner of this spamtrap email address, any email messages sent to this address are immediately considered unsolicited.

2. A formerly valid email address recycled by an ISP or anti-spam organization that has been invalid for more than 18 months. Without activity for an extended period of time, spamtrap owners can safely assume that the mailer hitting spamtraps purchased the list or does not have an ongoing relationship with the subscribers. Alternately, a spamtrap can be an email address that bounces for a period of time (if appropriately handled), bounce management would have removed it from a list. Mailing these types of spamtraps proves that a sender did not process bounces appropriately.

When a legitimate email marketer mails to a spamtrap, deliverability can take a steep plunge, often resulting in temporary or long-term blocks. Ongoing spamtrap hits are associated with a sender's IP, domain, and ultimately, reputation.

Deliverability Factor: Sender Authentication

As sender authentication does not currently exist in "standard" SMTP logic for email, spammers can easily disguise their identity and locale. As a result, many ISPs now check for sender authentication, such as Sender Policy Framework (SPF), Sender ID, or DomainKeys in determining whether to deliver your emails to the inbox, bulk folder, or to quarantine:

- *Sender Policy Framework (SPF):* The authentication standard that specifies what IP addresses can send mail for a given domain. Requires change to DNS records implement. Currently used by Bellsouth, AOL, Gmail, and MSN/Hotmail.
- *Sender ID:* The authentication standard based on SPF that expands the verification process to include the purported responsible address (PRA) included in the header. Requires change to DNS records to implement. Currently used by MSN/Hotmail (Figure 13.2).
- *Domain Keys:* Domain Keys is the authentication standard that "signs" each outgoing message with a private encrypted key to match a public key published in the sender's DNS record. Currently used by leading ISPs such as Gmail, Yahoo, SBCGlobal, British Telecom, Rogers Cable, Rocket Mail, and several international domains (Figure 13.3).
- *DKIM:* The enhanced encrypted authentication standard that combines Yahoo, Domain Keys, and Cisco's Identified Internet Mail standards. Requires changes in how

Figure 13.2
Sender ID Expands the Verification Process

| **msn** Hotmail | Today | Mail | Calendar | Contacts |

free13@hotmail-int.com

Reply | Reply All | Forward | ✕ Delete | Junk | Put in Folder ▾ | Print View | Save Address

The sender of this message could not be verified by Sender ID. Learn more about Sender ID.

From : <jay@yahoo.colm█m>
Sent : Friday, April 1, 2005 6:48 PM
To : free13@hotmail-int.com
Subject : asdfasdfasdf

Figure 13.3
Domain Keys "Signs" Each Outgoing Message
with a Private Encrypted Key

From: "MTA_Verification" <hlabib@mta-test.exacttarget.com> ✉ Add to Address Book 📱 Add Mobile Alert
Yahoo! DomainKeys has confirmed that this message was sent by mta-test.exacttarget.com. **Learn more.**

---

messages are constructed to implement. Not currently used by leading ISPs, but likely to be implemented by many ISPs using Domain Keys.

Sender Authentication employs various methods of checking to ensure that the mail sender is in fact the actual sender by authenticating the bounce host, the sending IP address, and the PRA (Purported Responsible Address).

Sender reputation cannot be established without Sender Authentication, which provides the following safeguards to your reputation:

- Helps prevent domain forgery and phishing. While sender authentication doesn't explicitly prevent spam or phishing scams, it does allow an ISP's easy detection of illegal activity, spoofing, and other harmful tactics spammers employ that can negatively affect your brand. Because a spammer can currently send an email that appears as if it were sent from your domain, your domain is at risk.
- Provides important data to ISPs, enabling them to make more informed choices with regard to mail acceptance and disposition. Though not a silver bullet in itself, Sender Authentication adds protection against domain forgery, which runs rampant in the spamming community. By implementing Sender Authentication strategies for your email, the email receiving community, including ISPs, spam filtering companies, and public blacklists, can more clearly distinguish between legitimate email senders and

spammers—and whether or not to deliver a message to the inbox, bulk folder, a quarantine, or even block/bounce the message.

Table 13.1 details the current sender authentication methods, results, and notification provided to email recipients at the leading ISPs.

Deliverability Factor: The Technical Side

"In terms of getting mail into the inbox, it's about half technical components and half marketing best practices," says Laura Atkins at Word to the Wise. While your company may have mastered marketing strategy and best practices, it's imperative to ensure that your technical team or Email Service Provider (ESP) has checked (and updated) the technical components that affect reputation. Eichner at Pivotal Veracity sees "technical deliverability issues more prevalent at senders using internal systems, rather than from a third-party ESP, mainly because internal IT resources don't understand the importance of proper configuration."

Ensure that your configurations are in line with the following technical components that improve or quickly degrade your online reputation:

- *IP address:* An IP address is the node of the mail server from which your email is sent. IP addresses are typically arranged in larger groups known as IP net blocks. Your mail may be sent from a range of IP addresses to maximize your online reputation, or from a dedicated (or private) IP address. Because your sending IP address is the origination of your email, it is inextricably tied to your online reputation. In order to qualify for whitelists, feedback loops, and reputation services, you must have an IP address with a history of low spam complaints, unsubscribe compliance, and correct set up for your domain. ISPs and the anti-spam community can block a

Table 13.1
Current Sender Authentication Methods and Results Provided to Email Recipients at the Leading ISPs

ISP	Status	Version	Filter	Notification		
				Pass	Fail	
AOL (aol.com)	Publishing	SPF/Sender-ID	No	None	None
CompuServe (compuserve.com)	Publishing	SPF/Sender-ID	No	None	None
Netscape (netscape.com)	Publishing	SPF/Sender-ID	No	None	None
Bellsouth (bellsouth.net)	Verifying	SPF	No	None	None
Charter (charter.net)	Publishing	SPF	No	None	None
Comcast (comcast.net)	Publishing	SPF	No	None	None
Cox (cox.net)	Testing	DKIM	No	None	None
EarthLink (earthlink.net, mindspring.com, peoplepc.com)	Publishing	DK	No	None	None
Google (gmail.com)	Verifying/Publishing/Signing	SPF/DK	Yes	Yes	Yes
Juno/NetZero (netzero.net, juno.com)	Publishing	SPF/Sender-ID	No	None	None

	Checking/Publishing		SPF/Sender-ID		
Microsoft (msn.com, hotmail.com)	Publishing	SPF	Yes	Yes	Yes
RoadRunner (rr.com)	Publishing	SPF	No	None	None
Verizon (verizon.net, gte.net, bellatlantic.net)[a]	Publishing	SPF	No	None	None
Yahoo (yahoo.com)	Verifying/Signing	DK	Yes	Yes	Yes
SBC Global (sbcglobal.net)[b]	Verifying/Signing	DK	Yes	Yes	Yes
British Telecom (btinternet.com)	Verifying/Signing	DK	Yes	Yes	Yes
Rogers Cable (rogers.com)	Verifying/Signing	DK	Yes	Yes	Yes
Rocket Mail (rocketmail.com)	Verifying/Signing	DK	Yes	Yes	Yes
International Domains (Yahoo UK, CA, Hong Kong, France, India, Twain, Mexico, China, Italy)	Verifying/Signing	DK	Yes	Yes	Yes

[a] A small number of accounts hosted by Yahoo are verifying and signing.
[b] A portion of legacy domains not verifying or signing at the time.
Source: ESPC.

sender's individual IP address or entire blocks of addresses depending on the perceived spam abuse originating there. Depending on the level of spam complaints, spamtrap hits, and bounce rates on an IP address, a sender can quickly develop a positive or negative reputation that will affect long-term deliverability.

- *Sending domain or subdomain:* Though it is considered an extremely "spammy" practice, senders can jump from IP address to IP address in attempt to avoid IP address blacklisting. Therefore, the anti-spam community watches both IP address and sending domain when deciding where to deliver mail. Because legitimate email marketers leverage a recognizable domain when sending to their customers, a sending domain with a bad online reputation can haunt a marketer with low deliverability rates.

  Domain registration (public or private) and domain age are also important in establishing and maintaining a positive deliverability reputation. Because spammers are known to move domains in attempt to avoid legacy blacklistings (rather than solve the issue causing the blacklisting), newly registered domains can be viewed as suspicious and detract from your online reputation score.

- *RFC compliance:* Request for Comments (RFCs: available at http://www.rfc-editor.org) are a series of numbered Internet informational documents, primarily governing standards. Most types of Internet traffic, including email, operate as defined by various RFCs. The two most important RFCs related to email reputation are:
  1. *RFC 2821:* Simple Mail Transfer Protocol provides governance on SMTP protocol. Ensure that your email (or your ESP) is in compliance with this RFC.
  2. *RFC 2822:* Internet Message Format specifies syntax for text messages that are sent between computer users, within the framework of "electronic mail" messages.

- *Reverse DNS (rDNS):* Checking reverse DNS is the process of looking up an IP address to identify the domain name associated with it. In the SMTP communication between a sending and receiving mail server, the only data that cannot be forged is the IP address. This is because the receiving computer is able to ascertain the IP address of the sending computer automatically.

    Reverse DNS on that IP is then referenced to identify the host (server) name of the sending mail server. When you conduct a forward and reverse DNS check on an IP address, you get two pieces of information. First, the reverse DNS gives you the PTR, which is the host (server) name associated with the IP. Then you match this to the "A" record, which is an IP address associated with the host (server) name, and it should match the original IP address you looked up.

    Leading email deliverability auditing firm Pivotal Veracity lists common reverse DNS-related deliverability problems:

    —*Reverse DNS is not enabled.* This means you have not enabled reverse DNS lookups on your mail server IP address. Not only is this an RFC violation, but many ISPs, including AOL, require that reverse DNS be enabled. You must contact your mail server host (e.g., your ISP) or your technical department if you host your own servers to enable this. Once you have enabled reverse DNS, ensure that you configure it properly—reverse DNS configuration problems are the topic of the next two sections.

    —*Reverse DNS PTR (domain) is configured improperly.* The PTR is the domain name that you get when you lookup the IP address using reverse DNS. In the example header following, the HELO is in bold and the PTR is underlined:

    X-Envelope-From: sam@company.com

    X-Envelope-To: name@domain.com

Received: from **main.company.com**
(main.company.com [64.73.28.76]) by
w.domain.com (8.13) with ESMTP id j8947 for
name@domain.com; Wed, 3 Aug 2005

14:00:05-0500

Received: from xyz.com ([987.654.32.1]) by abc.com
Microsoft SMTPSVC (6.0.3790.211) . . .

There are two things that you must ensure with respect
to the reverse DNS PTR:

1. The PTR must be a fully qualified domain name (i.e.,
   "mail.company.com" or "company.com") and not
   simply the IP address with in-addr-arpa at the end (i.e.,
   "25.2.0.192.in-addr.arpa"). The former is correctly set
   up, the latter means you enabled reverse DNS but did
   not configure it to return a fully qualified domain name.
2. The PTR record must match the HELO. In the
   previous example, that means the domain in bold
   should be identical to the domain that is underlined.
   One of the purposes of using reverse DNS is to
   ensure that the HELO provided by the sender mail
   server (the HELO is the domain name of the sending
   server and is provided by the sender server during
   the SMTP conversation between the sending and
   receiving servers) is the same as the domain name
   associated with the IP. When these two do not
   match, it appears you have forged the name of your
   mail server. Thus, to ensure that these match, you
   can either (a) change the name of your mail server
   so that it gives a HELO that matches the reverse DNS
   PTR or (b) change the PTR that is given when a
   reverse DNS lookup is conducted. The first can be
   done by altering the configuration of your sending
   MTA. The second must be done with the assistance
   of your ISP.

—*Reverse DNS "A" record (IP) is configured improperly:* When you conduct a reverse DNS on an IP, you get the PTR record that is the domain name, and you get the "A" record that is the IP associated with that domain. The IP address or "A" record that is returned in a reverse DNS should match the original IP address you looked up. If it does not, there is a problem. The "A" record is improperly configured on your reverse DNS and is not properly resolving. To fix this issue, you must contact your IT department or sending host.

- *Bounce compliance:* According to the Institute for Spam and Internet Public Policy (ISIPP), accepted bounce handling includes marking a subscriber's address as "dead" (the sender should remove the address from the delivery list and not attempt to deliver to the address until the sender has reason to believe that delivery rejection would not occur) if the following two conditions are both met:
  1. Three consecutive delivery rejections have occurred
  2. The time between the most recent consecutive delivery rejection and the initial consecutive delivery rejection is greater than 15 days

Deliverability Factor: Accreditation

According to the Email Sender and Provider Coalition (ESPC), accreditation consists of third party whitelist programs that certify that mail from certain senders has gone through a rigorous review process and has been "certified" as safe for delivery.

ISPs use accreditation programs to supplement their internal data in making decisions about whether or not to deliver a message. Depending on the accreditation service employed, subscribers can see icons in their inbox denoting this certification or ISPs use specific whitelists to override their typical filters. Common sender accreditation providers include:

Goodmail™

http://www.goodmailsystems.com

The Goodmail CertifiedEmail service offers legitimate, accredited senders the opportunity to ensure that their messages are reliably delivered and presented to consumers as authentic and safe to open. The CertifiedEmail service is available to senders who qualify with an excellent deliverability history at a per-message fee calculated based on volume.

In addition to CertifiedEmail bypassing content and volume filters to be delivered to the inbox, these emails also arrive with images displayed and links activated at ISPs that block images and disable links by default. David Atlas, vice president of Marketing at Goodmail Systems explains this advantage of CertifiedEmail as "the difference between seeing a TV advertisement with and without the picture." Preliminary case studies showing Goodmail Certified email clients earning a substantial increase in click-through rates and ROI.

ExactTarget works with a number of organizations that send high-value email and are currently testing CertifiedEmail to see if it generates ROI improvements at the ISPs adopting the technology.

LashBack

http://www.lashback.com

LashBack monitors unsubscribe performance and sends data to receivers (including ISPs) in order for them to make more informed delivery and filtering decisions. ISPs can leverage LashBack's solutions to review unsubscribe reputation for senders, ensure compliance, and protect consumer privacy and promote legally compliant unsubscribe practices.

Sender Score Certified

http://www.senderscorecertified.com

Sender Score Certified is a leading third-party email certification program run by ReturnPath. Formerly known as "Bonded Sender," receivers using the Sender Score Certified Program see improved deliverability rates by querying its whitelist. Sender Score Certified defines "the reputation of a mailer" as based "on a comprehensive set of information about the entity obtained from a variety of public and private sources." Sender Score requires a thorough deliverability audit before adding a sender to its whitelist queried by nearly 240 million email addresses and ISPs including MSN/Hotmail and RoadRunner.

SuretyMail

http://www.isipp.com/suretymail.php

SuretyMail is an accreditation service run by ISIPP. While not technically a whitelist, SuretyMail accredits senders who agree to state and follow their bulk email policy. Widely used by large ISPs and filters, senders with SuretyMail's accreditation see improved deliverability.

The Solution: How Do You Solve the Reputation Equation for Your Company?

Assessing reputation and maximizing deliverability requires resources—personnel, time, and yes, some financial investment. Eichner at Pivotal Veracity warns that the time needed to improve deliverability reputation is directly dependent upon "what the mailer is willing to do to correct the problem(s)." Atkins at Word to the Wise estimates that senders looking to improve deliverability will spend a few weeks before seeing deliverability improvements. Rebuilding a total sending reputation can take three to six months. As reputation will ultimately follow a brand and sending domain, not just an IP address, it's imperative for your team to act now to secure your company's online reputation and ensure long-term deliverability success.

Here are some recommended next steps for developing a solid email reputation for your company:

1. Conduct a deliverability reputation audit. Third party audits are available from companies such as Pivotal Veracity or Email Service Providers (ESPs) such as ExactTarget.
2. Identify which deliverability factors are your pain points. Create a plan to change and implement new practices.
3. Over time, your deliverability reputation will improve. Send to test addresses so that you can measure this improvement.
4. Continue to monitor each deliverability factor and conduct inbox testing on a regular basis.

In its simplest terms, a deliverability reputation can be distilled into an equation that any legitimate email marketer can solve by following best practices. With each factor of the "reputation equation" in place, long-term trust will resonate with the cyber-postmen that decide where to deliver your email messages—in the inbox, the bulk folder, or not at all.

WHAT ARE OTHER MARKETERS THINKING?

In their own words . . .

CAN YOU SEE YOURSELF AS YOUR CUSTOMERS SEE YOU?

By Chip House
Vice President of Marketing Services, ExactTarget

Spam is in the eye of the beholder. As email marketers, however, we often fail to put ourselves in the recipients' shoes. Ultimately, it is the way that your email is *perceived* that will mark its success or failure. That perception can only be controlled by the actions you take on behalf of your brand. Set expectations and live up to them. Your customers will pay you back in loyalty.

According to Wikipedia, "Spam occurs without the permission of the recipients." Therein is the rub. Permission can exist differently in the mind of each email recipient. For example, a subscriber might send a complaint to you, saying, "Okay, I may have checked the opt-in box, but you didn't say you would email me a promotional offer every day. I was expecting a monthly newsletter." In this case, permission may have been technically given (or you understood it to be), but you didn't have permission to send daily, promotional emails. In essence, you didn't have the recipient's permission to do what you did. So, this, per the definition, is spam.

Again, avoiding being a spammer is to flip email on its head and to look at it from the recipients' point of view. I've seen many mailers complain about the spam in their inbox and how they ignore and delete it, but they fail to see the correlation to their own email, which may be unwanted by some portion of their list. Again, spam is the failure to gain permission before sending email.

Given this definition of spam, permission-based email defines content, frequency, purpose ahead of time, and your potential subscribers each "raise their hand" to decide if it is for them. No gimmicks. No hitches. What they see is what they get.

This concept of "sending email only as you would have email sent to you" is what I call the Golden Rule of Email—and it is powerful. The balancing act between brand equity versus profits (or high-road versus low-road) is often difficult. Yet, the Golden Rule of Email holds true in nearly every client situation I've encountered—be it B-to-B or B-to-C, enterprise or small business. The Golden Rule of Email is really about something very simple—truly listening to the wants and needs of your customers, then acting primarily from that standpoint (*their* needs) rather than your own.

What you want to send versus what your subscribers want to receive is often different. And if their expectations are different, they'll likely complain to you, complain to their ISP, unsubscribe—maybe worse, just ignore you.

I AM NOT A SPAMMER!!!!! AND OTHER MYTHS THREATENING THE EFFICACY OF YOUR EMAIL COMMUNICATIONS

By Deirdre Baird
President and CEO, Pivotal Veracity
Website: www.pivotalveracity.com

Recently, I sat in on a meeting with our sales staff. They were discussing various prospects, using terms from their unique methodology for segmenting clients based on needs and perceptions. One of the terms that kept popping up was FSS. There were lots of these FSS prospects that represented different industries, different size companies, and different mailing objectives. Try though I did, I just couldn't figure out what it meant. So I finally asked.

FSS stands for False Sense of Security and refers to companies that, with unwavering confidence, say, "I don't spam, so I don't have those issues," when asked what they are doing to mitigate delivery issues, safeguard their reputation, and optimize the inbox delivery and the integrity of their critical email communications.

This brings me to the first myth that exists with respect to deliverability: I only mail customers who opt-in to receive my emails . . . ergo, I am not a spammer . . . therefore, I do not have deliverability issues.

Unfortunately, while we proudly and self-righteously stand on our soap boxes proclaiming, "I am not a spammer!" the emails our customers requested are being blocked, stripped of their links, images suppressed, redirected to spam folders, and randomly deleted.

A flagrant disregard for permission will certainly lead to deliverability issues. So will reliance on the myopic belief that permission is all that is required to prevent these issues. Unconvinced? Consider the following nonpermission-related issues that will and do impact the deliverability, credibility, and effectiveness of email communications every single day.

Simple content-specific issues can still result in your messages being filtered as spam. Maybe it's a combination of the color fonts you are using or your ratio of text to HTML or something as innocuous as the term "home mortgage" versus "mortgage." None of these attributes say anything at all about the permission you obtained from your customer, yet on any given day, your message may contain enough of these triggers such that major ISPs and/or spam filters flag your communication as spam. Those who eschew the significance that content filters play fail to recognize that every single major ISP and every major enterprise spam filter in the market still utilize some content-based rules in determining whether your message is spam.

If you mail high volume or at a fast rate, your mail can be blocked altogether. Many recipient hosts begin blocking or rejecting mail if you exceed volume thresholds. At ISPs such as AOL, these thresholds can be as low as 100 emails for nonwhitelisted mailers.

Permanent or 5XX bounces are not synonymous with a bad address. They occur for many reasons, which include spam blocks, message size, technical issues, and so on. Regardless of the fact that ISPs do not consistently provide the specific reason for a hard bounce, they expect you to remove these emails from your list, or you risk outright blocking of all your mail. Faced with the unenviable choice between removing valid and hard-earned customers from your list (mind you, customers who have asked for your email) or having all your email to a particular ISP blocked, what do most mailers do?

According to a 2006 Email Experience Council study, most mailers don't know what to do. They allow the entire decision as to when and how names are removed to rest in the hands of a third party or the black-box rule sets inherent in their CRM or MTA software. Perhaps this is the more prudent course, but if I told you I was going to delete as much as 3 percent to 7 percent of your good customer names every time you mail (or as we've seen before, an entire domain), wouldn't you want to have a say in the matter? Or at least think it a matter of strategic importance to understand why?

With respect to deliverability, the 1-99 rule is king. What is the 1-99 rule? If less than 1 percent of your customers click on that "report as spam" button, there is a good chance the remaining 99 percent will receive your communication. There has been an inordinate amount of press convincing consumers not to trust the unsubscribe functionality or to click on any links for that matter (after all, you may just be telling a spammer or someone posing as a legitimate company who you are). Is it any wonder that many recipients use the report as spam button as an alternative to unsubscribing? Regardless, major ISPs such as Hotmail and AOL use spam complaints as a critical metric in determining whether to block or filter your mail. AOL told my company to advise our clients to shoot for less than a 0.3 percent spam complaint rate. Imagine that—a tiny fraction of your customers are controlling your ability to communicate with the rest. That is today's reality . . . and yet, the companies that avidly insist they are "not spammers" often don't track or analyze spam complaints. After all, they are not spamming. So it is inconceivable that overaggressive mailing or nonrelevant communications might just compel a tiny fraction of their customers to click on that ever-handy and very conveniently placed "report as spam" button. Hmmmm. . . .

If you are "not a spammer," then the measures put in place to thwart spammers (and their ugly stepsisters of phishers and virus-propagators) should logically not impact you, right? That's the theory. Of course, it's wrong for many of the reasons already noted. Even if you manage to overcome all of the nonpermission barriers related to reaching your customer's inbox, you are still impacted.

For example, a growing trend in both desktop and web-based email software is the use of image suppression to prevent the effectiveness of image-based spam and to mitigate possible security risks. Outlook 2003, AOL 9, Hotmail, Gmail, Lotus Notes, and Mozilla Thunderbird are examples of email clients that turn off images by default. This means those pretty HTML emails show ugly gray boxes where your compelling pictures and buttons were supposed to be.

Another example is authentication, which is a great idea intended to thwart phishers. Unfortunately, there is still no industrywide consensus on which method to employ and various ISPs and email clients support different methods. And if you haven't implemented all of these methods (after all, why should you if you are not a phisher?), don't be surprised when clicks decline as your recipients are warned that your identity could not be verified.

So you are not a spammer, right? Just remember that a False Sense of Security (FSS) will not preserve the deliverability, credibility and effectiveness of your email communications. You must get informed and treat these issues with the strategic diligence you place on other aspects of your customer communications. Ultimately, the long-term viability of your critical email communications depends on it.

ARE YOU A SPAMMER?

By Madeline Hubbard
Email Specialist, MindComet
Blog: www.emailmarketingvoodoo.com

The CAN-SPAM Act of 2003 set the tone for legitimate digital communication practices, protecting consumers from unwanted and *unwarranted* email messages from advertisers, marketers, and pharmaceutical representatives packed into a basement, sending the latest medical advancements (if you get what I mean).

Since then, "making the good list" has become an ongoing battle made even fiercer with the empowerment of consumers to report spam messages. Even the savviest of web marketers can't avoid the bullets and are becoming branded as spammers. Once you've been slapped with the label, it's time-intensive and costly to reattain the customer. To prevent this event from occurring, you should question your label as a spammer and ask, "How did I end up here?"

While much of what constitutes spam was determined by the CAN-SPAM Act, it is important to realize that the recipient is the ultimate decision maker. Any communication should begin with a documented and traceable agreement to receive messages, known in the email world as the double opt-in. While not required, the "double opt-in" is noted as an email marketing best practice to ensure your list members are who they say they are, and that they have joined your list of their own initiative. The CAN-SPAM Act may only speak to complying with opt-out requests, but opting-in is an absolute way to demonstrate "expressed permission" instead of "implied consent" between you and your list members. If list members have a question as to how they were added to your list, your double opt-in records give you the ability to locate and confirm their sign-up date.

The double opt-in procedure will also protect your database against spamtraps. Spamtraps are dropped into your database by ISPs if your sign-up process is weak. Every time you send an email to a spamtrap, it is a mark against you in the eyes of the ISP. Some ISPs will even refrain from whitelisting you if there is not a double opt-in procedure in place. Whitelisting refers to the process of consumers deeming your messages as "safe," thus in the future they will not be placed in the junk folder or marked as spam.

Keep in mind that double opt-in is merely a safeguard for an email marketer but does little to prevent spam filters and junk folders. Obtaining permission to send the communication is only the first step, with several other factors including subject lines, headers, and footers affecting the overall assessment by the consumer.

The first opportunity to captivate is also one of the first spam determinates. Email marketers must take advantage of the subject line while avoiding automated spam calculators such as SpamAssassin. It scores emails on a scale from 0 to 5 based on its subject line and content. The higher your score, the more likely you are to be considered spam.

Avoid subject lines with words such as "free," "offer," "discount," and excessive punctuation such as exclamation points that may raise red flags for most email clients. Remember, there is a very fine line between "catchy" and "spammy."

In addition to the basics of the subject line, many email marketers forget to pay attention to their anchor real estate: the header and footer. The header and footer have the power to capture the user's attention, influence the brand, teach, and create a foundation of trust through consistency. Use the header and footer to make it evident that the email is being sent by someone trustworthy and a legitimate information source, who the message is from, offer options to change preferences, provide other options for viewing the email such as a hosted HTML version of your message, opt-out instructions, and emphasize CAN-SPAM compliance.

If you ensure that your messages are in line with these points and deliverability is still a concern, consider moving toward a dedicated IP. A dedicated IP provides the ISPs the ability to accurately measure a sender's reputation. Think of it like your credit score: it is unique to you. A bad credit score equals no loan approval. Analyze where your current deliverability issues are, prior to setting up your dedicated IP. Then with the new IP in place, ensure that reputation is a key focus so your best will be credited toward the new IP address.

CHAPTER 13 REVIEW

- With respect to email, reputation is the general opinion of the ISPs, the anti-spam community, and subscribers toward a sender's IP address, sending domain, or both. The "opinion" is a reputation score created by an ISP (or third-party reputation provider). If the sender's "score" falls within the ISPs thresholds, a sender's messages will be delivered to the inbox.

- Most email systems that send email over the Internet use SMTP, or Simple Mail Transfer Protocol, to send messages from one server to another. Unfortunately, SMTP was created without checks in place to ensure that the sender is authentic. That's why spammers exploit this weakness by spoofing legitimate emails (known as phishing).

- Due to spam problems that affect their bottom line, ISPs have moved away from individual filters (such as content or image filters) and now you use a holistic sender's reputation, composed of factors such as legal compliance, spam reports, spamtraps, sender authentication, and technical components.

- To ensure maximum list hygiene, which can help prevent delivery issues, you should always receive explicit permission to mail, practice double opt-in confirmations, and consider a routine reengagement campaign that gives subscribers a chance to decline future mailings.

- Now that you understand the deliverability equation, recommended next steps to developing a solid email reputation for your company include conducting a deliverability audit, identifying which deliverability factors are your pain points, testing email addresses, and ongoing monitoring.
- Remember that in the end, we can have the best email, the most compelling offer, the greatest audience, and the best intention, but if your email never gets to the inbox . . . the opportunity will always be lost.

INDEX